A10701 613535

S0-GGE-082

Antique Shaving Mugs of the United States

By

Robert Blake Powell

©Robert Blake Powell 1972

Library of Congress Catalog Card Number: 71-186119

Limited First Edition Reference Book

—All Rights Reserved—
No portion of this book may be reproduced in any form without written authorization from the author/publisher.

Additional copies of this book may be purchased directly from the author/publisher —

>Robert Blake Powell
>1333 Kathryn Street
>Hurst, Texas 76053
>U. S. A.

Price $17.95 per copy.

PRINTED IN THE UNITED STATES OF AMERICA.

This book is dedicated to —

Aunt Fan, Edie and the grandchildren — Jim, Chris, Vicki and Larry.

— Aunt Fan, who in 1927 was responsible for my interest in my first hobby (stamp collecting), and who thirty-five years later, was responsible for my present-day hobby — shaving mugs.

— my wife Edie, without whose patience, understanding, interest and enthusiasm, this book would never have been written.

— our grandchildren, the "now" generation, who are growing up in a technologically advanced generation and who will someday inherit their share of the world's problems, but with what I hope will be a well-proportioned sense of values for a happy and full life — which will include an interest in at least one hobby.

This fine unmarked Bavarian or Prussian china shaving mug was the start of a mug collection by the author. It was originally owned by the author's uncle, Fred Bernd, who brought it back from Europe at the end of World War I.

ACKNOWLEDGMENT

Thanks to the many collectors and dealers all over the country whose interest and contributions of even small bits of information and words of encouragement helped make this book a reality.

Grateful acknowledgment is extended to Mr. A. Lawrence Abel, M.S., M.D., F.R.C.S. of England, considered to be the world's foremost authority and collector of antique barber-surgeon shaving/bleeding bowls, for his assistance in furnishing detailed information tracing the history and practices of the barber-surgeon and of the early bowls or basins.

So little is known today of the old art and practices of shaving mug designing and decorating, of the mugs themselves, and of the men who established and applied this art, that the author feels especially indebted to the following, for their interest and cooperative assistance and for permission to reproduce treasured personal photos, and pages from old company catalogs, which not only furnishes authenticity to the book, but preserves the true image for future generations of collectors:

Mr. Hugo H. Davis, former President of the Koken Companies, Inc., who retired after more than half a century of service with the firm, for his outstanding cooperation and interest in furnishing the author with valuable information pertinent to this book.

Mrs. Olive (Koken) Yackey, Jr., for graciously extending her assistance and for the loan of certain treasured personal effects about her father, Ernest E. Koken, the founder of the Koken company nearly a hundred years ago.

Mr. Oliver T. Johnson, nephew of Ernest E. Koken, now in his nineties, and still a practicing attorney, for furnishing vivid recollections of the days of his youth and of Mr. Koken, during the years of his inventiveness and business acumen. His identification of many of the early workers and various departments of the company are also appreciated.

Dr. Justin Grimm, for providing cherished family photographs and previously unknown information about his father Curt Grimm, the late foreman of Koken's Mug Decorating Department, who retired in 1925 when the mug department was closed.

Mr. Edgar H. Wendel, now nearing eighty, who learned china painting and the art of decorating shaving mugs from his father, Robert Wendel, one time foreman of the Koken Mug Decorating Department. He is the last of the old-time mug decorators, and his recollections of the craft and the mugs themselves have proven to be of inestimable value in writing much of this book.

Thanks are also extended to the following persons and institutions for their part in assisting the author and for their permission to reproduce the illustrations beside their names in the book:

The Library of Congress, Washington, D. C.
Beauty and Barber Supply Institute of New York City
The New York Public Library
Mrs. Irene McCreery, The Toledo Public Library
Mrs. T. Edwin N. Jefferies, Rochester Public Library
Henry Ford Museum, and Greenfield Village, Dearborn, Michigan

Mr. A. Christian Revi, Editor, Spinning Wheel magazine
Lake County Historical Society, Mentor, Ohio
Rochester Museum and Science Center, Rochester, N.Y.
The Bostonian Society, Boston, Mass.
Crown Publishers, Inc.
Mr. Nicholas B. Wainwright, Director, The Historical Society of Pennsylvania (Founded 1824)
Journal of the American Medical Association
Antiques Magazine
Capt. Roger Gerry
The Soap and Detergent Association
Sandwich Historical Society
The Missouri Historical Society
Mr. Mitchell A. Wilder, Director, Amon Carter Museum of Western Art
Mr. Carroll Hopf, Curator, Pennsylvania Farm Museum of Landis Valley
Mr. Erik Lassen, Director, Det Danske Kunstindustrimuseum, Copenhagen, Denmark
Mr. Calvin S. Hathaway, Philadelphia Museum of Art
W. C. Heimerdinger Company, Inc.
Mr. and Mrs. L. M. Zigler
Ellen Donahue
Mr. Bernard J. Satz
Mr. C. F. Kalb
Olga K. Wood
The Lenox Company
Mr. and Mrs. Mike Mocio
Mr. and Mrs. Frank O. Dresner
Mrs. Oma Anderson
Mrs. Fern Trimm
Mrs. Omega Belle O'Connor
Dr. David Maeth, M.D.
Mr. and Mrs. Jay Riggs
Mr. and Mrs. Jim Keller
Mrs. Margaret Brown
Mr. K. W. Southall, Jr.
Mrs. Virginia Hines, Liscott Studio
Lt. Col. Bill Larkin, USAF
DeGolyer Foundation Library
Charles F. W. Seitz family
Mr. Richard F. Snow
Mr. Joe L. Bowen
Mr. James Matthews
Mr. Virgil G. McCloud
Mrs. Ruth M. Millener
Mr. William Donnelly
Mrs. Joan Webb
Mr. W. H. Alexander
Mr. Albert Newton
Warner Lambert Company
Nelson Lebo Company
Dorothy Lawless
Dover Publications, Inc.
Mr. Zane Field

FOREWORD

The Old World had its armorial patterns — its coats of arms painted or embossed upon the shields and embroidered upon its banners. The silversmiths had their hallmarks — guarantees of supreme excellence in skill and artistry. The grandees of Spain and Portugal (noblemen of the first rank) had their rubics — the flourishing manner in which they signed their names. The cattle barons of the old West had their cattle brands — which they lived and died for. Even the average American male of yesteryear had his own particular type of heraldry — in handsomely decorated and designed shaving mugs.

Shaving mugs began their journey into obsolescence half a century ago, have been unused and unknown for two generations and are now practically extinct. For three-quarters of a century the creative talents of designers and artists of the nineteenth century, in a practical way promoted the sale of the shaving mugs.

History owes a debt of gratitude to the amateur connoisseurs, the collectors who search out the items of our past and protect them from the ravages of time and deterioration. . .for the benefit of future generations.

Our museums of fine art are today filled with treasures of the past which were first recognized, collected and preserved in the private collections of the amateur connoisseur, when these objects became scarce through obsolescence.

Museums of the future will surely follow the pattern previously set and eventually contain many splendid examples of shaving mug art, form and beauty, created by the early china painters and mug decorators of America. For only in this way, can a true representation of the tangible history of our American history of civilization and way of life be made available for the enjoyment of our future generations.

Robert Blake Powell

Three views of a rare "Parian-type" quality china 3-mold embossed shaving mug, circa 1840. Motif accented by light blue shading of all three panels and pinkish tint of top and bottom rim decoration (applied from mold). Faint gold stripe on top rim. Inside glazed. Similar mugs also found without handles and in other solid colors. *Author's Collection.*

CONTENTS

Title Page I
Dedication II
Frontispiece IV
Acknowledgement .... V, V
Foreword VI
Introduction XI
Evolution of a Shaving Mug 1

PART I

Sec. 1 — In the Beginning — The Sign of the Barber 7
Sec. 2 — Early Shaving Soaps 32
Sec. 3 — American Primitive Pottery Shaving Mugs 42
Sec. 4 — Pewter, Brittania, Silverplate, Aluminum, etc. Mugs 44
Sec. 5 — Glass Shaving Mugs 54
Sec. 6 — Patented Shaving Mugs 63
Sec. 7 — Occupational Type Shaving Mugs 71
Sec. 8 — Secret Societies (Fraternities), Trade Unions Mugs 91
Sec. 9 — Glass Label Mugs, Photographic and Gilt Number Mugs 98
Sec. 10 — Lenox Shaving Mugs 105
Sec. 11 — Advertising Shaving Mugs 113
Sec. 12 — Decal Shaving Mugs 114
Sec. 13 — Scuttle Shaving Mugs 117
Sec. 14 — Character Shaving Mugs, Humorous or Comic Design Mugs ... 119
Sec. 15 — Barbershop Mug Sheets 128
Sec. 16 — Straight Razors 130
Sec. 17 — Barber Bottles 135
Sec. 18 — Display Cases, Wall Cases, Mug Cases 146
Sec. 19 — Barbershop Pottery and Glassware 151
Sec. 20 — Fakes and Reproductions 153

PART II

Sec. 1 — Evolution of The Koken Barber Supply Company 177
    Early life of E. E. Koken
    Establishment of a business
    Ninety-eight years of Business
    Curt Grimm, Shaving Mug Designer-Artist
    The Wendels — Two Generations of Mug Decorators
Sec. 2 — Barber Supply Companies, Marks 209
Sec. 3 — Barber Supply Company Decorated Shaving Mugs 212
    Alphabetical List of Mugs 215

PART III

Sec. 1 — Barbering Equipment, Supplies and Furniture 224
    Decorated Shaving Mugs 240
    Barber Poles 260

Two views of fine china mug made for The World's Fair in 1904 (St. Louis), with obverse side picturing the Palace of Varied Industries. Ornately decorated with both etched and beaded gold and handpainted flowers. *Author's Collection.*

Rare robin egg blue glass shaving paper vase with handpainted decoration. *Author's Collection.*

INTRODUCTION

This book is intended to be neither fiction nor biography, except as the history of antique shaving mugs might be considered biographical in nature, or in format. From the time I first decided to seriously begin collecting shaving mugs, I was aware of how little is generally known about them by dealers and collectors alike. I keep remembering how much easier it would have been for me, if there had been a book available — showing at least a representative portion of the various types which I might expect to locate.

Thus — my one serious objective in writing this book is to provide for collectors and dealers alike, as comprehensive a reference handbook of information on all categories of antique shaving mugs as is possible. If this is accomplished, then my satisfaction in having contributed toward making it easier for present-day and future generation collectors to know more about this interesting hobby will be reward enough for my efforts.

It is, of course, impossible for any one person to know all there is to be known about shaving mugs, because of the physical impossibility for one person to have seen all the old mugs. It is improbable that one person has been able to have located (at this late date) all the old barber supply catalogs which were published for so many years and which have long since vanished. I have studied many such old catalogs in the Missouri Historical Society Archives and in the Library of Congress during my vacation treks back to Washington to visit family and friends during the past few years. And I've compared notes with information appearing in old catalogs which I own, and with those owned by collector-friends. However there are many I am sure that I have not seen.

The old-time shaving mugs are closely akin to American history in a sense; some represent vividly the history of our country — in their decor, their reason for being manufactured and in their use, at different periods of time. In addition, there were many local customs connected with the old-time barber shops — depending on the area of the country and the period of time being considered. I have spent a great deal of time travelling in search of information to include in this book and for a better understanding of the hobby and have learned of many instances of such local mores. However only a few such customs are included in this book — those which are considered of any real significance.

Although this book may wander into the vernacular at times, and in other places contain listings compiled from my many notes, it has been my sole intention to give information about shaving mugs and closely related items — to the buff and dealer alike, which will enhance their knowledge of the subject, and which would otherwise be impossible to locate.

I have attempted to compile and arrange all information in this book in such a manner that it will be both interesting and useful to all who read it and use it. The chapter arrangement is somewhat chronological, but in no way should be interpreted to mean that the mugs listed first or last are the most or least worthy or valuable, because value is a relative thing. Basically value is actually what you are willing to pay to own something — what it is worth to you alone.

In recent years there have been many books written about antiques in general and about particular categories of antiques. A few of these have made slight mention of shaving mugs. But to my knowledge there has not been one published expressly for the shaving mug collectors and the dealers who sell them and which book attempts to cover all aspects of the many categories of shaving mugs.

I feel that I've gained a lot of knowledge from my correspondence and association with other collectors, and I hope that this book will serve in some measure to express my gratitude to them for the exchange of knowledge and to preserve the information for future collectors.

My description of a mug as being rare, quite rare, or similar terms, in no way should be interpreted to mean that this alone makes it quite valuable or expensive. Two entirely different types of mugs may be rare, and yet the price range for the two may vary considerably. Rarity alone does not determine the value or price one may expect to pay or receive for something. Rarity means literally that there aren't many of them in existence or on the market. In other words, the available supply on the market is limited. The demand of buyers basically affects the selling price, and that demand is often closely related to the eye appeal of a particular mug.

There are many mugs which are rare, quite rare or even extremely rare, and yet would not bring as high a sales price, as for example — a trade design mug (occupation), even though there may be fifty times the quantity of that particular occupation-type mug in existence as the other mug. One reason for this fact is that there has been publicity over the years, in magazines and newspapers, about the occupations, with little or no emphasis on the other types. Consequently little is known about them. And, in many instances, few collectors even know certain mugs are in existence. (So the demand has not yet developed.) These mugs which have not been in great demand, are the real bargains of today, for they have not reached their peak in popularity nor in price. If you can recognize these mugs for their true potential, then you will profit by your interest and investment in the long run, both from a hobby standpoint and from a monetary standpoint — should you ever decide to sell them.

Except as noted, all photographs, including color photographs in this book were made by the author. Being an amateur photographer, previously interested mainly in photographing my grandchildren and the flowers in my garden, I was determined to do the photographic work connected with the pictures of this book. And, for this I learned something to enrich my hobby of photography. To the unintiated, photographing glass or china with gold decorations of high or brillant gloss may not seem much of a task, but the problems of eliminating light reflections can be the most complicated and difficult thing imaginable. Credit lines are given where picutres were furnished for inclusion in the book.

There were many times during the writing of this book that I nearly gave up in despair. Despair over the insurmountable odds against finding the information required to make this book as comprehensive as I thought it should be.

When confronted with these situations, I found it necessary to re-evaluate the situation and the circumstances per se'. First it must be realized that it would be impossible to own or to see all the shaving mugs still in existence. And it must likewise be realized that few of the old Barber Supply catalogs are still in existence. These two facts presented the first of several problems; thus a compromise had to be made. It was necessary to categorize all shaving mugs into a few general classifications and to use a representative number of barber supply catalogs from a few of the oldest, largest and even smaller barber supply companies.

Another difficult situation is the fact that the barber supply companies did not list in their catalogs all the different types. (Generally the mugs listed were the popular mugs of that period — the trade designs, society emblems, fancy decorated and names or initials, and a few others.) The earlier types, such as pewter, Brittania or silver-plated mugs were seldom listed, if at all. (The pewter mug, for example, would be found listed only among other early pewter manufactured utensils of a particular pewterer. This was many years before barber supply companies came into existance.) The same holds true of mugs made of earthenware, redware, stoneware and glass to some extent.

Scuttle mugs were of a much later date and were mostly imported from Europe. They were generally used in the homes. I have never seen a catalog listing scuttles.

Silver mugs, both sterling and silverplate, were seldom listed in the barber supply catalogs. They were listed in the catalogs of the silver companies which manufactured them, or by the retail outlet, such as Montgomery Ward or Sears. (Look in one of these old catalogs to see pictures and prices of some varieties.)

Lenox shaving mugs were never sold through the barber supply companies. Consequently they will not be found listed or shown in any Barber Supply catalog. They were listed only in Lenox catalogs or lists, or perhaps by a retailer of Lenox wares.

Character shaving mugs were a novelty and were imported mostly from Bavaria and Austria. They were manufactured and painted or decorated in their country of origin. And were likewise not listed in Barber Supply catalogs.

In other words, all information is scanty and comes from many varied sources. The barber supply companies seldom kept their records or even catalogs but a few years, so the availability of catallogs is scarce. Only a handfull of old-timers are still living, who were connected in any way with this industry, and to locate them is not an ordinary task.

In many instances it was impossible to separate fact from fiction, so here again a compromise was made in order to tell the whole story in an orderly fashion.

However, on the other side of the ledger, I was encouraged each time I did find out a truth. And I was encouraged to be able to picture a representative number of varied shaving mugs, knowing that pictures tell more than words and would be an invaluable aid to all collectors and dealers.

It was most gratifying to me to get the cooperation from other collectors in permitting their collections to be photographed, for inclusion in the book.

And finally after all the facts and phrases of fiction were gathered together and sorted out in some semblance or order, my despair turned to desire. Desire to finish writing the book and to do a creditable job of it.

So here it is, for your pleasure or profit, and I hope you will judge it not by other books, but rather by its own merits in terms of usefullness to you as a collector or as a dealer in antiques.

The Author

EVOLUTION OF A SHAVING MUG

The shaving mug has undergone perhaps even more changes than the airplane in its history on the American scene. From the first time a barber sloshed soapy water on the customer's face from an oval or rounded bowl or basin which fit under his neck and also caught the excess lather or suds which rolled down his chin and neck, to the almost standard type which resembles a heavy coffee mug, man's idea of what a shaving mug should look like has undergone many transformations. In between these two extremes are found many interesting and varying types, many patented and many more copied or simply manufactured.

The original American, the American Indian, had little or no use at all for shaving accoutrements. Our early settlers however, brought Old World habits and customs with them when they came to the new world. These customs varied somewhat, depending on the country from which they had emigrated. But it is safe to assume that this marked the time when barber bowls or basins were first used in the United States. History reveals that for a period of time the first American settlers were dependent on many items of import from the Old World. Then as they became more self-reliant and productive, the surroundings in the new world necessitated many changes from the mores of Europe.

Exactly when the use of the European barber bowl was discontinued as a useful barbering accoutrement in America is a matter of conjecture. Its useful period in this country was no doubt dependent upon the people and the different areas of the country. It is believed that its widespread use in the United States was interrupted because of the rapidly changing times and conditions which was quite different from the countries and customs of everyday life in Europe.

Many parts of America however, were at this early time very self-reliant, and not often occasioned by visits from traders and sellers of merchandise manufactured elsewhere. In these areas there developed many crude household utensils, including basins and mugs used for shaving. Such examples locally produced were: Redware, stoneware and other earthenware and pottery, and many resembled the forms and shapes and even decorations known in Europe. Still others were even more crudely shaped, or shaped for a better utilitarian value. Refinements in styles came gradually.

For a time the early glass mugs resembled simply cups or glasses and even small pitchers — with a spout or extended neck for pouring off surplus suds and water. Innovations were introduced and manufacturers decorated these early glass mugs with design patterns molded into the glass mugs (such as the Viking pattern, also called Centennial or Bearded Man and the Hinged Handle and Scroll, Lion's Head, Robin and Wheat, and others).

Hard paste porcelain shaving mugs made their debut into America, having been brought to the United States by immigrants, and during the late 1880's were imported from Europe in great quantities. Most of these were highly decorated — also as pictures and designs from the mold, sometimes decorated in pastel colors from the molds themselves. Such mugs are quite rare and are considered of museum quality.

Many varied names have been used down through the years in speaking of what we today call a "shaving mug". It has been called a shaving cup, a shaving pot, a shaving glass and a shaving box. These terms were frequently used on early patents applications. But the most common one used was "shaving mug".

Man's Hair and Whiskers

One of the most controversial subjects of all times has been man's hair and his whiskers. It has played a dominant part in the development of civilization in every part of the world — from the most primitive of peoples to the other end of the balance scales. At one time or another, man's curious growth has been combed, cut, brushed, shaved, trimmed, dyed, braided, singed, curled, powdered, greased and plastered. It has been plucked out, transplanted, cultivated and scalped — fondled, fetished and feared. Even envied and adored.

All periods of world history, from Samson and Deliah down through the ages are indelibly marked with the habits of hair and whiskers upon the male sex, and the men who changed the styles.

In the United States the modes of American gentry before 1775 was a clean shaven face and the wearing of perukes, while farmers, tradesmen, merchants and the like favored natural hair styles.

About 1844 the American male began to develop the mutton-chop cheek whiskers, which in the next few years gradually extended their boundaries down under the chin and formed a light beard. Then mustaches sprang up everywhere and were trimmed to improve their shape and appearance.

By 1860 the beard in America had become such an appealing symbol that the clean shaven Abraham Lincoln followed the advice of a Republican Committee and cultivated whiskers and wore a standing collar as a more certain means of getting the popular vote in the Presidential election.

Following the Civil War, in the big cities where tonsorial parlors flourished, the younger American gentry began shaving off the chin growth, and the so-called handle-bar mustache, heavily waxed to perfection, became the symbol, although the old West continued to be settled by veterans with tobacco-stained mustaches and a chin full of whiskers. Long hair was seldom cut either, because in this western wilderness, away from the tame life of the big cities, where the settler or miner seldom saw anyone but Indians, he stuck to the ideals of his convictions as to how a man's face should look. Then as Army posts were established and communities and settlements grew into cities, the change in customs finally caught up with him. Civilization had trapped him into its changing times.

During the early 1870's the idea of personally decorated shaving mugs for American men caught on like wildfire and for the next forty years all American men were shaving mug conscious and provided themselves with the ultimate in handsomely adorned and decorated mugs. Although shaving mugs were decorated in Europe, even sometimes with the owner's name, the idea of the more personally decorated shaving mugs (with the owners' names) is considered strictly an American tradition, due no doubt to the Old American custom of keeping your shaving mug in your favorite barber shop and to the conscious efforts of the early barber supply companies in establishing shaving mug decorating departments to meet the ever-growing demands.

World War I Era

Next came the World War I era (1914-1918) and the United States' entry into the war in 1917. Once again a war would change the habits and appearance of the American male's beard and hair. This time Army barbers mass-produced the so-called "cootie haircut" (for reasons of sanitation and health) by close-cropping haircuts with mechanical hand clippers. Recruits were issued the ingenious Gillette safety razors. During the war many men who had usually had a daily or weekly shave at the town barber shop in civilian life, found from necessity that they could shave themselves. Many men liked the new safety razor, which had originally been marketed for $5.00 in 1903, but which now cost only 10¢.

The brushless lathers and lather developments and innovations that followed eventually spelled FINISH for the old barber shop individually owner-type named and decorated shaving mugs. Again the changing times had its effect on man's countenance.

In the 20th century America "23-skiddooed" into the period of time when women began entering man's domain. . .to have their hair shingled or bobbed. . .another death-blow to the sanctuary of the American male's barber shop fraternities.

World War II had little effect upon the American male from the standpoint of hair and whiskers, except that many men now seemed to like the "close cut" of the hair on the head, and continued to wear it thus, while others were only too eager to let their hair grow to the shape of their head, with an occasional trim and periodic regular hair cut.

During the Viet Nam War the Hippie movement in America once again called the world's attention to man's whiskers and long hair. The so-called "protesting youth" will probably be remembered in history more for their bewhiskered, psycodelic appearance than for their alleged purpose of protest. At the risk of sounding facetious, there are some people who think their real purpose is a rebellion against today's TV commercials on shaving accoutrements.

Latest Barbering Innovation

Next comes the very latest innovations for the most modern and up-to-date idea in men's hair styling fashions. It may never reach the once popular portentous proportions of perukes (before the latter 1770's in America), but it offers an escape from the ordinary for the American male during his visit to the barbershop. Before stepping into the Barber Chair, the customer is welcomed by a special hair stylist whose presence assures him of the professional advice on proper hair care and the correct style to make him look his very best. In order that he doesn't have to commit to memory or take notes on all that free advice, an artist sketches the new him so that the barber can copy from his sketch.

Now that the Knight of the Razor and Shears has transformed his appearance, he is once again welcomed into society, not with just a haircut, but he gets to keep the artist's sketch. So, if he's a traveling man, and ever needs a haircut when he is out of town, all he has to do is show the sketch to any barber, who will then give his hank of hair the attention it requires to once again transform it into the prescribed pseudo-peruke-like appearance.

Nevertheless the male population now is perhaps better off, whiskerwise, than ever before. If man doesn't like to use a straight razor, he can use a safety razor. If neither fits his whims or desires, he can use an electric shaver. Many men have both a safety razor and an electric shaver. A few old-timers still cling to the old straight razor idea of shaving but also have an electric shaver for convenience of a "quick shave". But here again man struggles in a losing game with feminine gender, for milady also is up to par with the masculine gender, with the latest in shaving equipment.

Pity the poor barber — a few years from now — when man will daily rub a lotion onto his face — watch the whiskers fall into the sink — then wash his face — take a pill to control the growth of hair on his head, and be off for the office, without fuss or fuzz.

Author's collection.

Left — *Robert Lawrence McGee collection.* Right — *James Blake Davis collection.*

First illustration of bloodletting on Greek vase (in the Louvre), circa 500 B.C. Surgeon appears to be a woman. Note cupping vessel.

Collection of Mr. A. Lawrence Abel, M.S., M.D., F.R.C.S.

Lower right: Pointed lancets, phlebotomes used in early bloodletting.

Early flint or glass splinters used in bloodletting.

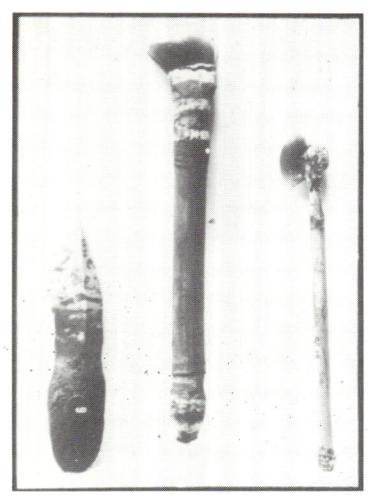

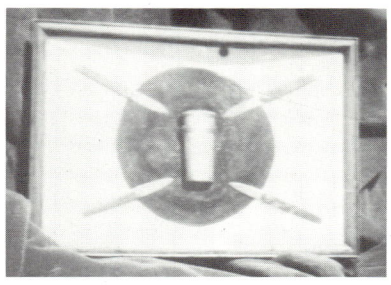

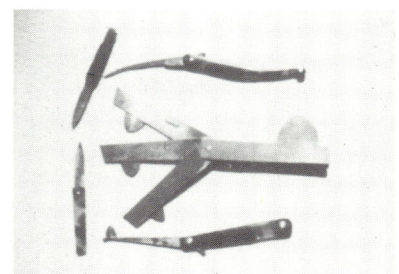

PART I

Section 1

"IN THE BEGINNING. . ." THE SIGN OF THE BARBER

The practice of barbery (barbering or shaving) is one of the world's oldest known professions—more ancient than the Roman Eagle or Golden Fleece. The word barber is derived from the Latin word "barba", which means beard.

Its beginning is shrouded in the mysteries of the beginning of civilization and the passing of time. Thus also are the earliest practices and implements or tools of the trade. Without a written record facts must be deducted from discoveries in later centuries, and like a jig-saw puzzle, some of the pieces become lost.

The fact that the barbering profession was closely akin to and a prominent part of the earliest practice of medicine, has already been established by archaeologists, scholars, and the like.

There is evidence that even in prehistoric times surgery (by the use of flints), including trephining the skull and for scarafication and other forms of blood-letting existed. Even today primitive tribes use shells, flint flakes and the like for bloodletting.

In ancient Egypt flints were used as knives and arrowheads up to and even after the advent of the Bronze Age—2500-1800 BC, after which razors and lances were made of bronze, as revealed by Egyptian and Mesopotamia excavations.

The first calendar was Egyptian and began in 4241 BC, but a thousand years passed before the development of the alphabet, papyrus, the brush and ink and for a literary class (including doctors) to emerge.

Five thousand years ago a doctor's work consisted of treating injuries—snake and scorpion bites, wounds from daggers and arrows, bilharzia and malaria and performing blood-letting and shaving. Palm leaves were used as splints and bandages. The juice of the poppy and of the mandrake plant were extracted to make general and local anaesthetics. The first barber-surgeon would suck out or cut out the venom of a snake bite and allow the wound to bleed. The Pharaohs, male members of the court and many other classes were clean-shaven.

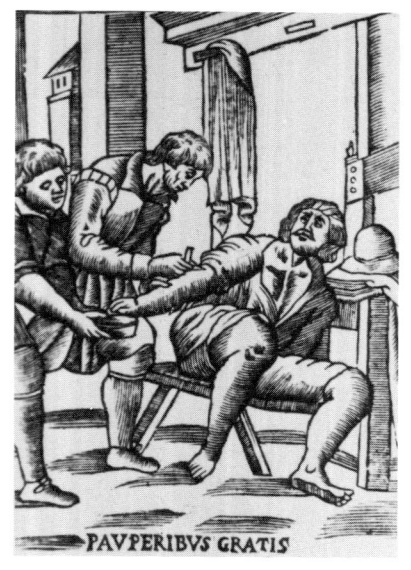
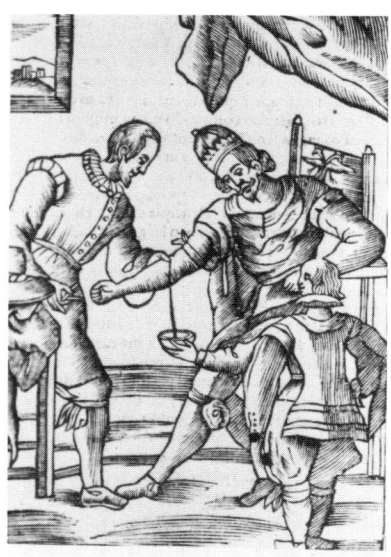

Top: Early century woodcut prints of bloodletting techniques. *Bottom left:* Early drawing showing phlebotomy techniques. *Bottom right:* North American woman being venesected for smallpox with a phlebotomy bow. *Collection and photos of Mr. A. Lawrence Abel, M.S., M.D., F.R.C.S.*

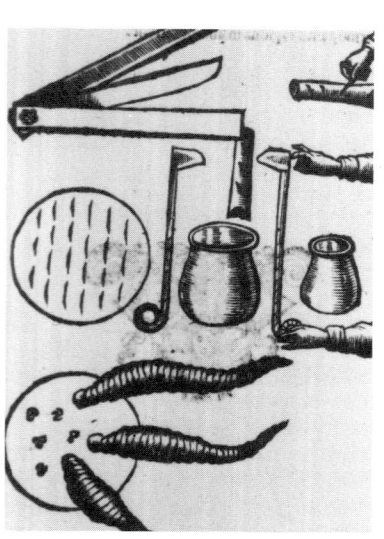

In 2,000 B. C. medicine flourished, and under the direction of the Pharaoh, medical practicioners sailed in the Royal Fleet to Crete and the Agean Islands. Each carried a staff or rod as a symbol of authority —a practice that has continued for thousands of years. It was also in the year 2,000 B.C. that Jacob, when he passed over Jordan, "carried his staff with him."

The surgeons and barber-surgeons went with the Egyptian navy to Greece and from them, the Greek, Asklepios, studied their teachings. His two sons (Machaon and Podelarius) were military surgeons with the Greek army when it beseiged Troy. They were present when Troy fell in 1194 B. C., and are seen in the ARMS OF THE ROYAL COLLEGE OF SURGEONS OF ENGLAND.

The Greeks made Asklepios their god of medicine and said he was the son of Apollo. From 1200 B.C. cure-resorts were set up in Greece and each was called an Asklepeion. Each had its snake pit (for Pharmacy) and a gymnasium (Physiotherapy Department). The attendants were known as Zatrolyptes and they were the barber-surgeons who dealt with barbering, bleeding and cupping.

The Holy Bible contains many passages in reference to shaving. In 600 B.C. the Prophet Ezekiel wrote "Thou, son of man, take thee a barber's razor and cause it to pass upon thine head and upon thy beard", (Ezekiel chapter 5, verse 1.)

In 500 B. C. the first European representation of bleeding was portrayed on a Greek vase, which is in the Louvre in Paris.

Hippocrates, the son of a doctor, was born in 460 B.C., some 800 years after Asklepios. And his two sons were also doctors. The true practice of medicine began with Hippocrates for it was he who separated the art of healing from superstition and magic. His treatment was based on commonsense, good nursing and rational diet, with the welfare of the patient his first consideration. Thus is he called the "Father of Medicine". The first written record of blood letting was by Hippocrates in the year 400 B. C.

A hundred years later, barber-surgeons went with the forces of ALEXANDER THE GREAT, treated his troops through many battles and lands far into Asia. Alexander returned to conquer North Africa in 332 B. C., and founded the city of Alexandria, with a university and medical shcool.

While CHRIST was still a youth, there was at Alexandria a student named LUCAN. He became a Ship's Surgeon, sailing round the eastern ports of the Mediterranean, and after the death of Christ he landed

Early woodcut prints of European monks and patients.

From the collection of Mr. A. Lawrence Abel, M.S., M.D., F.R.C.S.

Left: Ceiling hung with barber/surgeon basins in an early European shop.
Right: Early French barber shop. Note basin in use.

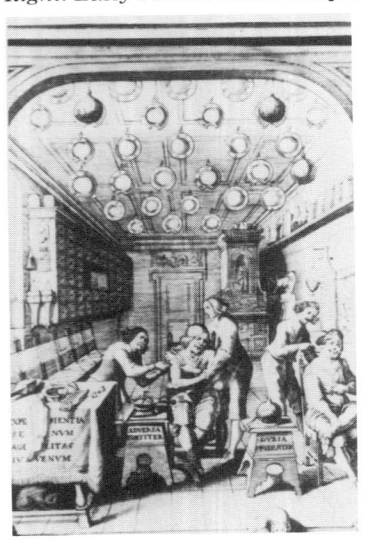

in Palestine and, impressed with the stories he heard, wrote the life of Christ with medical details, which we call the GOSPEL OF ST. LUKE.

The Greek physician and philosopher CLAUDIUS GALEN (about 200 A.D.) wrote an elaborate treatise on bleeding and on his authority the practice extended to almost every disease. The Arabs continued in Galen's tradition and the Anglo-Saxon Leech-Books prescribed bleeding for most conditions.

These ideas were handed on to Monasteries—the chief centres for medical practice for over 1,000 years. Thus for many centuries the care of the sick was in the hands of the clergy throughout Europe. The shedding of blood by monks was later forbidden, so most bleeding and surgery were carried out by laymen.

Bowls to catch blood were, for hundreds of years, made of metal-- copper, pewter or silver. Originally a large bowl was used.

Later small saucers were placed inside the large bowl to give a better idea of the quantity of blood removed.

Then the porringer with 2 handles or ears was introduced, but soon the blood bowl was given only one ear and sometimes had measuring marks on the inside.

Until early in the 16th Century, circular or oval household bowls were used for washing, shaving or bleeding. Then a NOTCH was fashioned in the circumference of the bowl to fit against the neck. The same notch fits the ANTECUBITAL FOSSA, and the barber-surgeons bleeding-shaving bowl came into being. It quickly became obvious that a bowl with a notch was more useful in shaving and bleeding than a circular bowl.

BARBER-SURGEONS BOWLS were used all over Western, Southern and Central Europe and introduced into Egypt, North Africa and North America. Thus for over 400 years a bowl with a notch has been used by barbers, barber-surgeons and surgeons, and we still use this type of bowl . . . . . . but now we call it a "KIDNEY DISH".

The commonest materials of which these bowls were made were: earthenware or metal. The earthenware was *TerraCotta Clay*, made by hand and fired—then dipped in lead glaze and re-fired.

From the mid-17th Century *Tin-Glaze* was used. These wares are *Majolica* or *Faience*. When finer clays are used the product is Porcelain.

Left: The "Royal Bowl", The Royal College of Surgeons for England. (Photo by Mr. C. Redman.) *Right:* European pewter. XVIII C.

Pair of Dutch bowls, glazed Delft. XVIII C.

Except for the "Royal Bowl", bowls and photos from the *collection of Mr. A. Lawrence Abel, M. S., M.D., F.R.C.S.*

Left: French. XVII C. *Right:* French XIX C. Made for "M. Emile Dethius, engine driver 1869".

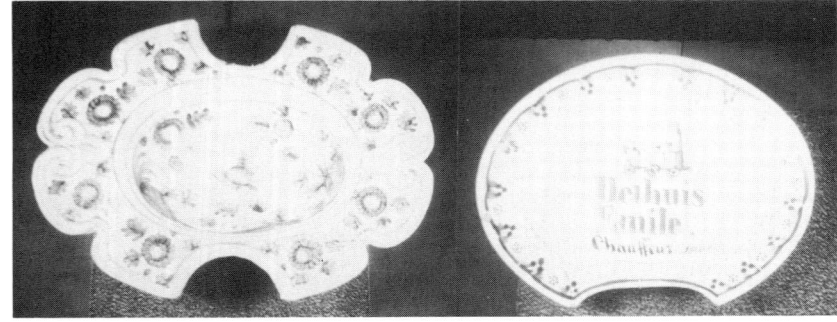

The main outline of the bowl was circular or oval, sometimes crenelated, with a notch cut in the broad rim. In this rim there was often a dent to hold the soap. Rarely the soap receptacle had perforations to drain the water from the soap and allow it to dry. There were a few with a small handle for holding the bowl. Similar bowls were made of metal-pewter, brass, tin-ware, copper, silver, etc., and these often had a ring or perforation for ease in holding the bowl while being used, or for hanging it up.

Pottery barber bowls were plain or decorated. Perhaps the most highly decorated were those made by the Chinese and Japanese for the European market in the 18th and 19th Centuries.

London or (Lambeth) English Delft dates from the 17th and 18th Centuries.

Bowls were also made of glass in Venice and in Bohemia. Others were made of skin—human or animal. More elaborate bowls had a notch on both sides.

Many of the 18th and 19th Century French glazed earthenware bowls were decorated with writing inscriptions.

Examples: 1. Here one is rejuvenated.
2. Don't cut my chin because it is the right length already.
3. Give my head a dry shave.
4. Long live my beautiful little piece of violet-scented soap.

According to Edwin Atlee Barber, in his book "Tulip Ware of the Pennsylvania German Potters", (first published in 1903), many of the German emigrants to Pennsylvania, used many of their old country German sayings and proverbs, quotations from the Bible, rhymes and mottoes, as well as decorative motifs, in the decorations of their pottery wares . . . . even on some of the shaving basins. These were done either as Sgraffito or Slip Decorations.

And sometimes, the bowls bore pictures of razors, combs, etc. . . . . . . and, even the name of the owner, or his family crest or a hand-painted picture of his occupation.

BARBERS' SIGNS

Barbery leads us to the barbers' signs—from the Twelfth century through the history of this profession and the many-sided controversial aspects of evolution to the present-day twentieth century striped barber pole, whose history many of us know little or nothing about and simply take for granted.

A pair of brass miniature barber bowls (5¼" dia.) originally a "sign" of the early barber/surgeon. *Author's collection.*

Left: Delft, 19th Century, polychrome, oval shape, floral decoration, with soap indentation. *Right:* French, 19th Century, high gloss porcelain, shallow, colorful, hand-painted center floral decoration. Rim and other design in gilt. *Author's Collection.*

Lower left: English Delft, round deep plain white basin, circa 1700-1758. *Lower right:* Rumanian aluminum barber basin. Circa 1890. *Author's Collection.*

Right: Dutch (Friesland.) XIX century. *Abel collection.*

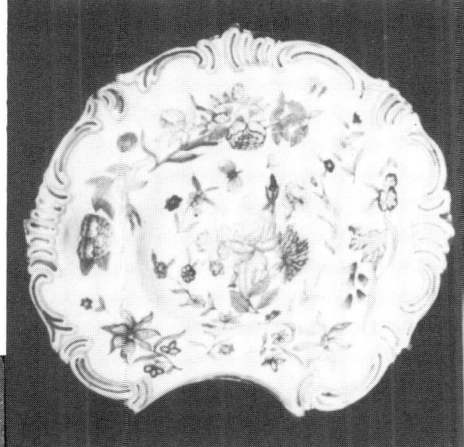

Left: Swiss (Thun, Canton Berne). XVIII century. *Abel collection.*

Right: Swiss, XIX century. "Aus Freundschaft" means "In Friendship." *Abel collection.*

Left: Swiss. 1800 (Schooren). (Words translated — "In the whole of this little town you are the most beautiful girl", a message from a customer to his lady barber. *Abel collection*

Little information has been written in modern times about barber signs, although down through the ages it has played a very important and dominant part in the development of our civilization. Today the barber pole is the last remaining vestige of what was in ancient history the sign of the barber.

To understand the reason why the barber's sign existed in the first place one must first realize that in the 12th through the 18th centuries few persons could either read or write. House signs proclaiming the owner's trade were indispensable in the cities. These signboards, bearing the accepted symbols of the populace, and regulated by the ruling monarchs, were easily recognized and understood by all.

Often painted, cut, carved or shaped in miniature or of exaggerated sizes, they set the standards for all to follow—until the 19th century, when the system of numbering houses were introduced, and every thoroughfare had its name painted at the beginning and end.

After this period of time, the original value of the signboards gradually lost its usefulness, but in some instances (even to this day) have lingered on. For in certain cities in Europe are to be found some of these early century reminders, adorning the store fronts.

The professions of barbers, doctors or surgeons, dentists, wigmakers and those who operated bath-houses in these early times were, in many instances intermixed, until laws regulating their practices were made and enforced by the ruling heads of state.

In addition to the early signboards, the barbers of early times used other methods of proclaiming their trade—exhibiting in the store-window all the decayed teeth which had been extracted from their patients. This would, by our standards of today, be considered most repulsive and disgusting—but to a man with a tooth-ache during that period of history, who could neither read or write, there was no doubt in his mind that he had found the right place when he saw the extracted teeth, and any repulsion he felt at their sight was soon turned to relief when the bad tooth was extracted.

The History of Signboards by Larwood and Hotten, printed in England in 1866, describes in verse from John Gay's Fables of 1727, the following multiple-profession of a dentist-barber-surgeon:

> *"His pole with pewter basin hung*
> *Black rotten teeth in order strung.*
> *Rang cups that in the window stood*
> *Lined with red rags to look like blood.*
> *Did well his threefold trade explain*
> *Who shaved, drew teeth and breathed a vein."*

Top (left): French XVIII C. (Translation — "You have a light touch".) *(right):* English Tin. XVIII C.

Second Row (left): Spanish. Aragon. XVI C. *(right):* Portuguese XVIII C. Pewter with pitcher. Collection of Mr. A. Lawrence Abel, M.S., M.D., F.R.C.S.

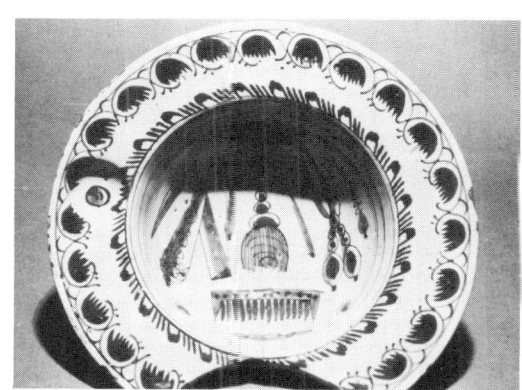

Mr. Henry Thompson's basin. Center decoration of barber tools.

An account is also given that "in Constantinople where the barber still acts as surgeon and dentist, the teeth drawn by him are worked in ornamental patterns inter-mixed with blue beads and hung as trophies in the window." The custom was also followed in London, where it was noted that a certain chemist dentist exhibited in his window a bottleful of decayed teeth. So it would seem that before laws prevailed, that there were many varied customs.

During the first half of the twelfth century in France, the clergy had been practicing barbery and surgery, but in 1163 the Council of Tours forbade them to draw blood, after which barbers assumed the role of surgeon, as did certain other tradesmen. But the barber played the more dominant role. It was not until 1371 however, that the barber-surgeons were organized in France. This was sixty-three years after Worshipful Company of Barbers was founded in England, in 1308.

In France surgeons were known as the "Surgeons of the Long Robe", and the barber-surgeons as the "Surgeons of the Short Robe". When the wealthy nobility disappeared, surgeons turned to the newly-formed middle-class and came into active competition with the barber-surgeons.

Fifty years ago an eminent Danish connoisseur wrote of many early century customs in Europe pertaining to the uses of barber's advertising signs and of the Danish brass Barberbaekkener (barber's bekkener or basin) still waving in the wind, latched to an iron spear in front of the barber shop.

Traditionally the brass bekken was shined daily and hung out each morning, then taken in each evening at 6 o'clock, regardless of the season or the weather. Its use as a sign is still backed with great prestige, and remains in service as an advertising sign, even though many of the other types of trade signs have disappeared from the front of old trade shops of today.

The barber pole as we know it today, originates from the early century *barber skare* or *blood tapper rod* (also called a *spear rod*), representative of the early custom of physicians, surgeons and barber-surgeons of carrying a rod or staff of office or authority (also called a mace).

The Paris Barber Association Law of the year 1371 mentions that the brass basin was still being used as a tool in the barber shop and in front of the shop with the same spear rod but with three basins instead of one, because in Paris in the year 1536 the barbers are said to have performed small operations on people's faces. They therefore

Painted Faience Barber's Basin of a Bishop. French, XVIII Century. Oval dish with undulating rim indented one side. Painted in cobalt and orange, showing Bishop in landscape, titled "S. T. Hugues, 1777". In W. Porter Ware collection from 1942-1971. Length 12½ inches. Bottom photo shows inscribed on back "M. Hugues Lesvignes, Vicare de Bois, 1777." *Author's Collection.*

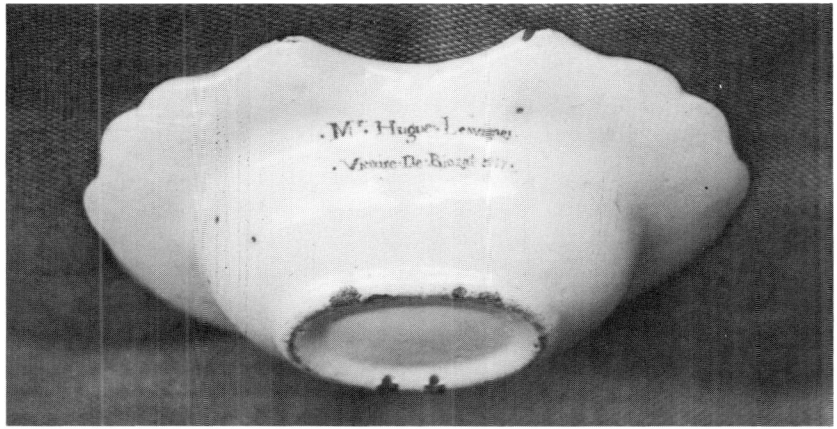

called themselves surgeons and added the picture of the patron saint —Saint Cosmas and Saint Damianus and three salvejars which became the surgeons' advertising sign in 1611.

The law in Paris in 1718 specified that the surgeon should advertise with the brass basin and three salvejars on the outside door and that barbers and wigmakers should advertise with a white basin.

In England barbers were practicioners in the surgery and dentistry of the day and were often called barber-surgeons; they practiced both the trades (as we know them now) until the reign of Henry VIII, when barbers in England were forbidden to perform at both trades, except to let blood or to extract teeth. Surgeons were likewise forbidden to practice barbery, and about 1750 dentistry ceased to be a regular part of their vocation.

In England surgeons were itinerant and were attached to the higher nobility. In London surgeons who took the "Guild Oath" wore a special cap and gown and were called "Master" or "Magister". The Surgeon's Guild in London had eight members in 1491, twelve in 1513, and never more than twenty. In the provinces there were even fewer.

Early barber-surgeons' shaving basins are also called bleeding basins or bleeding bowls, because of their dual purpose. Early barber-surgeons are known to have practiced phlebotomy.

According to Mr. A. Lawrence Abel, M.S., M.D, FRSC, the noted British physician, collector and authority of medical history, in his comprehensive narrative on "Blood Letting", (Journal of the American Medical Association, Vol. 214, No. 5, dated November 2, 1970), "At the time of the birth of Christ, barber-surgeons practiced in ancient Rome; they were called tonsores and cut hair, drew teeth and bled at the public baths."

Mr. Abel further states that "these treatments continued for hundreds of years. Galen in 200 AD prepared an elaborate treatise on bleeding and on his authority the practice extended to almost every disease and every country." He reports further that in Europe the monasteries became the chief centers for medical practices for more than 1,000 years, but "later the shedding of blood by monks was forbidden, so most bleeding and surgery were carried out by laymen."

The advent of the notch in the outer rim of the bowl did not occur until soon after 1500 AD, when it was realized that a notched bowl (to fit against the neck and antecubital fossa) was much more useful then a circular bowl. Mr. Abel states that "these bowls were used over Europe and later introduced into North Africa and North America and

Delft, 17th Century. Decorated both sides with dragons and floral motif in cobalt. Back side shows stem and leaf decoration also in cobalt. Outer rim is brown. Depression for soap ball. Previously in W. Porter Ware Collection. *Author's Collection*.

were forerunners of the modern kidney dish." He further explains that prior to the development of the notched bowl "a large bowl did not provide an accurate measure of the quantity of blood removed, so often a small bowl or saucer was used inside the larger one."

Early records (around 1550) of utensils used for this purpose, show they were made in nests (graduated sizes) and in addition, had ounce rings or graduated markings on the inside, for the chircurgeon to see how much blood had been let. In England they were sometimes called bleeding-dishes ear-dishes and bowls, as well as porringers or blood porringers.

The English blood-porringer is about four inches in diameter, about the same size as another porringer, which in English history, was called a "taster" and was used in every royal household at a time in history when poisoning was not uncommon. The "taster" utensil had no markings on the inside.

The barber, wigmaker and surgeon tradesmen of Paris had rivals in their trade with the tradesmen in Lubeck, Germany, where the Barber Association was formed in the year 1480. These tradesmen used the same sign as in Paris, and the barber was also a vein surgeon, licensed to tap blood from people's veins. A large white skin was added to the basin which hung on the spear rod outside—to advertise blood tapping. A bath towel was also added to the sign to indicate the availability of bathing facilities. Nearly seventy-five years later the ram, scale, hunter or waterman was added to the original advertising sign in Germany.

Vein tapping or the drawing of boood was also widely practiced as a measure for good health. The patient would grasp the spear rod firmly to make the blood run faster through the veins. These rods thus became spattered with blood and later were painted red and wound with a white skin. Later on the rods were painted with red, white and blue stripes, symbolically and with the brass basin attached at the top, served as advertising signs.

All over Europe, from the twelfth through the seventeenth centuries, bitter legal battles were waged in the old courtrooms for the right to advertise by the use of the shiny brass basin, but in the end it was the barbers who won the fight. According to "The History of Signboards", it was stated by Lord Thurlow in the House of Peers, July 17, 1797, when he opposed the Surgeon's Incorporation Bill, that "by a statute still in force the barbers and surgeons were each to use a pole. The barbers were to have theirs blue and white striped, with no appendage, but the surgeons (which were the same in other respects) were to have a gallipot and a red flag in addition, to denote the particular nature of their vocation." The blood tappers, surgeons, bath

French faience pottery barber basin. Circa 1830-1840. Colorful floral, bird, insect design in cobalt, red, yellow, green and brown. Formerly in W. Porter Ware collection. *Author's collection.*

Delft faience barber basin of the early 1800's. Formerly in the Ware collection. *Author's collection.*

owners and wig makers all were defeated in their attempts for the right to use the shiny brass bekkener (basin or bowl) to advertise their own shops.

SHAVING BASINS IN AMERICA

One of the great contributions in the preservation and adoption of the European shaving basin for the American culture was made by the Pennsylvania Germans and the Pennsylvania Dutch.

According to Edwin Atlee Barber, in his book "Tulip Ware of the Pennsylvania German Potters", first published in 1903, German emigrants began to arrive in Pennsylvania as early as 1683. Many of their old country German sayings and proverbs, quotations from the Bible, rhymes and mottoes and time-honored methods and decorative motifs were used, according to Mr. Barber, in the decorations of their pottery wares, even on some of the shaving basins.

In the absence of a popular literature during the 18th century, Mr. Barber further states that this "ceramic literature" was also a method of transmitting ideas resorted to for the amusement of the common people.

A noteworthy feature of their customs is that much of this early pottery was not only decorated but was embellished with the date the items were made, either in sgraffito or slip decoration.

In 1903, Mr. Barber reported that "the oldest known piece of slip ware found in Pennsylvania is dated 1733. This is a barber's basin, made to fit the neck of the person shaving during the process of lathering."

He further reports "A white faience jug of German origin, owned by a collector in Baden, bears on its front a colored design representing a barber shop. A customer is seated on a stool holding a shaving basin to his throat, while a Knight of the Razor stands beside him applying the lather. Above the picture is the inscription in block lettering," translated which says "God is the physician, and I his servant-When he helps me I heal right."

"The barber in those days was the doctor or chirurgeon, and was always ready to shave, bleed or leech his patients. The ceramic illustration described is of interest in showing the manner of using this ancient utensil."

Early-century use of the barber basin was widespread in all European countries and is evidenced by relics of those times and by

Top row (left to right): Oriental Export barber basin, 19th C., bearing the decoration of the old Ottoman Empire (Turkey). Spanish pottery barber basin, circa 1800-1850. Orange, green and brown decoration. *Author's Collection.*

Middle row (left to right): Chinese, Canton, XVII C. Enameled on metal. Spanish, XVIII C. Vitreous lustre; design in browning-red-gold with purplish tinge. *Bottom row:* French, XVIII century. Venus and cupid. Spanish XIX century. Shell-shaped basin. Reverse has 3 small cockle-shells for legs. *Mr. A. Lawrence Abel Collection.*

Top: Pennsylvania pottery (USA) 19th century, Tulip design, slip decorated.
Middle: Very rare shaped Spanish copper basin. Circa 1800. Inside is silver.
Author's collection.

Bottom: Aluminum itinerant barber basin. Circa 1890. Made in Temesvar, Rumania. Impressed in the metal is "Kegskemeti Sandor Temesvar". *Author's collection.*

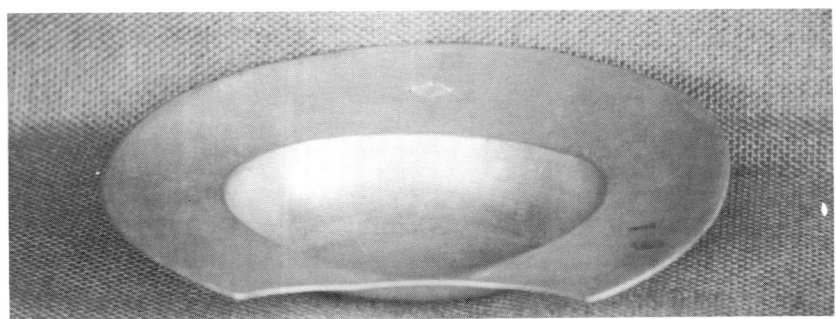

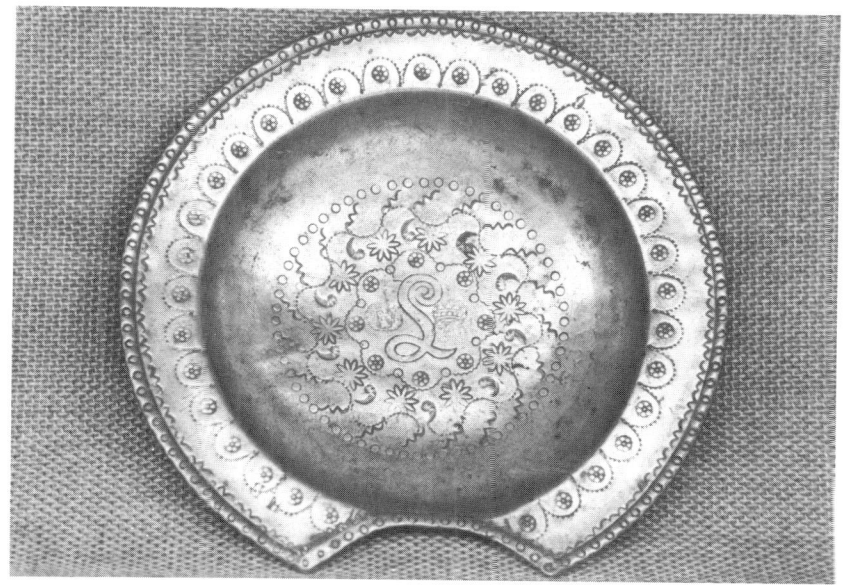

Top: Rare Pewter barber basin (9½" dia.) once belonging to the William Randolph Hearst collection. Purchased by W. Porter Ware in 1942 when Gimbels (NYC) was agent for disposing of many Hearst antiques. Reputedly the original owner was one of the Pope Leos. All designs hand-impressed. Makers mark inside. *Author's collection.*

French pottery, circa 1850, cobalt dot design, with soap indentation. *Author's collection.*

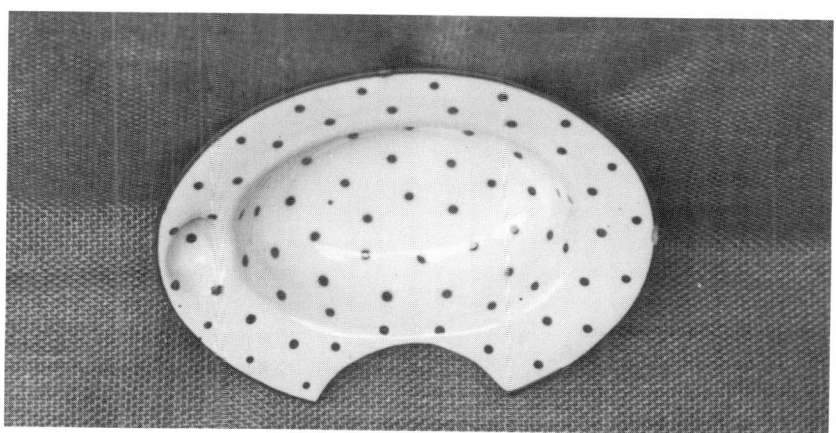

Left: Nineteenth century silver-over-brass basin. *Right:* Spanish brass basin, circa 1850. *Center:* Small aluminum basin (8" widest dia.), Rumania, circa 1890. *Author's Collection.*

Two 19th century European pewter basins. Smaller basis in 7½ inches (widest dia.) and came from Augsburg, Germany. Larger basin measures 14¼" diameter. *Author's Collection.*

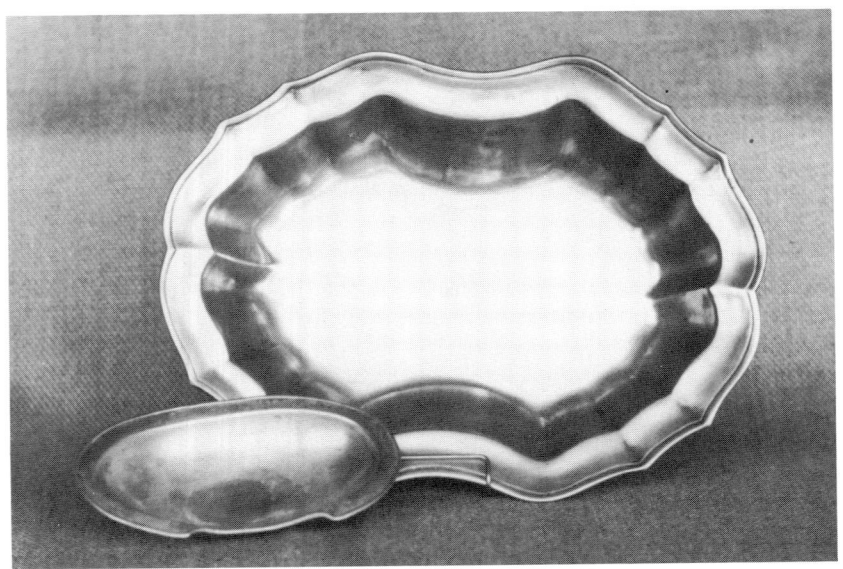

early engravings, woodcuts, and paintings picturing its uses. But in the United States, which was colonized several centuries later, little has been written or documented about their Americanized uses.

The first settlers in America were three different groups of colonists, establishing themselves in three widely separated locations. In 1607 there were the Virginia colonists who settled in Jamestown; in 1620 the New England colonists who settled in Plymouth, and the Pennsylvanian Dutch, under William Penn, in 1681.

The customs of all three colonies were no doubt quite different, both because of their ancestral traits and because of the varied climatical and physical environments in the new world. Although American history reveals little documented fact that early colonists used wooden shaving basins or mugs, it is only a reasonable deduction to assume that in some localities they did make these utensils from wood. There are too many overwhelming reasons that they should, as evidenced by the numerous wooden household utensils from that era.

In addition to the early settlers, emigrants from other nations, including England, France, Italy and other European countries likewise brought customs of shaving and the barber basins to the United States. Spendid examples of these basins are to be found in both museums and in private collections throughout the country. Also there were barber basins from the Orient—both Japanese and Chinese Export items.

They are also to be found in pewter, tin, brass, silver, copper and other metals, in addition to earthenware and porcelains, and according to Mr. A. Lawrence Abel, noted British physician-collector, were made of glass (Venice, Bohemia) and even papier mache and of skin (human or animal).

The shapes and sizes of old barber basins are as varied as their countries of origin. Some are round; others are oval. Some are deep while others are shallow. Others have a scalloped edge or rim; but most have a plain edge.

The usual distinguishing feature of those made after the early 1500's is the half-moon indentation on the rim of the basin. This was to enable the basin to be held close to the neck to catch all the surplus suds, during the lathering process. Some have a double indentation—on opposite sides of the basin (a double utility value). A few even have a small depression near the rim which could hold a small bit of soap, or was convenient for holding the basin, with the thumb in the depression. Still others had no depression on the rim, but had a small soap dish on the inside of the basin (with or without a drain hole). The Pennsylvania Germans made this type utensil in their Redware Pottery.

Top: White enamelware deep basin, cobalt rim, pedestal base, 10½ inches dia., 4 inches high. Probably late 19th century. *Lower: (left):* Swiss 18th C. basin, 8¼ inches dia. *Right:* Rare Pennsylvania redware, circa 1800 U.S.A., no indentation. Inside soap dish with drain hole. *Author's Collection.*

Very few of the basins had handles, although many basins had a small hole on the underneath side of the base or lower part of the basin, from which to hang the basin on the ceiling or wall when not in use. The metal basins usually had a small ring attached to the under side of the rim for that purpose. Still others were not intended to hang from the wall, and so were made with a sort of pedestal base that would allow the basin to set upright on a table or shelf.

Some basins also had a companion matching water pitcher from which probably evolved the later basin and pitcher toilet sets which became so common to everyone during the 18th and 19th centuries.

Among the much sought after basins are those which have two holes through the outer top rim, through which a long cord was threaded. The cord was extended behind the neck and tied, thus holding the basin in a convenient upright position in front of and below the chin.

Large French Majolica bowl dated 1793, colorfully decorated depicting a poor French peasant carrying a big load of church and state regalia and the inscription which translated says "I am tired of carrying this load". In the background is the Bastille and a lowly peasant's hovel. On the lower border decoration is the red Freedom cap (Phrygian cap) of the Revolution. The small bowl is brass, 5 inches in diameter, from upper New York state, and according to its owner dates to about 1840 and was for use on children. *Collection of Dr. David Maeth, M.D.*

Detail from a steel engraving, Arlequin Tooveraar en Barbier, showing a barbers' bowl in use; engraved by Peter Tanje' after a painting by Cornelis Troost; published by P. Fouquet, Jr., Amsterdam, dated 1758. *Courtesy ANTIQUES magazine, from the Roger Gerry Collection.*

PART I
Section 2

EARLY SHAVING SOAPS

Few people stop to realize the important and integral part that soap has played in the development and modernization of the United States, and particularly shaving soaps and their effects on the American male's countenance — that is, until the current bearded movement got underway.

Until the early part of the 19th century most of the soaps used in the United States were important from Europe, mainly from England and France. All soaps were not the same, for there were a variety of soap compounds manufactured for various purposes, such as mill soap, laundry soap, and of course shaving soap. The earliest American soap makers were generally known then as *"Soap and Candle Manufacturers"*, as listed in the early records, and some were listed as *"Fancy Soap Manufacturers"*.

Originally the popular name for shaving soap was *"saponaceous shaving compound"*, later as *shaving compound, shaving soap* and *shaving cream*. By the mid 1800's most of our shaving soaps were manufactured in the United States by various firms, many of which were located in Philadelphia. Some of the better known firms were Jules Hauel, X. Bazin, H. P. and W. C. Taylor, Wright, and Roussel.

But the best known manufacturer, a company still in business today, is The J. B. Williams Company, a name associated with men's shaving soap for well over 100 years the world over, and whose early recognition for the necessity of progressive advertising through methods of packaging, were evident almost from the firm's beginning.

Early shaving compounds in Europe were packaged in round lidded porcelain boxes or containers, in 2, 3 and 4-ounce sizes and usually bore transfer designs on the lids identifying the product and the manufacturer.

In the early 1840's the Williams Company is believed to have first imported these European lidded boxes for packaging their shaving soaps for the American market, although the firm today was unaware of this type of early packaging. Circumstances of continuously operating a large business for over a century and a quarter, not to mention the ravages time has on records, has shrouded much of the firm's early history. Interested collectors often turn up unique items of historical significance and interest through the perseverence of avidly following their hobbies.

Early J. B. Williams porcelain shaving cream container, bearing two-color (violet and brown) slip transfer design. *Author's collection.*

Rare "personalized" porcelain shaving soap box with owner's name hand-painted in gold. *Author's collection.*

Taylor's Shaving Compound porcelain box. Circa 1851-62. *Author's collection.*

First American-Made Shaving Soap

Thus it was the Williams Company that is credited with producing the first American shaving soaps for the general populace. And their early products were proclaimed as *"shaving cream"*, or the added emphasis of *"Swiss Violet Shaving Cream"* was used, as evidenced by the early container pictured. This added a new dimension of meaning in challenging the American male to try it and judge for himself its merits. And who could resist such a temptation to try the new product made by an American firm which was even now making such great inroads into the European trade market of men's shaving soaps?

The success of The Williams Company in this field was quickly realized, and during the ensuring two decades there arose an abundance of competitors in several of the larger cities and populated areas of the country. Packaging-advertising methods were copied by all in their over zealous attempts for customer recognition and acceptance, in order to gain a foothold in this fast-developing new American business. Each firm seemingly outdid the other, in producing shaving soaps packaged in the mode of the day, which was porcelain or china containers with the lids decorated with great eye-appealing colorful scenic slip transfers or wet-point engravings and worded messages proclaiming the high merits or many prize-winning virtues at Fairs and other competitive exhibitions.

By the early 1870's the enterprising barber supply companies, with their own china decorators specializing in the art of shaving mug decorating, in their own zealous attempt to create new markets, quickly dealt the death blow to lidded procelain shaving soap boxes. For as the business in barber shops developed, the need for this type of packaging became obsolete, except possible for home use. Soap manufacturers soon realized that they could sell their wares to the multitude of barber shops sans the box and thus realize a larger profit. Hence the form of packaging changed to printed paper wrappers for individually small orders or simply were unwrapped in large quantities.

In addition to the usual lidded type soap box with its decorated lid, *personalized soap boxes* with the owner's name lettered in gilt on the side, made their brief appearance in a few barber shops and for home use. This was almost simultaneous with the period of time of the rapid development and preferred use of the more colorful, handpainted and personalized barber shop type (trade emblems, secret societies, etc.) shaving mugs.

Thus their use in the United States spanned but a few brief years compared to the half to three-quarters century that barber shop shaving mugs were in vogue. Only a very few are known to exist today, and they occupy special niches in private collections, usually of shaving mug buffs. And, there are possibly some in museums around the country.

It is interesting to note, that, contrary to popular opinion, the term "shaving cream" is not just a recent innovation of TV advertising, but was used a hundred years ago.

"Williams Genuine Yankee Soap"
First Shaving Soap Manufactured in America

J. B. Williams — a name associated with shaving soap the world over, for well over a century, is reputed to have manufactured the first shaving soap in America, according to records and history of the present-day company. It was called "Williams Genuine Yankee Soap".

James Baker Williams attended the East Hartford Academy in 1833-34. When he was sixteen years of age in 1834, he left school to work as a clerk in the drugstore of F. & H. C. Woodbridge at Manchester Green, Connecticut.

Four years later, in 1838, when he was twenty, he became a part-owner of the drugstore and the name of the drugstore was changed to "Kenney & Williams."

Here he remained for two years, until 1840, when he sold his share of the drugstore, with the exception of the drug department. He next formed a partnership with his brother George W. Williams, calling the new business "Williams Brothers." It was here the two brothers began the manufacture of a variety of compounds, which at the time were sold by apothecaries.

Convinced of a great and increasing demand for a better quality of shaving soap than that being imported from Europe, the brothers began experimenting with soaps. Thus it was that their first marketed shaving soap, "Williams Genuine Yankee Soap", became a success, in the early 1840's.

In the beginning and for many years, the soap products manufactured by the Williams brothers were sold from house to house. In 1847 the business was divided, with George W. Williams taking the drug department and James B. Williams the shaving soap business.

In 1848 James B. Williams took another brother, William Stuart Williams into partnership and re-named the firm "J. B. Williams and Company". The original Yankee Soap, which at first was manufactured in square form, was later changed to a round cake to fit the

Top left to right. Wright's Gold Metal Rose Shaving Cream porcelain 2-oz. box, slip transfer design; X. Bazin 4-oz. box. *Author's Collection.*

Above and to right: Colorful multi-color slip transfer lid (performing bear) and bottom of Bear Grease (for the hair) porcelain box. *Author's collection.*

shaving mug, as business in barber shops developed, and special shaving soaps were introduced. Barbers' Bars containing so many cakes to the pound roll, were offered to the barber shops.

In 1876 the original Yankee Soap was registered, and together with shoe blacking and ink, formed the first products of J. B. Williams and Company. Company records do not reveal why this "Yankee Soap" was not registered until 1876. But this was the year of the Centennial, an important date to all Americans,· and countless items were registered, seemingly in an effort to become associated with the Centennial and thus gain an advantage (through advertising) over competitors. This also was the year that the "Yankee Shaving Mug" was made, as evidenced by the *mold-mark* on the bottom side. This mug, which more resembles a small cream pitcher, was made of white opaque glass and contained some degree of opalescence. (See picture in Glass Mugs Section.)

Here again present company officials are unable to locate old records as verification, but it is believed that this mug was made as a form of advertising for the *Yankee Soap* and the *Centennial*. It may also have been made of china or porcelain, although up until now I have been unable to locate one or to verify this suspicion.

About 1880, David W. Williams, a son of James B. Williams, established a factory across the street from J. B. Williams and Company. The younger Williams manufactured laundry and mill soap. This firm was called D. W. Williams and Company, and its principal product was a laundry soap powder called *Ivorine*. The name *Ivorine* was later sold to Proctor and Gamble, and in 1885 David Williams' company was absorbed into J. B. Williams and Company. Then in 1885 the name was changed to "The J. B. Williams Company," and James Baker Williams remained at the head of the business until his retirement, just a few years before his death in 1907 at the age of 89.

First Williams Shaving Stick

In 1890 the first Williams Shaving Stick appeared on the market. It was called "Travelers Leatherette" and was succeeded by the Hingecap Shaving Stick, the Doublecap Shaving Stick (patented 8-15-16) in an aluminum container, and the Holder Top Stick, which at first was in a nickle-plated case; the case was later made of plastic. The Holder Top Stick reigned supreme among progressive shavers for twenty years.

Lather Shaving Cream

Then came Lather Shaving Cream in *tubes*. Many years earlier Williams sold a shaving cream that was packaged in an imported

Below: J. B. Williams page ad from 1892 Koken catalog.

Above: Page from 1892 Koken catalog.

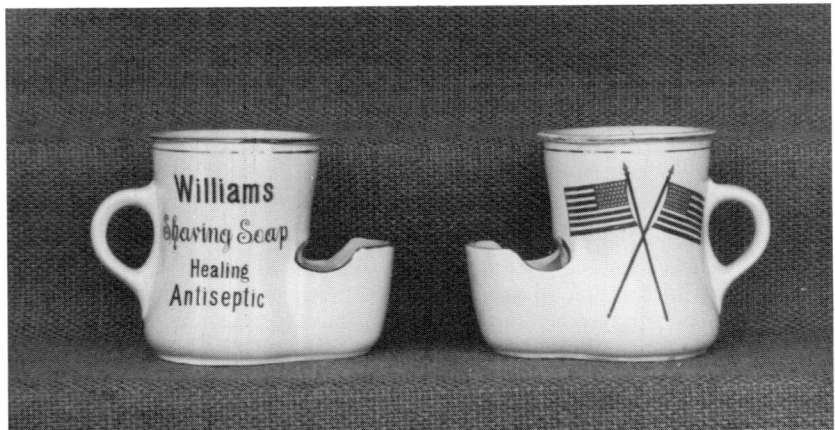

Early J. B. Williams Co. advertising type scuttle shaving mug. *Collection of Mr. and Mrs. Frank O. Dresner.*

porcelain jar, but it did not prosper. Then about 1905, a more modern, convenient, collapsible tube hit the popular fancy of the shaving public.

Aqua Velva Lotion

In 1918, one of the most noteworthy products of The J. B. Williams Company, was introduced and soon became the second largest volume product of the company. It was Aqua Velva — a lotion engineered expressly for *after shaving*, which has withstood the test of time and consumer whims for over fifty years now.

Brushless Shave Creams

In 1933 another radical innovation — Williams Glider No-Brush Shave — was introduced. Brushless shave creams eventually became a well-established form of shaving preparation.

Williams Lectric Shave was developed about 1939, and in a few years it became the number one J. B. Williams product. In 1953, following the trend of the new aerosol shaving creams, Williams added Instant Lather as its contribution.

Many other additions to the shaving preparation line have been made down through the years, including a broad selection of high grade toilet soaps, talcum powders, after shave talc, toilet waters, vanity cases, face powder, hair oils, hair dressings, pomades, etc.

J. B. Williams Company is a world-wide company. The foreign business is handled by its International Division through wholly or partially owned subsidiaries and branches. Some of the Williams products have not been developed in the Williams laboratories, but have been secured by merger with such companines as the Skol Company, the Conti Products Corporation, and Kreml, to name a few.

The J. B. Williams Company of Glastonbury, Connecticut — started by the efforts of a young lad of sixteen in 1834, when he went to work in a drugstore — was purchased in 1957 by Pharmaceuticals, Inc. of New Jersey. Pharmaceuticals, Inc. and soon changed its name to The J. B. Williams Company, Inc., and in 1961 it purchased a large appliance firm, Universal (L.F.C.). Thus James Baker Williams' name became the name of a company which operated widely in toiletries, pharmaceuticals, and appliances.

Author's collection.

Taylor Shaving Soap Boxes

In the early 19th century *saponaceous shaving compound* was to the barbering profession what the horse was to the carriage. This fancy phrase for soap played as integral a part in the development and modernization of the American male's countenance as did the straight razor and bay rum.

One of the early manufacturers of "saponaceous compound for shaving" was the H. P. & C. R. Taylor Company of Philadelphia, Penna., established in that city in 1820. The firm listed as "J. D. Taylor, Soaps & Candle Manufacturer at 11 Poplar Street" in the 1844 Philadelphia City Directory, became known as the "H. P. & C. W. Taylor Company, manufacturer of fancy soap" in 1845 and later as *"perfumers* on Logan Street above Wallace", and from 1851 to 1862 was located at 641 North 9th Street. Henry P. and Charles W. Taylor were the proprietors, along with William C. Taylor.

In 1862 the firm was first listed as the H. P. & C. R. Taylor Company, and operated under that name until 1872. From 1873 until 1883 the company was known as the C. R. Taylor Company and listed the location first at 500 Franklin Street and later at 703 Buttonwood Street. The firm is not listed in any of the books that give historical sketches of Philadelphia firms, according to The Historical Society of Pennsylvania; consequently nothing is known of the company after 1883.

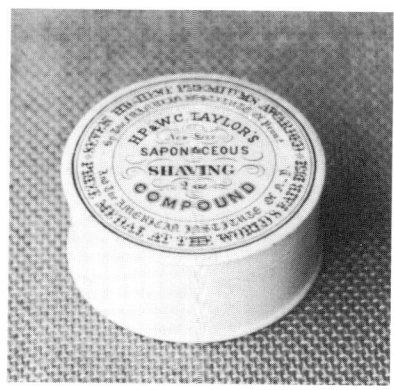 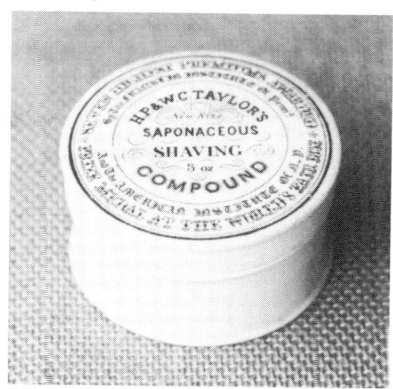

Taylor 2-oz. porcelain soap box. *Author's collection.*

Taylor 3-oz. porcelain soap box *Author's collection.*

In business for just over sixty years, the firm's product, packaged in porcelain containers and decorated with early transfer prints, (some in color and some in black & white) played an important part in the development of shaving habits in America.

This firm's porcelain containers of Saponaceous Compound for Shaving are much sought after by both collectors and museums. Such soap boxes are considered by some buffs to be the forerunner of the porcelain shaving mug.

The container picturing the man before a mirror applying soap to his face in preparation to shaving is white porcelain, and the lid is decorated with a lavender-colored slip transfer. It is a 3-ounce container and the wording "3-oz." is impressed in the bottom side. (Note: all boxes are not so impressed.)

The larger 4-ounce size is 2" high and 4' in diameter and the lid is completely covered with Old English and fancy lettering in a circle around the outside edge, extolling the virties of this "new size, 4 oz. saponaceous shaving compound..' This wording reads "Seven Highest Premiums Awarded — By The Franklin Institute of Penna. And the American Institute of N.Y. — Prize Medal At the World's Fair 1851." (Note: The Franklin Institute Fair was in Philadelphia in 1846.)

There doubtless exists other soap containers, similar to these two examples, made by this firm which was in the manufacturing business for well over a half century; they could bear any of the aforementioned company names.

Section 3
American Primitive Pottery Shaving Mugs

Left: "Rockingham type" shaving mug; yellow ware base with dark brown slip applied over to produce mottled effect, Circa 1850; probably New Jersey origin, 4 inches height, 4½ inches dia. *Right:* Redware shaving mug; red clay base with dark brown slip coat applied over; Circa 1860, Pennsylvania origin, 3¾ inches height, 4½ inches dia. *Courtesy Pennsylvania Farm Museum of Landis Valley.*

Rockingham type shaving mug made at Bennett Bros., Baltimore, Md., circa 1853. *Collection of Mrs. Fern Trimm.*

Extra large shaving mug. Height 4⅝ inches, top dia. 6¼ inches. Light yellow ware base with light tan slip applied, probably Virginia origin, Circa early 1800's. *Author's collection.*

Top row left to right: Early Redware base with light brown slip, sgraffito decoration, probably Pennsylvania origin, Circa 1800. Stoneware shaving mug with dark brown slip on outside, Circa 1800-1850. Unmarked Bennington circa 1850.

Second row left to right: Common brown slip-ware shaving mug, Circa 1800-1825. Redware with brown slip glaze inside and outside. Probably Ohio origin. Circa 1800. Spongeware Mug. *Collection of Mrs. Fern Trimm.*

Early stoneware, handle-less shaving mug. Grey base with cobalt decoration and name "E. M. Williams", salt glaze clear slip, dark brown slip applied inside. Unknown origin, Circa early 1800's. Ht. 2⅝ inches, top dia. 3½ inches. *Author's collection.*

PART I
Section 4
Pewter, Brittania, Silverplate, Tin and Aluminum Mugs

Of all the shaving mugs known to have been made of metal there is perhaps none as scarce nor as expensive as the genuine old pewter ones. Good old pewter is scarce and expensive regardless of whether it is a large charger, a beaker or whatever. And the genuine old pewter shaving mugs, particularly those made by early American pewterers, are the most difficult to find.

In recent years with most genuine old pewter items already gathered together in collections, there has been a tendency for many people to associate Brittania or German White Metal with pewter. And as a consequence many of the latter items are often advertised and sold as pewter. This may be done by design or unknowingly. So, if you own a pewter mug (or suspect it is pewter) or you are earnestly looking for a genuine old pewter shaving mug, it would be to your benefit to become acquainted with the differences by seeking the advice of a pewter collector or a reputable dealer who specializes in pewter would also prove advantageous, and probably save you money in the end. But by all means do a little research to know what the possible consequences are before you embark upon a determined effort to clean it up or shine it. You may be sorry if you realize too late that you overcleaned it. No one in his right mind would strip down a rare antique table to its original bare wood, and neither should all traces of character and patina be removed from your pewter mug.

During the 1870's, when silverplated wares had reached their popularity in the United States, countless varieties of shaving mugs and shaving stands were silver-plated, and were no doubt highly prized possessions of many an American male. Silverplating of shaving mugs continued in vogue for many years, even into the early twentieth century, as evidenced by the quantities still available at antique shops around the country.

Many of them were made in the United States by American silversmiths, and their circa can be checked in any good book on silver marks. They were also produced in Europe, especially in Germany for the growing American market. The cheaper ones as well as the more expensive ones were readily available in all of the early mail order catalogs.

There were also sterling silver and coin silver mugs made in America. And even gold-plated ones, for the most discriminating male, or for the man who had everything. Some were nickel-plated. There were tin shaving mugs and mugs made of aluminum as well.

Quadruple Silverplate shaving mug made by James W. Tufts, Boston. Soap compartment with brush holder is detachable. Engraved "George Schoen from his Clerks 1893". *Author's collection.*

Quadruple Plate shaving mug made by Adelph Silverplate Co., New York, Copyrighted 1892. Decoration floral with six cherubs. *Author's collection.*

Front and Side View "The Utility Shaving Cup", made by James W. Tufts, Boston. Silverplated, features soap storage drawer, straight razor storage (between cup and handle), inside water and soap compartments. *Collection of Mrs. Fern Trimm.*

Quadruple plated, made by Biggins-Rogers Co., Walingford, Ct., Patented Jan. 18, 1910. Sterling Handle brush. *Author's collection.*

Silverplate shaving mugs from *James A. Keller collection.*

Gold-Plated Shaving Mug and brush (milk glass insert). *Author's collection.*

Early pewter shaving mug. English origin, circa 1790-1820. Brittania handled brush. Carved bone handle razor (original owner G. F. Powell, the author's grandfather). Mug height without lid 4⅝ inches (with lid 5¾ inches), inside dia. of top 3⅛ inches. *Author's collection.*

Two views of English Brittania Shaving mug marked "James Dixon and Sons Sheffield," Circa 1810. *Collection of Mr. and Mrs. Frank O. Dresner.*

Silverplate shaving mugs from *Author's collection.*

During their heyday, the metal mugs (particularly the silverplated ones) were as popular as the highly decorated procelain mugs, and were mass-produced in great quantities in literally hundreds of shapes and sizes Some were patented and had mirrors attached. Many were in the shapes of shaving stands, either with or without a lid covering the soap dish. Some had a brush rest. Many were plain, but many were also very fancy in decoration, and others were quite unique.

Metal shaving mugs, shaving pots and shaving stands are one of the most overlooked or neglected areas by mug collectors today. They are still available and in certain locations even abundant, although in many instances the silver is badly worn.This likely accounts for the fact that the prices are still quite modest compared to other types of mugs. But for the buff who wants to assemble a worthwhile collection at a moderate cost here is a golden opportunity. Re-silvering is generally acceptable and not very expensive, especially if small items are grouped together in a one-lot job. And the total amount spent for the collection, plus the cost of re-silvering (if needed) is usually nominal.

Even a small collection of varied shapes and sizes has great eye appeal when displayed in a proper surrounding.

Civil War Tin Shaving Mugs. *Author's collection.*

CIVIL WAR TIN SHAVING MUGS

There are many types, styles or shapes of "tin shaving mugs" in existence today. Traditionally they are called "Civil War Tin Shaving Mugs" or just plain "Civil War Shaving Mugs". But not much has been said about them heretofore.

However, according to Lt. Colonel Bill Larkin (USAF), who is both a student of Military History and a considered expert on the Civil War, they are rightfully placed in this category and are genuine old relics of that era, having been made by a number of different firms who had contracts for the manufacture of hundreds of items for the armies of both sides during the great war between the states. They are listed in documents of these manufacturers.

At least one book on Civil War collector items pictures a few examples of these tin shaving mugs. And there are Civil War buffs who claim that the taller types of mugs were used by the officers, while the smaller ones were used by the enlisted men. Although not a student nor an expert on the history of the Civil War, it is the considered opinion of the author that the soldiers used whatever was available at the time — in many cases a tin drinking cup was probably pressed into service as a substitute.

Civil War Tin Shaving Mugs. *Collection of Mrs. Fern Trimm.*

Civil War Tin Shaving Mugs. *Courtesy Pennsylvania Farm Museum of Landis Valley.*

Although this author is not an expert on Civil War, it is believed that the sizes (and perhaps even the shapes) of these old tin mugs were more or less determined by the manufacturers, and since there were many firms with contracts for furnishing military accoutrements there were many different sizes and shapes made, without too much regard for specifications, as long as they were furnished. For if the Civil War boots were made "squared-toed" (to fit either foot), and the rifles were not made for "left-handed" soldiers (a left-handed soldier firing the rifle or musket from his left shoulder would have received, and probably did, a bad powder burn when the gun was fired,) it isn't likely that either army was so concerned with having a cheap tin shaving cup made just for the comfort of the common left-handed soldier.

As a general rule these tin mugs are found in surprisingly good condition, practically rust-free — this condition due no doubt to the heavier tin content and because the Union soldier, upon returning home after the war, usually placed his tin shaving mug, together with his rifle, uniform, etc., in storage in the basement or attic, where they lay undisturbed for generations.

These mugs have until recently, been rather plentiful, but are becoming more difficult to locate because of the growing interest in antiques, especially Civil War buffs and amateur tole-painters around the country, who like to decorate them with their own ideas of flowered motifs. (it is doubtful that during the Civil War any of these tin mugs were decorated with more than mud from the battlefields — or the blood some soldier spilled for his country while shaving with a long razor. And the writer has heard some accounts of these tin mugs being pressed into service as a coffee cup or whiskey mug during the war.)

All have pouring spouts (which could also have been used as a razor receptacle) fashioned in various shapes — large, small, wedge-shaped, square and even cylindrical or conical — soldered to the mug itself, which is cylindrical or conical (and perhaps even square). Handles of varying sizes and descriptions may also be found on the mugs — in varying positions relative to the spouts. Originally it is believed that all such mugs had a shallow tin insert (which fits into the top of the mug). This would have been used to hold the soap when mixing the lather.

It is doubtful that these items have been "reproduced" because few people even know of their existence, and they can still be bought for a modest price.

Although the writer has never seen a tin mug that is dated (by the mold), this is an interesting point to bear in mind, because many old tin items are dated, and it is entirely likely that some of them were dated — with a date of manufacture, and possibly even the name or initials of the manufacturer.

Aluminum shaving mugs. *Author's collection.*

Aluminum Shaving Mugs

Although the chemical identity of aluminum was not known until 1746 and for decades men attempted to isolate aluminum to create pure aluminum, the first American patent for making aluminum was applied for in 1886.

However it was not until the 1890's that consumer acceptance of this metal suddenly caught on. Among the many items made of aluminum were of course — shaving mugs, in various and sundry sizes and shapes. For awhile the aluminum shaving mug was quite popular among barbers — one of the reasons being that because the metal was a good conductor of heat (applied directly to it), the aluminum shaving cup or mug kept lots of warm soap lather available. This was very important during that period of time, when you realize that the barber shops of those days did not have the plumbing facilities of hot running water such as today's modern equipped shop. Then the barber often heated water in a kettle, usually on a wood burning or oil burning lamp stove, or any one of several types of small burners.

Aluminum mugs were used in the home and in barber shops. Their use in barber shops was generally as a bench mug, where they were owned by the barber (as opposed to being owned by a customer), and were kept on the barber's work bench with other tools of his trade, rather than in the mug rack with mugs belonging to the regular customers.

Section 5

Glass Shaving Mugs

Although the early records of many American glass manufacturers may be vague or incomplete and very difficult to locate, the fact that these early glassmakers did make glass shaving mugs or shaving cups, just as they made other household utensils, is evidenced by the presence of the mugs themselves. The exact date they were first made is impossible to trace. On some the date appears as part of the mold itself, or as a patent date. Earlier than that however, it is near impossible to establish definite dates from limited records.

Early references to "shaving glasses" in the larger cities and centers of society, lend credulity to the belief that these references were in fact references to glass cups or similar containers used for shaving.

The Sandwich Historical Society, although it has no records of shaving mugs having been made at Sandwich, reports that one of its members has a clear glass shaving mug that was made in the old factory. It is small — about the size of an over-grown punch cup with a small handle, but with sides that slant in. And it was made by one of the best workmen in the factory for his son. It has always been used as a shaving mug and for no other purpose.

P. T. Barnum's shaving mug, made of French Opaline Glass has to be one of the *greatest on earth*, especially if you are a mug collector, a collector of circus items, or an art glass collector.

The author purchased it in the winter of 1965 from Ellen Donahue, who upon learning of my intentions to feature it in a book some day succeeded in tracing information from its former owner, Mr. Bernard J. Satz, concerning the mug. Mr. Satz interestingly wrote that sometime in 1941 or 1942 "Ruth and I attended a Broadway Show" in which Alfred Lunt and Lynn Fontaine played in "There Shall Be No Night".

"In the program, there was an ad of a sale for *BUNDLES FOR BRITAIN* in a vacant store off Fifth Avenue, around 45th to 48th Street, in New York City. We taxied up next A.M., found the place being run by some very lovely high class Englishwomen. I spotted the mug, and being in show biz, I grabbed it. Could have sold it that minute as another man was making up his mind to purchase it. The saleslady told me not to lose the letter that went with the mug." (This letter referred to, states that "it was given to me by the widow of P. T. Barnum as her husband's shaving mug.")

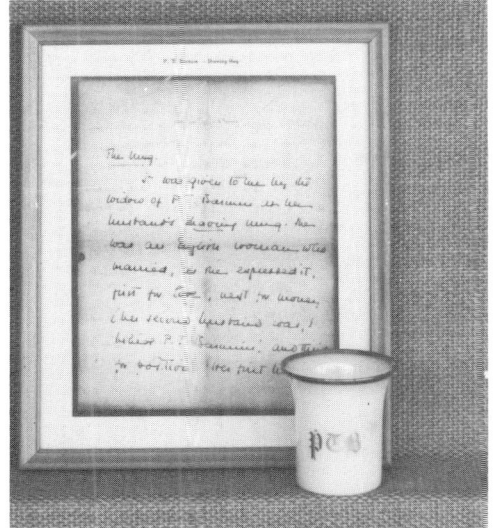

P. T. Barnum's shaving mug and letter of authentication. Brilliant French Opaline Glass, 3 inches ht., flared top rim dia 2¾ inches, gold rim and initials. *Author's collection.*

Pair of 1867 patented shaving mugs, made of milk glass. Pattern of mug on left is known as Viking Pattern or Centennial Pattern. *Author's collection.*

The next mugs pictured are the patented milk glass mugs of 1867 which have the inscription "Patent Shaveing Mug, July 16, 1867" on the bottom, from the original mold. Note the spelling "Shaveing".

The same patent mug was also used for making the "Viking Pattern" milk glass mug pictured. (Refer to the chapter on "Patented Mugs" for details on this pattern.) The quality of this glass varies from a strong white opacity to a glass which has distinctive opalescence. The opalescent mugs are believed to be the "white opal ware" glass referred to in the early barber supply catalogs. Although I have not seen other patterns on this particular early shaving mug, it is entirely possible that they do exist.

Left to right: White opaque glass (milk glass) shaving mug patented Sept. 20, 1870; "Yankee Shaving Mug" of 1876 made of white opalescent glass. *Author's collection.*

The pitcher-type milk glass mug with the head of a lion on the side bears the wording "PAT. SEP 20, 1870" on the bottom. The mug originally came with a 2⅜ inch glass insert for the soap compartment. Several types of mugs bearing this patent date are evident, but this is the only one known to exist in milk glass.

The "Yankee Shaving Mug", resembling a cream pitcher, is undoubtedly the "white opal ware" listed in early catalogs. (Today called milk glass.) The mold mark on the bottom reads "Yankee Shaving Mug — 1876". A fan-shaped design and light scrolls decorate the front portion under the spout. On each side the molded head of what appears to be the "head of the Gorgon Medusa", a winged monster from Greek Mythology, which had serpents for hair, although the detailed features leave a lot to be desired.

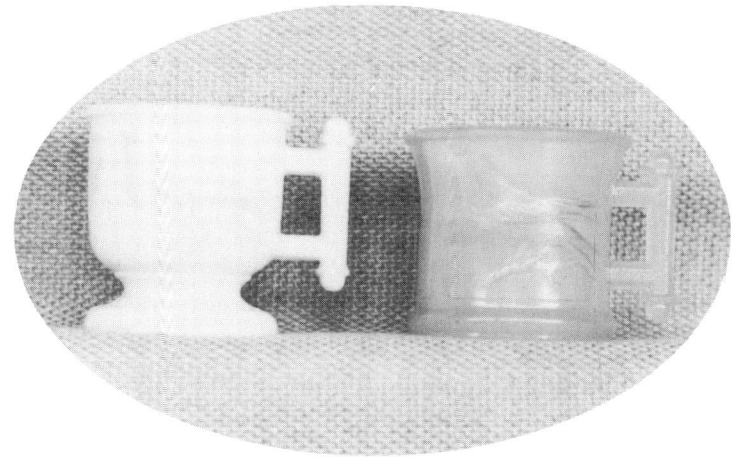

Shaving mugs — Robin and Wheat pattern. *Left:* White opaque milk glass. *Right:* pink clambroth glass. Barber pole handles. Circa 1870. *Author's collection.*

The 2-mold milk glass shaving mug with a pedestal base and a "barber pole" handle is another early mug but has no date or name on the bottom to help identify it. It does have a "Robin and Wheat" pattern on the sides, and is white, very opaque and has a bluish color or caste when held to the light. Other shades might also be found. (Amber-colored glass mugs of this pattern have been seen, in several sizes, and it is not known if the amber ones are genuine old mugs.)

White opaque milk glass, swan design shaving mug. Circa 1870. *Author's collection.*

Historical type opaque milk glass shaving mug. President James A. Garfield is featured on one side; Mrs. Garfield on the reverse. *Author's collection.*

An extremely rare early glass shaving mug is the peculiar "toilet shaped" heavy glass mug reported to have been made by Adams and Company in 1880 as a Presidential campaign novelty. Slightly only more than 2½ inches high, it features a remarkable extruded likeness of President James A. Garfield (side view, showing a full business or professional man's beard trim, sometimes called the "Van Dyke" or "Napoleon" beard"), and a 6-leaf sprig of ivy on each side of his head. It is a 2-compartment mug with the handle under the smaller compartment. This mug was made in both white opaque (milk glass) glass and also in clamwater glass (sometimes called clambroth glass). It is also reported to have been made in pink clamwater glass. These mugs may also be found as plain, unadorned mugs. In the clamwater glass mug, the smaller compartment is round instead of oval.

Another variety of this mug exists, and it bears the likeness (full face view) of Mrs. Garfield, framed in sprays of laurel, on the opposite side.

President Garfield, who served as President for only four months before his assassination in 1881, was honored by memorial items made in glass. And it is supposed that some of these varieties in shaving mugs were memorial items also. Garfield was the first United States Presidential candidate to appear before the populace and speak in his own behalf, a present-day custom among all politicians.

Historical type clambroth glass shaving mug. President Garfield on one side; other side blank. *Author's collection.*

Another early glass mug is the "Cherub and Arches" pattern, which is a beautiful white opalescent glass featuring six arched panels, each with a different cherub surrounded by graceful vines of grapes, with a stippled background. On some of these mugs, the arches were originally decorated in gold to accentuate the details of design.

Left: Brilliant white opalescent glass shaving mug (Cherubs and Arches): *Right:* White opaque milk glass shaving mug known as the "Unique", "Mephistopheles" and "Devil Head" mug. Circa 1875-1885. *Author's collection.*

Author's collection.

The likeness of George Washington also appears on both sides of a clear glass mug. The head of Washington is encircled by beads between two laurel branches.

Still another early glass shaving mug is the "Litho Label or Glass Label" mug in a beautiful shade of light blue glass, sometimes called blue milk glass. There is a recessed area on the side which accomodates the lithographic label and thin glass covering, which are both glued onto the mug.

Left: Clambroth glass with silver-deposit initials, design and date (1924). *Right:* "Holzsager Antiseptic Shaving Cup", Pat'd. Nov. 3, 1908, made of Ruby Glass. *Collection of Mr. and Mrs. Frank O. Dresner.*

Author's collection.

Then there's the large clear glass Amole Cup shaving mug with the patented device in the bottom for holding the cake of soap, to prevent it from slipping while making lather. It is decorated with a gold "Amole Cup" emblem or medallion on the side. On the reverse side is the molded raised wording "Licensed For Use Only With Amole Shaving Soap". Near the bottom is the wording "Pat. May 14, 1907" molded in the glass.

Clambroth glass shaving mug with silver-deposit design and enameled "red" cross. Circa 1920's. Front view of 1867 patented shaving mug showing the 1876 patent design "Centennial" or "Viking". *Author's collection.*

61

About this same year we find highly decorated clamwater mugs, of regular size and shape but with silver overlay designs, such as the one pictured. In addition to the sterling overlay it has a red cross, trimmed in black, hand-painted on the front of the mug opposite the handle.

Later there was a variety of plain white opaque (milk glass) mugs, and plain clear glass mugs, both with and without decoration. These mugs are now beginning to become scarce, although they can still be bought for a very nominal amount, compared to the older more unique glass mugs. Some mugs have a raised bottom (from the base), which is supposed to have certain "thermal" qualities for keeping the lather warm.

Stylish shaving mug with brush rest. Made of white opal ware (glass). Called "Leader" in catalogs of the 1880's.

Top row: Opaque white milk glass shaving mugs. *Middle row:* different shades of clambroth glass mugs. *Bottom row: (left)* milk glass with decal, circa 1930-40; *(3rd from left)* 10-sided milk glass mug marked "J. Handel - Pat'd. Feb. 9, '09 No. 911878". *Author's collection.*

Section 6
Patented Shaving Mugs

The United States Constitution gives each American the right to patent his inventions. Congress created a patent commission in 1790 for the promotion of useful arts and sciences. It originally consisted of the Attorney General, the Secretary of State and the Secretary of War. In 1836 the American Patent System was established and the Patent Office built. The Patent Office of today is under the jurisdiction of and is an integral part of the Department of Commerce, and issues some 50,000 patents yearly.

The first patent was granted on July 31, 1790; it was signed by George Washington as President and Thomas Jefferson as Secretary of State. Some seventy years from that date, more than 66,000 individual patents had been granted before the first shaving mug patent was issued in 1860 to Thomas E. Hughes of Birmingham, Penna., for a metal mug which had a movable soap compartment and a hinged lid which contained a mirror. In the ensuing twenty-odd years many porcelain mugs with mirrors glued into the sides were made in Germany, probably under this same patent. And although rare and difficult to locate, these mirrored porcelain mugs are not as valuable as the original first metal patented mugs.

During the ensuing 100 years another 96 patents for shaving cups or shaving mugs were granted by the U. S. Patent Office. The total through September, 1959 was 97 patents.

Centuries ago English Kings gave to some of their subjects written documents granting special privileges or favors. These were called "letters patent". However the United States set a standard for all the world to follow in creating its system of patents with special emphasis upon the rights of the inventor. The United States has always led the world in the resulting success and importance of inventions, and through international agreement with many of the countries of the world, has shared these patent rights. Consequently one will find that many of the Patented shaving cups and shaving mugs were originated in foreign lands, although the greater portion were issued to people in the United States.

Few collectors or dealers realize that so many varied patents for shaving mugs ever existed. And although the information is a matter of public record among countless archives and documents in our Nation's Capitol, it is an endless task to search out information on all of them. There is no quick way of learning about all of them or of which ones were ever actually put to practical use as manufactured items.

This then largely accounts for the fact that patented shaving mugs, as collectibles, have never reached their proper status. When an item is shunned by collectors, most dealers likewise are disinterested, and such items retire to obscurity until more knowledge becomes available and a new interest is created among the collectors. When this occurs, the resurrected patented shaving mugs will be brought from obscurity to a more prominent place on the dealers' shelves and show windows. The patented mugs may never reach the high peak of popularity of the colorful trade designs mugs, but they are even now an untapped source as collectibles for shaving mug collectors.

Perhaps the information contained in this book, limited though it may be, will create the stimulus needed, to start the resurrection. Only a few of the many patents issued for shaving mugs are contained herein. Some of them are known definitely to exist, because they are in the author's collection or have been seen in collections of other collectors. Others have not yet been found but are believed to exist as manufactured items. And, some are doubtful items of manufacture. But this is what really makes for the real challenge and excitement of collecting — never knowing exactly what unusual patented shaving mug may turn up.

The second patent ever granted by the United States goverment for a shaving mug was on July 16, 1867 — issued to George P. Brooks and James McGrady, both of Boston, Mass. The patent claim was for an "improvement in shaving mugs. . .combining a soap receptacle with a mug" — with the soap compartment in a convenient position above the water compartment.

It was six years (on September 13, 1873) before the next patent was issued. This one was for separate "receptacles" (3 compartments) for "the shaving brush, soap, and water", and was granted to William Sawyer of Boston, Mass. Two years later (April 14, 1875) a patent for a "shaving-cup made of detachable sections" (handle detaches from cup) was granted to David Heston of Philadelphia, Penna.

During this period of time many varieties of shaving mugs were manufactured under the patent of July 16, 1867. They were made of glass, china, pottery and silverplate. Those made of glass were what we call "milk glass" today, although most glass manufacturers of the 1880 period referred to the glass as "white opal", "opal", or as "hot cast porcelain", according to Mr. A. Christian Revi's book "American Pressed Glass and Figure Bottles" and "Spinning Wheel" magazine. Atterbury & Company of Pittsburgh, Penna., and most of the other mid-western glass manufacturers made white opal glassware in the latter part of the 19th century, while New England glass manufacturers also used it as early as 1840 and as late as 1890, according to Mr. Revi. Early barber supply catalogs of the same period listed such glass shaving mugs as "white opal ware". All glass mugs manufactured under this patent are believed to contain the patent date on the bottom as a part of the mold. (The date is raised or "embossed".)

The first of these milk glass mugs was plain, without any decoration or ornamentation — until sometime after November 21, 1876, when, according to Mr. Revi (The Spinning Wheel for October, 1961), a *patent design* was issued to John H. Hobbs, Wheeling, West Virginia. This design featured a "bearded and helmeted head of a Roman warrior". The factory name of this pattern was "Centennial", possibly in tribute to the Centennial Year Anniversary of the nation's independence, while the common nomenclature was "Viking".

It was obvious then, that these mugs containing the patented "Viking Pattern", were not manufactured until 1876, even though they bear the shaving mug patent date of "1867" on the bottom. And these Viking shaving mugs must surely have been made by Hobbs, Brochunier and Company, which began as Hobbs, Barnes and Company of Wheeling, W. Va., in 1845, since they bear that firm's patented "Centennial" design, and it is known that the firm began production of pressed glass as early as 1865.

Under this same patent (July 16, 1867) we find shaving mugs made of white ironstone china — all of the same shape, but in various sizes. Note their similarity in appearance to the glass mugs manufactured under the same patent.

Left to right: Ironstone Shaving Mug bearing the mark "Patented July 16, 1867 Howland & Jones Importers, Boston". White opaque glass (milk glass) made under the same patent. *Author's collection.*

Three sizes of the July 16, 1867 patent shaving mug, made of ironstone. *Author's collection.*

Early hand-painted porcelain mug patterned after the patent mugs above. *Author's collection.*

Three different sizes of the ironstone mugs are in the author's collection. All bear the wording "Patented July 16, 1867" stamped under the glaze on the bottom. In addition, one such mug bears the inscription of one of Boston's early importers — "Howland & Jones, Importers, Boston", while another bears the name "Combination Mug" and the patent date. Still another was the "Excelsior" mug, which was manufactured under the patent date of September 20, 1870. The patentees were apparently well supplied with distributors for their patent. The names "Combination Mug," "Excelsior," and possibly others, refers to trade names or marks used by various distributors, as wholesalers (merchants) often had their "marks" or names placed on items they sold.

Then of course there were obviously similar shaving mugs manufactured, which were "copies" from the originals, or which failed to use the "patent date" reference. An example of this would be the heavy china mug pictured.

Smith Brothers

The Centennial Year of 1876 was a noteworthy occasion for the Smith Brothers of Boston and Cambridge, Massachusetts because it not only marked a hundred years for the United States, but it was the year John W. Smith was granted his first patent for a shaving mug and the seventh year in business for himself and brother James. On his patent application, filed November 24, 1876, he listed as assigner both himself and his brother James Smith of Cambridge.

'Prior to 1870, when the firm of Smith Brothers, Cutlers, was first established, James Smith had worked as a blacksmith from 1843, and in 1853 formed a partnership in the cutlery business with a man named Schachtebek (who had been in the cutlery business since 1846). The firm was known as Schachtebek and Smith, Cutlers, Boston, Massachusetts.

The firm's address was at 19 Hawley Street, Boston, from 1855 until 1864, when James Smith was listed as a "surgical instrument maker" in the city directory.

From 1870 when the firm of Smith Brothers, Cutlers was founded, until 1880, the location was at 152 Washington Street, when the offices were moved to a larger location to accomodate expanded business activities; in 1880 their business was "cutlery and hairdressers' supplies (barber supplies).

An old supply catalog of the firm, issued in 1888, lists their address at 349 Washington Street and specified that the company was "manufacturers, importers and dealers" in all kinds of Barber Supplies, cutlery, toilet articles and Fancy Goods — with the accent on *Barbers' Supplies.*

Ten pages of the catalog were devoted to Koken's Barber chairs, the first one pictured being "Koken's Patent Reclining Chair (Pat. Oct. 5, 1881) with cane seat and back, made of black walnut with nickel-plated trimmings plus arms and headrest, priced at $30." Later models of "Reclining and Revolving" chairs were also pictured, which had "foot pedals" for changing from a sitting to a reclining position. The catalog also contained the announcement that although Smith Brothers had "sold many of the Koken chairs during the past few years" and because of the "satisfactory proofs of their excellence", had now become the sole agent for Koken chairs in Pennsylvania, New York, the New England States and Canada.

By 1887 only John W. Smith was listed with the firm, and in 1905 the firm was reduced to a second floor room. The last mention of John

Smith in the Boston directory was in 1909, with the company apparently dissolved then or the following year.

Patented Shaving Mugs

The patented shaving mugs designed by John Smith were quite unique and very worthwhile from a utility standpoint. The claims for the first patent in 1876 were "having its soap receptacle permanently fixed to and arranged aside of its water reservoir" and "having a discharging nose or spout to project from the water reservoir over the soap receptacle."

The following year, in a patent filed on November 12, 1877, the additional claim was for having "extending upward from its upper edge two projections" for the purpose of "supporting a brush handle when laid between them". The partition between the soap and water receptacles was likewise notched, for holding the brush. (A close examination of several such mugs in the author's collection reveals little difference, if any, between the actual shapes of the mugs manufactured under the two separate patents, and it is therefore concluded that the latter patent claim was to protect a utility value (of holding the brush — laying between the two compartments) that had gone un-noticed when the first patent had been granted).

The decorations are varied on these patented mugs. Some are applied transfer prints (decals) of flowers and some are hand-painted floral decorations. In addition, some have gold stripes and/or bands on the top rim and lower base. Others are plain, except for gold stripes or bands. They are all quite rare, regardless of the type of decoration. Not all of them have the patent dates on the bottom. These that do however, are usually transfer prints in the color or colors used for the side decoration. All are under the glaze. These mugs are porcelain, and usually have a "crazed" effect due to age and the base materials used in their manufacture.

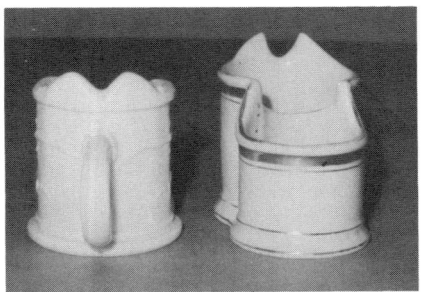

Front and Rear View of 1876-77 mugs. *Author's collection.*

As in the case of the earlier patent of 1876, the patentees of this particular patent evidently leased the patent rights, for we find, in addition, another mug manufactured under this patent with the name "The Requisite" appearing on the bottom.

Glass Mugs

These mugs were also made in white opaque glass (termed milk glass by collectors today). At least two patterns are known to exist in this white opaque glass on these patented shaving mugs.

One pattern I call *"Hinged Handle and Scroll"* because the extruded hinge design is located at the top of the mug, extending from the handle to the mug itself, and this seems to be a good descriptive name. Belknap s book "MILK GLASS", published by Crown Publishers, Inc., refers to this pattern as "Hinge and Scroll", and it is also known as the "Hinge Pattern" by some collectors of pattern glass.

Hinged Handle and Scroll design white opal ware glass (Opalescent), with mold mark on bottom "Pat Dec 26 1876". *Author's collection.*

The other pattern I call *"Centennial Flower"* purely as a means of future identification purposes, since it fits the period of time (1876-77) during which it was obviously made and used. To my knowledge this pattern is different from other similar flower type patterns, and has yet to be found pictured in any old glass company catalogs or listed in any book on pattern glass.

The opaque white glass mugs bear the patent dates from the original molds, embossed on the bottom-side of the mugs. The oldest mark shows "PAT DEC 26 1876", and the later one shows the working "PAT. DEC. 26 1976 AND DEC. 18 1877", forming a 2-inch circle.

Three varieties of opaqueness in these mugs are known to exist. The first and oldest is made of *white opal ware*. (This term is mentioned in early barber supply catalogs as late as the 1880's and is believed to have existed at least as early as the 1860's or earlier.)

The other two varieties are both much more opaque and whiter in appearance than the "white opal ware", but have a greenish caste or tint or the appearance of *white agate glass*.

Although all mugs made under these two early patents are quite rare, those made of glass are usually more difficult to find and are usually more expensive to buy than those made of porcelain, due to the fact that they are sought by collectors of milk glass and pattern glass, as well as shaving mug collectors.

Three hand-painted and slip decorated patented 1876 shaving mugs. *Author's collection.*

Patent mark on bottom of Smith Bros. mugs.

Section 7 Occupational Types

The terms "occupationals" and "Trade Designs" have the same literal meaning in reference to shaving mugs. The latter term (trade designs) was the original wording used in all the early barber supply catalogs while the term "occupational" is relatively newer, having been coined by writers of stories on these mugs during the late 1930's and early 1940's. Since that time the older descriptive phrase has been dropped from usage by the current generation of mug collectors.

There were many variances of these so-called trade design mugs, depending upon the whims of the owner and upon the ability of the particular mug decorator. Each barber supply company had its own standard designs as pictured in their catalogs, and they also "duplicated designs pictured in any catalog". Many designs were painted from photographs or printed pictures (usually of newspaper or magazine advertisements" as furnished by the customer, according to a former employee of the Mug Decorating Department at the Koken company.

Some examples of the varieties made just for one trade (or profession), that of a Doctor are: a Doctor attending a patient (and there are varieties even of this); the skull and crossbones emblem (several varieties); the Doctor's name on any specially requested design, such as a shield; the Fancy Decorated mug (design chosen from other mugs pictured in the catalog) also showing the Doctor's name. There are perhaps countless other varieties in this one profession alone. Similar variances in all different trade designs were also evident. Many of them were actually one-of-a-kind decorations.

Author's collection.

Sulky, Horse-drawn steam fire engine. *Author's collection.*

Some of the photographic mugs (with the photo developed onto the side of the mug) would also be considered as "occupationals". Example: a locomotive engineer's mug, showing a photo (instead of a hand-painting) of the locomotive engine he operated, or a photo of a farmer plowing.

The classification of some occupational (trade designs) shaving mugs is often a controversial subject among collectors. This no doubt stems from the fact that some of the old barber supply catalogs made no great effort to distinguish between what was then considered to be a *trade design* mug and a *fancy decorated* mug. (Note: At least one old catalog even lists a butterfly decoration among the trade designs.)

In the strictest sense of the word an occupational mug depicts action — the owner *working at his trade*. (Blacksmith at anvil, brickmason laying brick, etc.) Then there are the occupation mugs which depict the working tools or emblem of the tradesman. (Mortar and pestle of the druggist, the anvil, hammer and tongs of the blacksmith, etc.) These designs do not depict *action* of the tradesman.

Occupations are generally classified as either *indoor trades* (Printer, Jeweler, Barber, Baker, etc.) or as *outdoor trades* (Farmer, Surveyor, Policeman, Carpenter, Bricklayer, etc.

Author's collection.

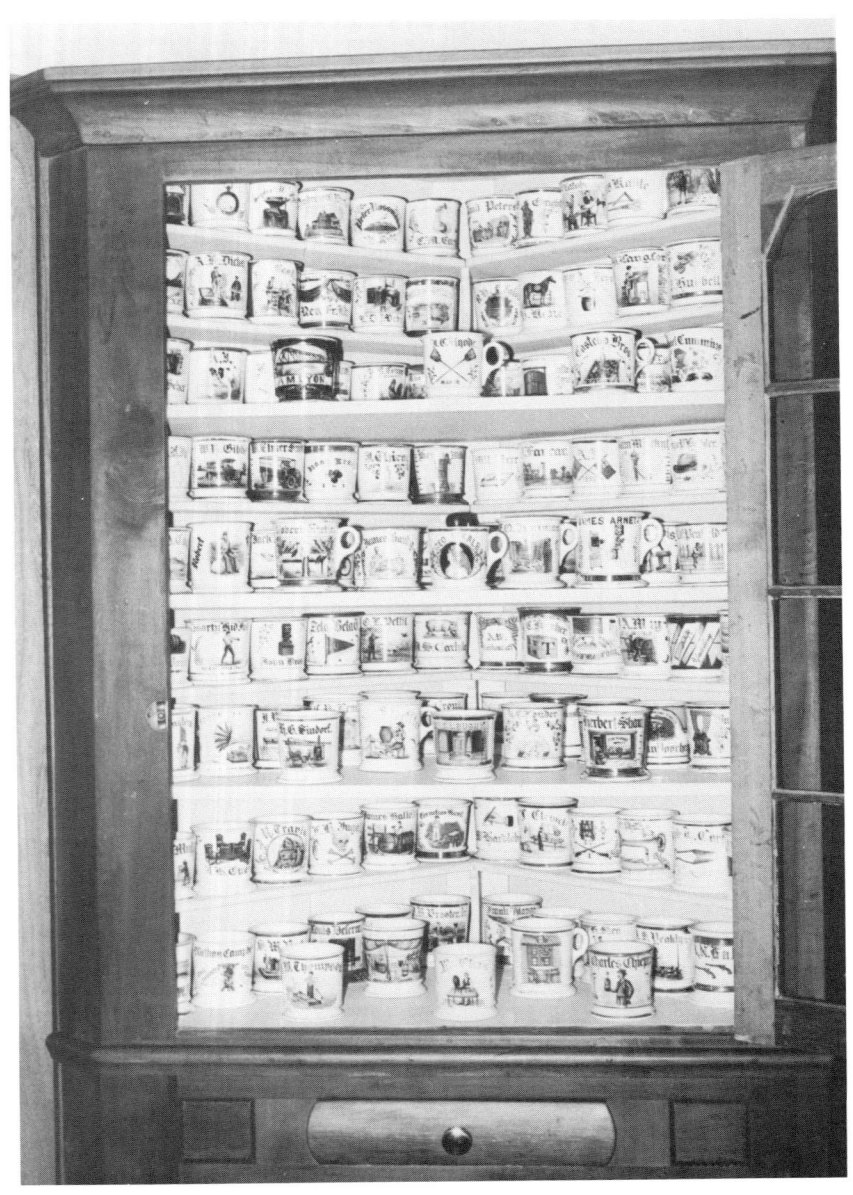

Collection of Mr. C. F. Kalb.

Collection of Mr. C. F. Kalb.

Collection of Mr. and Mrs. Frank O. Dresner.

Collection of Mr. W. H. Alexander.

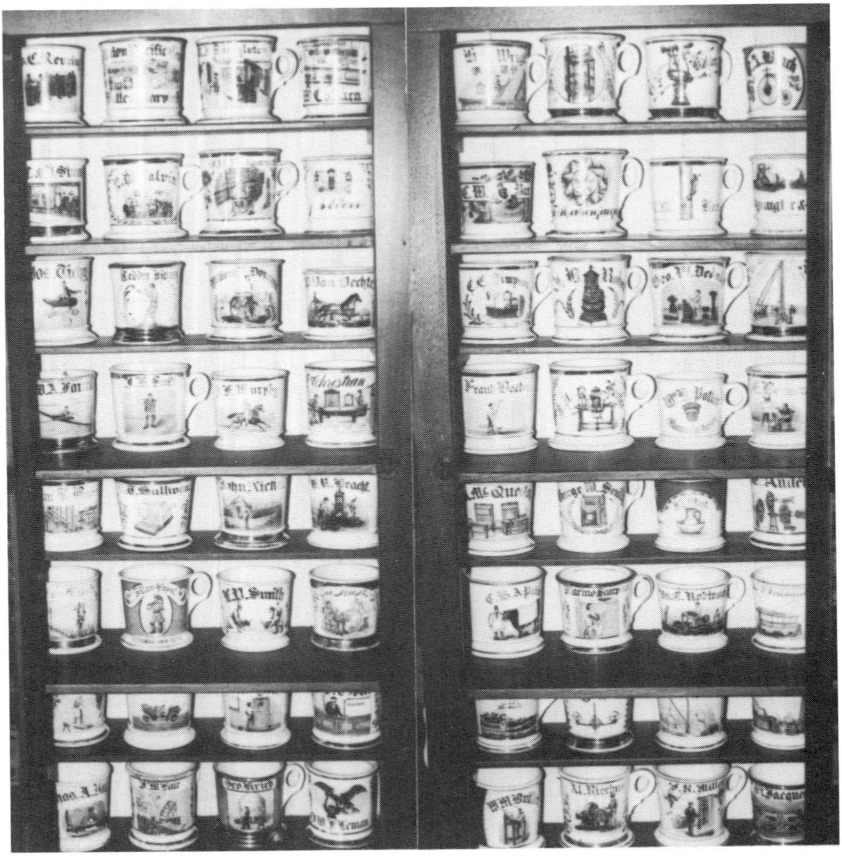

Collection of Mr. C. F. Kalb.

Collection of Mr. Virgil G. McCloud.

Collection of Mr. C. F. Kalb.

Collection of Mr. C. F. Kalb.

Collection of Mrs. Ruth M. Millener.

Collection of Mr. Virgil G. McCloud.

Author's Collection.

Rare one-of-a-kind shaving mug. Original owner was operator of Phillips' Arch Iron Pier - Seaside Station - Rockaway Beach, N.Y. *Collection of Mr. Joe L. Bowen.*

Left: Undertaker mug showing horse-drawn hearse. *Right:* Oil Field Derrick scene. *Collection of Mr. Richard F. Snow.*

Collection of Mr. Richard F Snow.

Collection of Mr. and Mrs. Mike Mocio.

Collection of Mr. and Mrs. Mike Mocio.

Collection of Mr. K. W. Southall, Jr.

Collection of Mr. and Mrs. Jay Riggs.

Collection of Mr. and Mrs. Jim Keller.

Collection of Mr. and Mrs. Mike Mocio.

Author's Collection.

Collection of Mr. Albert Newton

Collection of Mr. Ulric S. Messier

Collection of Mr. James J. Butler

Collection of Mr. Wm. H. Alexander.

J. B. Williams Americana Shaving Mug. Hand cast and hand polished, these mugs are made by the Wilson Brass Co., of Columbia, Penna. for the Williams Co. in honor of America's 200th Anniversary. The mug offer is current for $3.75 (1972)- and is contained in Williams cup soap at retail outlets over the country. They are handsome replicas (in shape) and are of heavy metal, practically unbreakable. *Author's Collection.*

Author's Collection.

Collection of Mr. Zane Field

Section 8

Secret Societies (Fraternities), Trade Unions

The period of development and popularity of fraternal organizations (originally called secret societies) and trade unions in the United States probably reached its early climax during the time when barber shop shaves were not only popular but were a way of life among America's gentry, in the cities and townships.

Although Trade Unions or Craft Unions existed in the United States as early as 1792, it was not until the end of the Civil War that the Industrial revolution in America furnished the incentive for the American laboring man to unite in a national effort. One of the first such national organizations was the Noble Order of the Knights of Labor, organized secretly in 1869, and which by 1890 had a membership of some 700,000. By 1917 this organization disbanded.

Many of the early trade unions were organized as "secret societies" — thus the listing in the old Barber Supply catalogs as "secret societies".

Another of the oldest labor groups was the Grand International Brotherhood of Locomotive Engineers, founded in 1863. By 1883 we find also organized labor groups of conductors, trainmen and firemen (of the railroads.)

Fraternal Orders (or Fraternities) as we know them today, were also considered "secret societies", although the word "Fraternals" has come to be accepted today among most shaving mug collectors and dealers alike, as meaning a mug with the emblem of Masonry, Elks, Moose, Woodmen of the World, etc.

History has proven in many instances that with time, interpretative meanings of words change. Consequently no effort has been made in the list below to distinguish between what we consider today to be a Fraternal shaving mug, a Secret Society shaving mug or a Craft or Trade Union shaving mug. This list has simply been assembled from several catalogs for the convenience of a quick or ready reference to make your hobby more interesting. Whether or not each listing (mentioning an "Emblem") was a truly established trade or craft union would entail much more time-consuming research. The fact that they were listed in many of the old catalogs, were so decorated by the china painters, and bought and used by the customers, is reason enough for most buffs to be interested.

The following is believed to be the most comprehensive list of fraternal orders in America. Many of the listings were shown in an old catalog of "Emblems" of the Irons and Russell Company, which was established in 1861. Some listings may be duplicated in the listings or of mugs from the old Barber Supply catalogs, others will not be shown elsewhere in this book.

A few of the better known emblems, among today's generation, are: the emblem of the Free and Accepted Masons, the oldest fraternity in the world; the emblem of the Knights Templar, originally a military order, founded about 1818 at Crusaders' Palace, Jerusalem, and later a higher degree of Masonry; the emblem of the Mystic Shrine (A.A.O.N.M.S. — Ancient Arabic Order of Nobles of the Mystic Shrine), founded in 1871 with membership open only to Knight Templars and 32nd Degree Masons; the emblem of the I.O.O.F. (Independent Order Odd Fellows), founded about 1745 and started in the United States in 1819; the emblem of the Knights of Pythias, founded at Washington, D. C. on February 15, 1864; the emblem of the B.P.O.E. (the Benevolent Protective Order of Elks) founded in New York City, September 15, 1868.

Others include the Knights of Columbus, founded in New Haven, Conn., in 1882, a Catholic mens fraternity; the emblem of the Fraternal Order of Eagles (F.O.E.), founded in 1898; the emblem of the Loyal Order of Moose (LOOM), founded in Cincinnati, Ohio in 1888; the emblem of the Improved Order of Red Men, tracing its origin to the Sons of Liberty, a secret society of early Colonial days, was founded at Baltimore, Md., in 1833, claimed to be the oldest patriotic fraternity in the United States.

The list of Secret Society or Fraternal Order Emblems pictured and listed herewith is included for the purpose of aiding in identification of emblems which were used to decorate old shaving mugs. It would be next to impossible to reproduce here all the emblems found in America, because there are to many variations in design in many of them. (In the Masonic order alone there are perhaps a hundred or more variations, showing different symbols of the order.) In these cases only the most popular emblems are pictured. One should remember too, that in the days when secret societies emblems were popular as a decoration for shaving mugs, the man ordering the "special motif" or decoration often submitted his own sketch or sent a printed picture of the emblem with his particular order, or he requested certain changes (because of his own whims) from the sample picture on the Barber Shop Wall Poster or Mug Catalog. These special instructions were in some instances no doubt followed implicitly by some decorators, and in other cases were a different interpretation, depending upon the resourcefulness or creativeness of the decorator.

In some cases the emblem on a particular mug was actually a "combination emblem". An example of this would be a Masonic emblem of the Square and Compass enclosing the letter G and below this would be "3 links of a chain", which is the symbol of the I.O.O.F. I have seen a few mugs with more than one fraternity emblem thereon, and on one occasion I saw a mug with 5 separate fraternity emblems painted on the sides of the mug, a fact which no doubt distinguished the owner from most of his fellow men.

I have also seen a few mugs with emblems which I have been unable to identify. In fact I have one such mug in my own collection, and it is one of my most beautiful emblem-decorated mugs.

While on the subject of emblems, it should be mentioned that in some instances the "coat of arms" of the various states were likewise placed as decoration on shaving mugs. These I believe to be quite rare; at least I have only seen a few such mugs among thousands of mugs in private collections.

Author's collection.

Fraternal Shaving Mugs

A.A.O.N.M.S. (Ancient Arabic Order Nomads Mystic Shrine)
American Legion of Honor
American Protective Association
Ancient Order Hibernians
Ancient Order United Workmen (AOUW)
Ancient Free and Accepted Masons (AF&AM)
D.O.K.K.
Free and Accepted Masons (F&AM)
Foresters (I.O.F.)
Foresters (F.O.A.) with flags
Grand Army of the Republic (GAR)
B. of R.R.T. (Trainmen)
B.P.O.E. (Elks)
B. of L.E. (Brotherhood of Locomotive Engineers) — monogram
B. of L. F. (Firemen's Monogram)
B. of L. F. & E.)
L.O.O.M. (Loyal Order of Moose)
K.P. (Knights of Pythias)
F.O.E. (Friendly Order of Eagles)
I.O.O.F. (Independent Order Odd Fellows)
I.O.G.T.
I.O.O.R. (Independent Order of Redmen)
I.O.R.M. (Improved Order of Redmen (America's oldest patriotic fraternity)
K.C. (Knights of Columbus)
K.K.K. (Ku Klux Klan — founded after Civil War. Modern Secret society was founded later in 1915. Several varieties, usually has a "burning cross".
K.T. (Knight Templar)
Knights of the Golden Eagle
Knights of Honor
Knights of Labor
Knights of Ladies of Honor
Knights of Maccabee
Knights of Tented Maccabees (K.O.T.M.)
Knights of Malta
Knights of St. George
Knights of St. John
Orangemen Emblem
Order of Iron Hall
I.K.T.
Order of Owls
Order of Tonti
Q.U.A.M.
Patriotic Order Sons of America
Royal Arcanum
Royal Arch Masons (various emblems, Masonic)
Royal League
Royal and Select Masters (various emblems, Masonic)
Sons of Herman
Sons of St. George
Sons of Temperance
Sons of Veterans
T.P.A. (Travelers Protective Assoc.)
Woodmen of the World (W.O.W.)
Modern Woodmen (M.W.A.)
U.C.T.U.

Patriotic Order Sons of America	Orangemen	Order of Eagles		Woodmen of the World	Knights of Pythias

Masonic Blue Lodge	Masonic Chapter Royal Arch	Masonic Scottish Rite	Dramatic Order Knights of Khorassan	Jr. Order United American Mechanics

Modern Woodmen of America

	Knights of Golden Eagle	Order of Railway Telegraphers	Order of Railroad Conductors

Loyal Order of Moose

Knights of Columbus

Order of Owls

Brotherhood of Railroad Trainmen

B of L F & E

A.A.O.N.M.S. (Shrine)

Brotherhood of Locomotive Engineers

Order of Elks

Knights Templar

IMPROVED ORDER OF RED MEN	Royal Arcanum	Independent Order of Odd Fellows

SWITCHMEN'S UNION OF NORTH AMERICA	BROTHERHOOD OF RAILWAY CLERKS	BROTHERHOOD OF RAILWAY CARMEN OF AMERICA

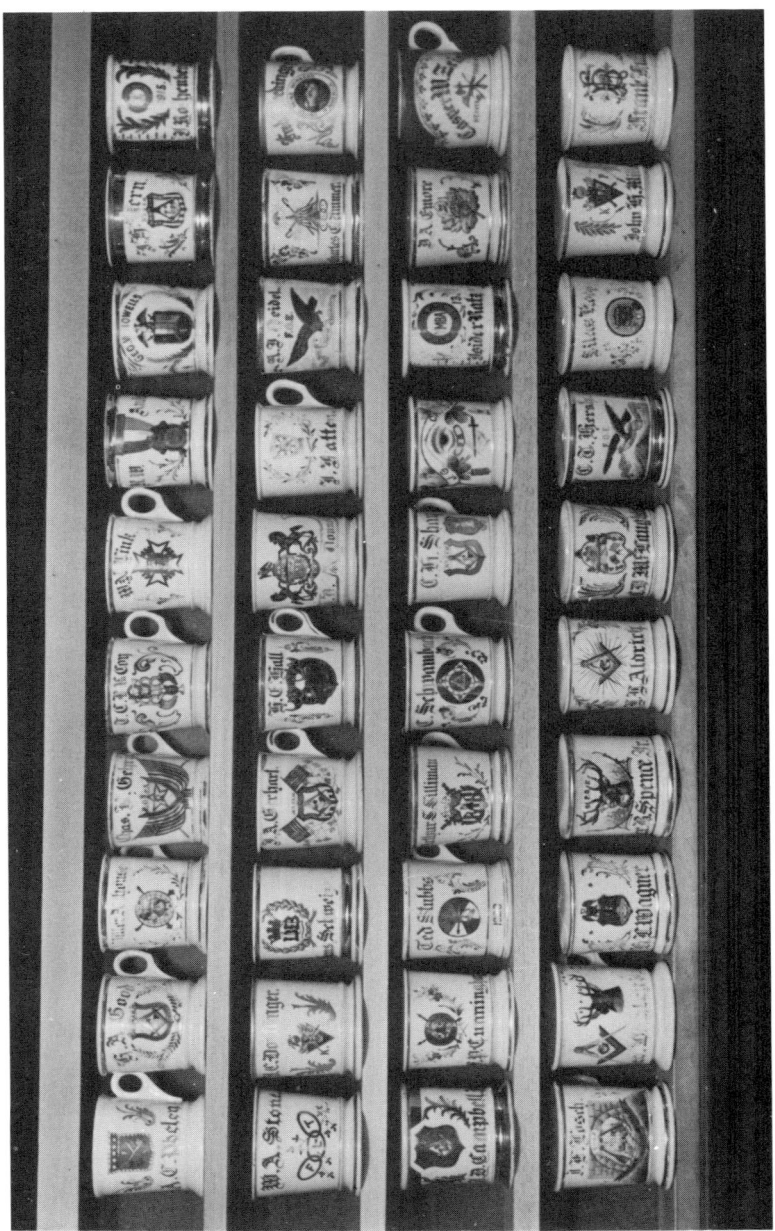

Forty mugs, including Secret Societies (fraternals), social clubs, societies and unions. *From the William Donnelly Collection.*

Collection of Mr. and Mrs. Frank O. Dresner.

Collection of Mrs. Fern Trimm.

Section 9
Glass Label Shaving Mugs

The old glass label porcelain shaving mugs date back to the early 1870's, about the time Ernest E. Koken first established himself in the business of decorating shaving mugs for the barber shops in St. Louis, Mo. And the idea for "reverse painted" glass label shaving mug is thus attributed to him.

At the time of his entry into the shaving mug decorating business, when he established his company, one of his best customers was a St. Louis firm that manufactured glass apothecary bottles for the retail druggists all over the country. These bottles were made in a variety of sizes, but each bottle contained a thin glass label, contoured to fit the shape of the bottle and glued onto the bottle. It is believed that at one time these early labels were decorated with gold-leaf, applied to the underside in much the same manner that a sign painter would meticulously apply gold-leaf to the inside of a storefront window or office door.

Whether Koken did gold-leaf art work is not known, but it is known that he did reverse painting on the apothecary bottles during his early years in business. And, from this work it doubtless was here that he conceived the idea for glass labels and the reverse painting process for them to be used on shaving mugs.

His shaving mug decorating business thrived, but the "glass label" mugs were not popular, once it was realized that the thin layer of glass was easily broken, or the constant use of water and soap, spilling over the sides of the mugs, caused a deterioration of the glue which held

Collection of Mr. and Mrs. Mike Mocio.

Author's collection.

the glass onto the side of the mug, causing discoloration of the label which was unsightly and unsanitary.

The glass label mugs' popularity ended sometime in the early 1880's, but during these few years, a variety of different types were developed.

Litho Label

One of the varieties was a lithographed paper on cardboard label, which was covered with the glass label to protect it. Some of these were *embossed* with different standard designs, and the owner's name printed thereon.

Others had the owner's name printed under a photograph, which was covered with the glass layer and glued onto the mug. Glass labels were also affixed to glass shaving mugs.

Any glass label shaving mug, especially one in good condition, is today a rare find, because they were made only a few years, before their manufacture was discontinued in the early 1880's, and if they were used regularly, then their condition is usually fair to poor. And often the thin glass layer is cracked or broken.

It is interesting to note too that some barber bottles also were made in the glass label manner, and continued in use for a much longer period of time than did the glass label shaving mugs. This was due no doubt to the fact that the bottles did not receive the rough treatment which was accorded the mugs, and consequently were more practical.

Photographic Shaving Mugs

Like the crown jewels of an ancient monarch, the photographic shaving mug of the late 1880's and early 1900's held the unique distinction of being the *highest priced* porcelain shaving mug listed in all the barber supply catalogs. But the main distinction it had, both then and in today's realm of mug collecting, is that it is the most personalized shaving mug ever designed or produced in the United States.

What could be more personalized than a photo of it's owner, burnt right into the mug, decorated with hand-painted floral designs, and with the owner's name in gold lettering?

The photographic process of "developing" the image of a picture onto the side of a procelain shaving mug was not related strictly to shaving mugs, for this was done on other pieces of china and porcelain, such as plates and other dinnerware — even on individual coffee or tea cups. (These were usually adorned with a photo of milady.)

No information has been found concerning who actually introduced this idea or exactly when they first came into use, but several of the different barber supply firms in St. Louis and Chicago advertised them as early as the 1890's. It is not believed to have been a patented procedure. The Theo. A. Kochs' catalog for the year 1896 prominently displayed a photographic mug, bearing the picture and name of President Grover Cleveland. (Note: Mugs with decals of President Cleveland and also President Woodrow Wilson were likewise made, and are fine collector items today, although are not photographic mugs.) The mug illustration is actual size and underneath it reads the following description: "We can reproduce upon these mugs any photograph or tin-type, without defacing or injuring the photograph in any manner. The work is a perfect mechanical reproduction and the result upon the mug is always exactly as good as the photograph which is furnished. If a good photograph is sent, we guarantee a good reproduction upon the mug. The photograph and decoration are thoroughly burned and cannot be effaced."

Another company advertised that any picture of any kind, such as a "building, locomotive or machinery or other design could be burnt right in the mug." Consequently the photographic shaving mug may thus be a *trade design* or *occupation* or even a *secret society* or *fraternal mug* as well as a photographic mug. All photographic mugs are considered rare, and mugs in this category are much sought after by mug collectors.

Some of these mugs bear only the photograph and the owner's name in gilt, while others are also lavishly decorated with hand-painted

Photographic shaving mugs. *Author's collection.*

Photographic shaving mug of Tarrant County Court House, Fort Worth, Texas. *Collection of Mrs. Margaret Brown.*

flowers. A few will have a date hand-painted with the name, oftentimes with the owner's birth date or the date of a special occasion.

Three Dimensional Effect

Some photographic shaving mugs have a three dimensional appearance of the photograph, due to the photograph being touched-up by the china painter. I have seen only a few of these. One was a locomotive, showing a three-quarter view, which had been hand-painted, giving it a fine quality appearance of depth. The photograph had details that even the most expert mug decorator would not be able to duplicate, and yet was accented by additional china painting, making it as realistic as a colored photograph. Two other mugs made in this manner have been seen. One was a passenger coach and the other a caboose, which were both equally superior in quality to most railroad mugs.

Photographic shaving mugs. Mug on right shows roughnecks at an oil well drilling rig. *Collection of Mr. and Mrs. Frank O. Dresner.*

Gilt Numbered Mugs

If you have been collecting very long you no doubt have seen a few of the old gilt numbered mugs, or you may have a few in your collection. But most people are not at all knowledgeable regarding them.

They are listed and pictured in many of the old barber supply catalongs as far back as the 1880's and were usually priced *by the dozen* ($2.50 to $4.50), although they could be bought singly at 30¢ to 40¢ apiece.

Gilt numbered mugs originally were made for use in large hotel barber shops in the larger cities, but later were often sold to any shop which ordered them. At least one collector I met a few years ago claims his numbered mugs came from the old barber shop in the Waldorf-Astoria Hotel in New York City. However they were no different from many other numbered mugs I've seen. There was no way to identify that they had come from that shop.

Most of these mugs were imported French or German blanks decorated by the mug decorators in American barber supply companies. And they were either the large or medium size mugs. These are the heavy-looking, thick porcelain mugs, as distinguished from American-made mugs that were used during the later period of about 1917-1927.

Gilt Number shaving mugs. *Author's collection.*

"Gilt numbered mugs were generally ordered in large quantities to completely fill barber shop mug racks which held from 36 to 100 mugs", relates Edgar Wendel., old-time mug decorator for the Koken Company. "And we kept hundreds of these numbered mugs on hand most of the time so we could ship the mugs upon receipt of the orders. Occasionally an order would contain instructions for some additional decoration such as flowers. And sometimes an order would be received for only one or two mugs, probably to replace broken mugs."

Mr. Wendel recalls that the numbered mugs were usually the ones "ordered when a new barber shop was opened — before the regular customers bought their own individual shaving mugs."

Not all mugs decorated at Kokens had the Koken mark on the bottom "because we decorated mugs for many of the other barber supply companies, and on those we stamped their own name on the bottom." The Heimerdinger Barber Supply Company of Louisville, Kentucky was one such company which never employed their own mug decorators, according to the President of that firm which has been in business for over 100 years, and the Koken Company decorated all their mugs for them. This early practice is one of the little known facts of the trade, although the Heimerdinger company did publish their own catalogs, picturing the decorated shaving mugs.

Section 10
LENOX SHAVING MUGS

America's oldest famous manufacturer of fine china is LENOX, INC., founded by Walter Scott Lenox who was born in Trenton, New Jersey in 1859. His life story and that of this company is truly a remarkable modern epic of idealism, for his life was the consecration to the sole ideal of elevating American ceramic art to a place of primary importance. Through his ideal and perserverance, he became America's foremost potter—to rank with the Palissys and Wedgwoods and master potters of former times.

Walter Scott Lenox was but a schoolboy when the potter's wheel aroused in him a never-ending interest in the evolution of dull clay into shapes and forms of beauty, as he daily passed a small pottery going to and from school. He spent many hours simply watching the process. It was here perhaps that his desire, ambition and drive to excel, was first established—even before he become an apprentice potter.

He served his apprenticeship in the Ott and Brewer factory and in the Willets pottery of Trenton, mastering the practical details of the work while studying decorative art in his leisure time. As his artistic talents developed be became more interested in decorative and creative efforts and eventually became art director of the Ott and Brewer factory.

Picture from early Lenox catalog. *Permission of The Lenox Company.*

No. 201 4 in.

Lenox Belleek shaving mug. Rare handpainted design (factory decorated). *Author's Collection.*

Rare pink Lenox Belleek with Silver overlay. *Collection of Mr. and Mrs. Mike Mocio.*

Center — Pink Lenox Belleek with silver overlay. *Collection of Mr. and Mrs. Mike Mocio.* Other two mugs are rare cobalt blue Lenox with silver overlay. *Author's Collection*

Author's collection of Lenox Belleek shaving mugs. Mug second from left (2nd row) is from the *Mocio collection.*

During this period of time American ceramic products were lacking in artistry. Designs were crude and expression exaggerated. Lenox perceived that only by establishing his own factory, could he attain his own ideals of producing a grade of china equal to the finest created in Europe.

Ceramic Art Company Established

In 1889, he had saved $4,000 to become a partner with **Jonothan Coxon, Sr.**, in the Ceramic Art Company, which they operated until 1894, when Lenox acquired the interest of his partner. From 1894 until 1906 he operated the business alone.

When the Ceramic Art Company was formed in 1889, Lenox first began his struggle to produce fine china wares which would compete with the highest grade products then being produced by famous factories of Europe. His chances of ever doing this were considered very slim indeed, by most Americans. For years he had tried unsuccessfully to produce a china such as was produced in limited quantities in Belleek, Ireland. He even imported two Belleek potters, to assist him in creating this beautiful, creamy, ivory-tinted ware, marked by rich lustrous glaze. Finally failure gave way to perfection with the resultant richness and quality of the master pieces of other lands.

Then in 1895, at the very moment when success was beginning to crown his efforts, he was stricken with both paralysis and blindness, unable to walk or see for the remainder of his life. But his indominatable spirit and courage pushed him onward even in the face of such great odds. This gallant artisan was more determined than ever, and with the "eyes.. of his trusted associate, Harry A. Brown, the factory continued to function and prosper.

The blind potter had accomplished two great achievements. He had effectively eliminated American prejudice against American-made china, and he had established the artistic prestige of American-made goods. Both in quality of composition and design, Lenox wares, possessing a character, a tone and a charm all its own, rivals the really fine ceramic products of the world, today as it did then.

The men in charge of Lenox today are all proteges of Walter Scott Lenox, and none would ever sacrifice quality or compromise the high standards set by Lenox.

FIRST AMERICAN BELLEEK SHAVING MUGS

Just nine years after the Ceramic Art Company was formed, and three years after Walter Lenox was struck with blindness and paralysis, the company first began making shaving mugs. That was in 1898, and although Lenox himself was now blind, he still had the sensitive fingers of the potter for the touch and feel of form and beauty, and through the "eyes" of his assistant and all the men who had trained under him, the company produced china shaving mugs in the Lenox tradition.

These mugs, like many other useful china wares of Lenox, were destined to become equal or superior in richness and quality to the masterpieces of other lands. Here was produced America's first Belleek shaving mugs.

In 1898 countless thousands of blank shaving mugs were regularly being imported by the Barber Supply companies, where they were "personalized"—with the owner's names and various hand-painted designs. These mugs, although made in either large or medium sizes generally were all identical in shape and form—regardless of country of origin, and although the quality of china sometimes differed slightly—they were likewise about the same quality.

Shaving mugs produced at the Lenox factory were truly of a distinct character in both form (or shape), quality and beauty. For the first time an American potter had produced a shaving mug of the same quality and beauty of the dinnerware that would later grace the tables of the White House. (In 1918 President Woodrow Wilson ordered a 1,700 piece dinner set costing $16 000 from Lenox. Until that time no American-made china was considered worthy of use in the White House.)

Although Lenox shaving mugs never replaced the personalized type of mugs kept in the old barber shops, the symmetry and grace of the Lenox mugs added a new dimension heretofore unknown to the shaving mug. To this was added the high standards of detailed decoration, under the personal supervision of William H. Clayton, who as a boy had apprenticed to Walter Scott Lenox, and learned the art of china decoration under this great master.

But all factory-decorated Lenox shaving mugs was totally the handiwork of two distinguished china painters—H. Nosek and William Morley, the latter perhaps the most famous of American china painters, who died in 1934 but whose artistic merits are still recognized by the Lenox Company. Much of his china painting was signed "Wm. Morley". The author has a collection of six game bird plates which were painted in pastels and signed by Morley. So there is a good possibility that he also signed some shaving mugs. Such mugs would indeed be very rare collector items.

Lenox Belleek shaving mugs, decorated at the factory, like the tablewares, incorporated the highest standards with the highest quality control. All imperfect pieces were immediately destroyed—a tradition begun by Lenox when he first opened his business. Consequently you will never find a Lenox shaving mug that is not perfect in form and composition.

"Blank China" Mugs Sold

There was however a period of time when Lenox sold white ware or "blank china"—for the amateur china painters to decorate themselves. On these pieces (which includes shaving mugs) the craftsmanship of the painted decoration may be less than perfect, depending upon the talents of the individual amateur artist, but they are easily recognized by both the Lenox *white ware* mark (see mark expanation) and oftentimes the amateur artist's name, if not by the quality of the painting. You need only to have seen a factory-decorated mug to tell the difference.

Only Styles Made

Lenox made shaving mugs in only the three stock molds shown on the next page (from an early Lenox catalog).

Style Number 1, the most popular mug, was available however with a choice of two different handles. It was also made with or without a soap compartment. Those mugs with a soap compartment had two drain holes at opposite corners of the compartment. And there was sometimes a variation of small embossed design near the base of the mugs. The overall size and body shape never changed, but there was a variety of decorations available and any special handpainted design, including initials, or name, or portrait or scene could be ordered—even silver overlay engraved to suit the most discriminating taste of the new owner.

Exports To Europe

Early Lenox wares were exported to England and Europe, and at least one English silversmith decorated Lenox Beleek with silver overlay. So it would not be impossible to even find a Lenox shaving mug with a European silvermark, for in recent years many Lenox tea sets bearing English silvermarks, have made the return trip to America along with other European antiques, for sale in the American antiques market.

201   1128   1319
       4 in.   4 in.

In addition to the Lenox mark on these mugs, you may also find the mark of the Tiffany Company or other firms who retailed Lenox china, for an early custom of Lenox included placing the name of their wholesale buyer on the bottom. (In some instances the name and the city was also included.)

The shapes of the handles varied, to be artistically compatible with the different designs and motifs of decoration, as will be seen in the pictures.

SILVER OVERLAY MUGS

From 1903 to 1906 some Lenox shaving mugs were also decorated with engraved silver overlay. The artwork of applying or overlaying the silver was accomplished by the old Mt. Vernon Company, Silversmiths, Inc., of Mt. Vernon, N.Y., which was founded in 1903 through the merger of several firms and was later purchased by the Gorham Corporation in 1913.

On the bottom of these mugs will be found, in addition to the early Lenox mark, a "unicorn-type" mark which was the mark of the silversmith.

Only two different silver designs have come to light through research, but may be found on either cobalt blue or rich pink china shaving mugs. However, during this same period Lenox and Mt. Vernon also produced tableware in a chocolate brown color with silver overlay, and it is an educated guess that overlay in the chocolate color was likewise used to produce shaving mugs. And possibly even many other colors as well, especially in the rich, creamy, ivory-tinted Lenox Belleek.

In 1906 Walter Scott Lenox formed LENOX, INC., the name that has been synonomous with the finest in china ever since. The firm's business has grown from considerably less than $1,000,000 annually in the 1930's to a multimillion dollar operation, through advanced technology, modern production and business methods. But the company's manufacture of shaving mugs was discontinued sometime before 1915.

Considering the effects of the ravages of time on company records of more than three-quarters of a century past, the Lenox Company can only furnish the following accurate information with respect to Lenox marks stamped on their early wares. (This does not necessarily mean that other early marks may not have been used or that certain colored marks were not used to indicate manufacture only during certain years.)

 Mark used from 1889-1896 on factory-decorated china.

Mark used from 1889-1906 on white wares (not factory decorated).

 Mark used from 1896-1906 on factory-decorated china.

Mark used from 1906-1924 on white wares (not factory decorated).

 Mark used from 1906-1924 on factory-decorated china.

Mark used from 1924- on factory-decorated & white wares.

Mark used from 1930- on factory-decorated & white wares.

Section 11
Advertising Shaving Mugs

Most trade-design shaving mugs were in a sense "advertising" mugs, for they advertised the owner's trade or profession in various ways, but to be considered a *pure* advertising mug, a mug would have to advertise a particular *name brand product*. Generally pure advertising mugs were given away, sometimes to special customers and sometimes the mug was free if you purchased the shaving soap or other product of the manufacturer.

Without knowing the exact circumstances surrounding a particular mug's history, it would be impossible in some instances to know for certain whether that particular mug would be classified as an industrial type occupational mug or as an advertising mug. An example of this nature would be a mug, decorated with a man's shirt, neatly ironed and folded, and the name "White's Laundry" lettered on the mug. A mug such as this could have belonged to the owner of the laundry, or it could have been one of many that was given to the laundry's customers.

If a shaving mug contains an advertising message such as "Compliments of (name of a firm) and/or mentions a particular product, then it is obviously an advertising mug.

And if a mug advertises a particular product by slogan and/or picture on the side, it is an advertising mug. Examples of this type are mugs bearing the slogan "Use Tonique de Luxe. . .the Liquid Headrest" (advertising the Koken Barber Supply Company's famous hair tonic), or the "Wild Root" double compartment shaving mug pictured, or the "Williams Shaving Soap" mug also pictured.

Author's collection

Section 12
DECAL MUGS

Some people avidly collect decal-type shaving mugs, and others wouldn't knowingly have one in their collection. But are you really sure you could recognize them without being deceived?

If you are interested in learning to detect the difference between a decal and a handpainted mug, it is suggested that you invest in a good pocket magnifying glass and carry it with you to closely examine every mug decoration you may have doubts about.

Many decal mugs are genuinely old, having been imported from Germany from around 1900-1919, or even before 1890. As a general rule all German decal mugs imported after 1890 bear a stamped "Germany" mark and a number (such as 141,150,etc) under the glaze on the bottom. Others bear more complete marks such as "Three Crown - Germany" or other similar factory marks. However one of the most distinguishing characteristics of the German decal mug is the shape of the handle and the mug itself. (See examples of typical imported German decal type mugs, showing form and shape.)

Imported From Germany

During this period in history most imported mugs came from Germany, although England exported scuttle mugs, many of which bore decals or slip transfers, as they were called. In more recent years many old English mugs have been imported for the antique trade here. By the same token new English mugs are likewise now being imported by antique wholesalers as evidence of the growing market among antique collectors.

Author's collection.

Author's collection.

Another distinguishing characteristic of the Old German decal mug is the decal decoration itself. The mug adornment followed a popular trend of that era in providing reproductions of well known works of art by artists familiar to all, in decals of paintings such as "The Angelus", "The Gleaners" and many others. World reknown personages such as Napoleon, Sitting Bull, etc. were also featured decorations. Horses, dogs and other animals were also popular.

This was during the time when paintings by Christy and Dana Gibson were quite popular in America. And many of these paintings were also reproduced on decal shaving mugs. In today's antique markets these mugs generally are very scarce and bring a much higher price than most of the other more common decal mugs.

After considering the size and shape of the mug and its handle, the usual type of pictures featured and the German mark on the bottom, if you are still not convinced it is a decal then use your magnifying glass for a closer examination.

Some decals show their age by flaking, peeling or cracking. Under the magnifier it may have the appearance that certain areas of the decal has shrunk, leaving small irregular spots with decal. Or part of the decal may have slipped out of place when applied. Often the edge of the decal will be visible and sometimes if there is a small printed name (such as the Sitting Bull decal) it will be in reverse.

You should take into consideration that all decal mugs will not show their defects to the same degree. It is not intended to discredit decal mugs. Their popularity will rise or fall on their own merits. Originally they were the cheaper variety of mugs, compared to those hand-painted by china decorators. Decal mugs were sold for years by the large mail-order firms such as Sear-Roebuck and Montgomery-Ward.

Semi-Vitreous china mug made by Trenton Potteries Co., Trenton, N.J., in 1907. Note colorful decal of a Christy painting of the early telephone. *Author's Collection.*

Author's collection.

Section 13
Scuttle Shaving Mugs

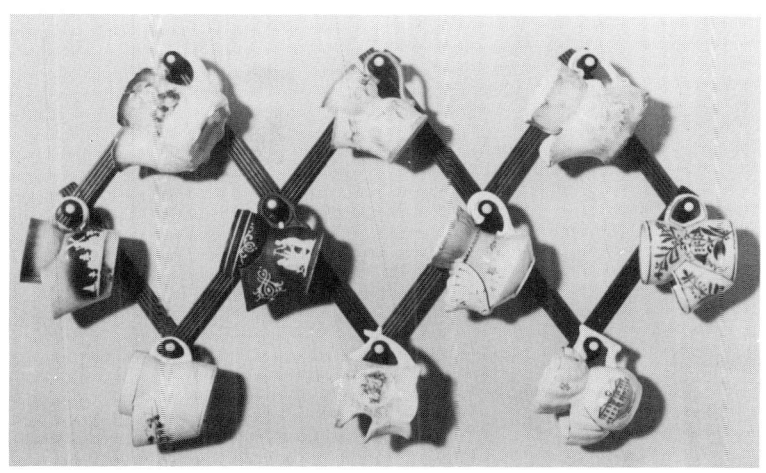

Collection of Mr. Kenneth W. Southall, Jr.

Author's collection.

Collection of Mr. and Mrs. Mike Mocio.

Section 14

Character Shaving Mugs

The collecting of character shaving mugs has been one of the great overlooked fields in shaving mug collecting. The scarcity of these mugs, together with the fact that there are so few different kinds of characters available, in all probability, accounts for this fact.

The characters occupy a special niche in any collection, large or small, and are in fact, just as much a part of the so-called aristocracy (though not as old) of the antique shaving mugs, as are the occupations. And they are often even more difficult to find than many of the occupations.

Some collectors have collected novelty china items for years, and character shaving mugs are to be found among such novelty collections as Toby mugs, tobacco humidors, cream pitchers, etc., wherein lies the paradox, for example, of what is a character shaving mug and what is a cream pitcher. If it has a soap compartment with drain holes, then it is definitely a shaving mug. But, then all shaving mugs didn't have soap compartments, so . . . . again paradox!

In recent years many more people have begun collecting novelty china items; in fact many people have simply started collecting, and what would catch the eye quicker than a finely detailed novelty such as this? Of course this causes the serious shaving mug collector to shudder at the thought of all the new competition in his chosen field, because these items are already difficult to find. And the obvious rise in prices is sure to follow.

Character shaving mugs are believed to have been introduced in the United States about 1900, although some mugs bear no mark of the country of origin (which would date them after 1891). For the most part, they were manufactured in Bavaria and in Austria. This fact is established by the marks. One of the most common marks found on such mugs is that of a castle and crown with the letters P.M. Bavaria.

Many of the early American importers often had their own marks on imported wares which were sold by department or variety stores and by jewelry stores.

Most imports from Europe ceased about the time of World War I, and it is presumed that the characters were no exception.

Quality-wise the characters vary considerably—from the finest bisque-like appearance and feel, with the most exacting details of shape

Two top rows: Author's collection. Two lower rows: Collection of Mr. and Mrs. Frank O. Dresner.

Top row: Collection of Mrs. Margaret Brown. Two lower rows: Author's collection.

and decoration-to the opposite end of the balance scales. And quality plays an important consideration in the price you normally would be willing to pay. But remember, you may be competing with collectors of novelty items as well as other shaving mug collectors, so you must take that into consideration when judging the price asked for the mug.

On occasion you may find a character shaving mug in its original box, complete with a ceramic handled shaving brush. One such set known to exist, is a "Devil's Head", with the brush handle of china in the shape of a little devil (entire body). Another set is an "Indian Head" and the brush is a totem pole.

There are several varieties (shapes) of most of the characters. And, there are differences in the quality and detailed decoration as well. It is believed that some were imported blank mugs, decorated in this country by amateur china painters. But this is not confirmed.

The Chinaman Head mug is believed to have been made of only one variety, as pictured in this chapter, since I have examined at least a dozen such mugs, and the shapes, quality of china and decoration have all been the same. On the other hand the same number of Pig Head or Boar Head mugs have been closely examined, and hardly two alike have been found. One was pure white with only faint coloring to denote features (barely distinguishable) and of a high glaze finish. Another, seemingly from the same mold, is off-white in color and sheen with more accented coloring or tonal features, yet with the same high gloss finish. A third is light pinkish or flesh-colored. These three mentioned do not have tusks, so would be called pig-heads. In addition, there is a variety with tusks and features that resemble a wild boar. Some have longer snouts than others. There is at least one type which is of bisque-like quality. More varieties have been noted in these and the "skulls" and "Fish-heads" than in other types.

The Dog Head mug (Boxer Dog) pictured herein, has been made in only one variety, to my knowledge. All mugs examined seem to be of identical properties from the same mold and have the same mark on the bottom, which is described as a "PM Castle" mark from Bavaria.

The elephant head shaving mugs have fine detail, and although the mugs are of a heavier quality china, the shading and coloring is excellent. The raised trunk serves as the handle.

The two-headed mug (again paradox) had no handle, is of very fine china, white, thin and with a high glaze or sheen. The inside is colored pink, also glossy. One side is the head of a monacled Englishman with long mustache and high collar, mouth opened wide, and a low brimmed skimmer for a hat. When it is turned upside down, the face

Author's collection

of an ape is apparent. The details of this mug are perhaps as fine in quality of workmanship as will be found. There is no manufacturer mark.

There are several types of Fish Heads and Fish, and most of these are of a heavier composition, and lack fine details of manufacture.

Japanese Reproductions

About 1966 some of the Fish Mugs was reproduced by the Japanese. These mugs were slightly smaller than the genuine old ones. And they were sold through retail outlets (including one of the largest nationwide department chain stores in the United States). The cost was less than $5. The colors known to have been used on these reproductions were a dark green and a dark brown. (The old ones were all white, with handpainted decorations for the features or the eyes, fins and scales.) And, these reproductions, like the reproductions of everything else being made in Japan, originally bore a small paper label.

Semi Characters

One unusual mug in the author's collection has a separate soap compartment with a hole in the vertical part of the divider. The hole is in the shape of a man's mouth and surrounded by a handle-bar mustache and goatee or chin whiskers. This mug might be termed a semi-character, and you must look inside the mug to see all this. The features are molded, but on some examples may also be handpainted to accentuate the features.

Other semi-characters include mugs with handles in unusual shapes such as: lizard handle, snake handle, barber pole handle, razor handle, etc., with the latter two perhaps being the most popular.

CHARACTER SHAVING MUGS

1. Bulldog Head (Boxer dog head)
2. Chinaman Head
3. Dachshund (entire dog)
4. Pig Head or Boar Head — 4 known varieties
5. Man's Head — 3 known varieties
6. Man's Skull (4 known varieties. One has ruby colored glass eyes, and is part of a case, complete with shaving utensils)
7. Indian Head (Indian chief or warrior) — two known varieties. One has a totem pole brush.
8. Rhino Head
9. Tiger Head
10. Man's High Button Collar
11. Two-Headed (no handle) — Englishman with monacle; turn it upside down, and it has Ape's head at other end. (Paradox)
12. Shirt Cuff — 3 known varieties (plain white with gold; floral decorated, or both.)
13. Man's Shoe
14. Fish Head — 3 known varieties. Same apparent mold, but various tones of shading in the decoration.
15. Fish
16. Sea Shell
17. Elephant Head with Trunk handle — two known varieties, light to dark grey coloring or shading.
18. Flying Birds (a definite scuttle-type)
19. Scuttle-type with snake coiled around mug. Handle is formed by the snake.
20. Swan — 3 known varieties, including white milk glass, porcelain with various handpainted details.
21. Rooster's Head — green shading.
22. Monkey Head — numerous varieties both in shapes and coloring.
23. Witch Head — green shading.
24. Goat Head
25. Devil Head
26. Hippo Head
27. Woman's Head
28. Negro boy or man Head — numerous varieties — several different molds — coloring from light chocolate brown to black — different facial expressions. One wears red jockey cap. One wears wide-brimmed hat. One smiling. One serious facial expression.
29. Buffalo Head

Top row: Author's collection. Lower: Two views "Before" and "After" (a shave). *Collection of Mr. and Mrs. Frank O. Dresner.*

Humorous or Comic Designs

Humorous or comic designs on shaving mugs were once a popular novelty and no doubt the object of many a barber shop joke for many of them are listed in the old catalogs just before the turn of the century. The Theo. A. Kochs Company of Chicago catalog of 1896 pictures several. They are listed either as "comic design" or "character design". And perhaps the most popular ones of this era were the comic frogs.

Frog humor among the populace was high, as evidenced by these humorous designs which appeared not only on shaving mugs but even on plates, cups, and all forms of porcelain and china. Here was a young America, showing its sense of humor, poking fun at itself through the characterization of frogs portraying people — doing the everyday things that the average citizen did or could do. They rode bicycles, fished, smoked pipes, and even got shaved.

The frogs usually were dressed in clothes of the day, typifying man at his best, whether it be in a high hat driving a team of horses, or leisurely fishing from the banks of his favorite stream. Below is a partial listing of designs listed in old catalogs or in private collections:

1. Frogs Smoking
2. Frogs Dressing up in Men's Suits
3. Frogs Inebriated
4. Frogs Fishing
5. Frog sitting on Quarter Moon
6. Frogs Getting Married
7. Frog Getting a Shave
8. Frog Wearing a Top Hat
9. Frogs Dancing
10. Frogs Leaping
11. Frog Taking a Nap (sitting under a tree)
12. Frog Riding a High-Wheel Bicycle

13. Frogs Boating (canoeing)
14. Frog Riding a Horse
15. Frogs Eating a Meal (at table)
16. Frogs Posing for Photograph
17. Frog Reading a book
18. Frog Painting a Picture

Other forms of comic decorations were also evident on shaving mugs, such as the caricature of woman wearing a sunbonnet, with outstretched arms holding a banner bearing the owner's name. She looks like a mountaineer woman from a Lil Abner comic in Sunday's newspaper.

In some the humor is more subtle, and these could easily be mistaken for occupation shaving mugs, such as the one listed under "comic design", picturing a negro playing a large bass drum. Or one listed as "humorous blacksmith design" which pictures a blacksmith shoeing a horse and two men watching the task. All this is within a large horseshoe and with floral decorations and the owner's name diagnoally across both sides of the horseshoe. Perhaps the humor was there seventy-five years ago, but it is not evident by today's standards of humor.

Other humorous designs were a variety of rabbit situations (similar to the frogs' antics) and a mug known to many collectors by the name "A Close Shave". The "Close Shave" mug depicts two negro men in a razor fight, one dressed in a suit and wearing spats, while the other in his shirtsleeves wears wide suspenders.

Each has an open straight-razor in his hand, and from the picture it appears the fight is a "draw", with no blood spilled since the long-armed man has one hand on the throat of the other, yet is held his distance by the "French-fighting" technique of the other contestant whose foot rests under the chin of his opponent. Another variation in design of the "Close Shave" mug depicts two negroes with razors ready, stalking each other. Other variations are suspected to have been made.

Other forms of humor from a turn of the century catalog.

Collection of Mr. Kenneth W. Southall, Jr.

Left: Collection of Mr. Kenneth W. Southall, Jr. Right: Collection of Mr. and Mrs. Mike Mocio.

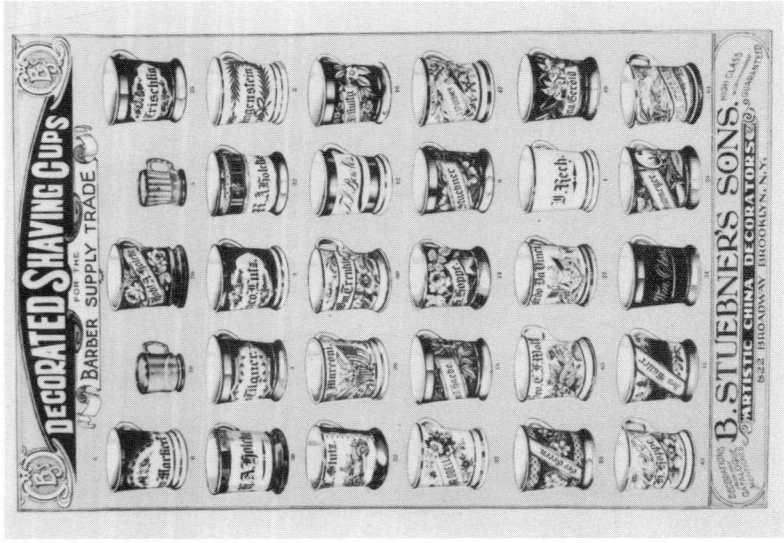

Author's collection.

Section 15

Barber Shop Mug Sheets

From the early 1870's to the mid 1920's competition for mug business among the Barber Supply companies in the United States was just as keen as between today's rivals in any American enterprise. This fact is evident from the statements found in many of the old Barber Supply Catalogs, such as "All Trade Designs and Secret Society Emblems Can Be Made (Represented) on Mugs" and "We Will Make Any Mugs Shown in Other Catalogs or Mug Sheets, at the Prices Quoted Therein", and "Decorations From Any Catalog Mentioned".

As further witness to the fact, many such Barber Supply Companies mailed out printed mug sheets of varying sizes (from 8½x10½ to 22 x 28 inches and larger) both in black and white, or brown and white, and even the more expensive ones of many colors. These larger ones were for hanging on the Barber Shop wall to solicit business. The smaller ones were supplements to the previous catalogs.

Most of these sheets had a space below each pictured mug, where the barber could write-in the price charged to the customer, which was generally marked up slightly to give the barber a small profit.

Some of the larger posters were very ornately designed and printed such as one from Koken's showing the large impressive buildings of the manufacturing plant as well as the mugs. And some extolled the virtues of many other departments in the plant such as the razor grinding department, the tannery (razor strop department), laboratory (for tonics, creams, etc.) and the accessory department (for towels, soaps, etc.). A few even showed the manufacturing plant offices. All were keyed to help the barber (who for many years was the dealer in all these items) sell the merchandise.

It is difficult to find these Mug Sheets or Posters today, because as new catalogs or posters were received, the old ones were usually discarded. And those that were kept are generally in poor condition when found today, due to the fact that they were exposed to the elements of time without a protective glass cover.

Section 16

Straight Razors

Photo from "The Crystal Palace Exhibition Illustrated Catalog — London (1851). *Permission — Dover Publications, Inc., New York, N.Y.*

According to archaeologists the first razors were made of bronze and date back to Roman days when many of them were shaped like spearheads, which suggests that the soldiers used the sharp edge of their spears for the secondary purpose of shaving.

For eight hundred years, from the 12th century when the early barbering profession first began to flourish, to the 20th century, until the invention of the ingenious Gillette Safety Razor by King C. Gillette, the breed of razors changed its shape very little.

During most of America's early period of history the word "razor" had but one meaning. It meant *straight razor*, and it was used by every adult man in the country — his most prized personal possession. It oftentimes lasted him a lifetime, and at his death was handed down to his son and so on for several generations.

Razors of course originally were brought to America by early settlers, having been made in Europe by the cutlers, generally in either Germany or Britain. Exactly when or where the first cutlery business in America was established is not known. The manufacture of razors was closely akin to surgical and dental instruments which werepikewise made by the cutlers. The term "cutler" is seldom used by the present generation of Americans, since from it has evolved more specialized trade names and manufacturing companies.

Early population explosions in America created new demands, and new barber shops sprang up to meet the needs of a growing male population. Many early cutlers transformed themselves and became known as barber supply companies. Other cutlery firms remained in that business with some of them beginning to specialize in the manufacture of razors. Still others imported razors in great quantities from around the world, with the larger portion of razor imports coming from England, Germany and Sweden. Other firms branched out into other related trades, and a few of the less enterprising ones faded into obscurity.

But by that time the large trade areas in America had been firmly established and rivalry grew, with each manufacturer trying to out-do the other, not only in the quality of steel in the razors, but in designs, etchings and engravings as well, both on the blades and handles. Razors began to be known by the *names* engraved on the blade, as well as by the manufacturer's names or trademarks. These *names* often were slogans, intended to be eye-catching and easy to remember. In some names one can even denote a likely intention of wit or humor evident among the male populace for certain periods in our history.

Important people and great events of the times were engraved upon the blades of many, such as George Washington, The Great Bertholdi Statute (Statute of Liberty), U. S. Presidents (including Lincoln, McKinley, and Garfield — the assinated Presidents), other well-known personages such as Admirals, etc.

During the next several years there followed practically every conceivable innovation of a design or decorative nature, used to adorn the blades and handles — all with the same purpose in mind — to sell razors. On many blades were the very finest of steel engravings, some even gold-washed, some with even the name of the owner engraved on the blade. This was the very ultimate in personalizing the American razor, and could be bought for $2 in 1908, from the Sears, Roebuck & Company catalog. These razors were made by The Wilbert Cutlery Company of Chicago, with the engraving "Made Expressly for" and the desired name. A choice of several blade widths, hollow or square point, black rubber or translucent wine-colored handle, was available, and the name engraved on the blade was in *gold*.

Razor handles are known to have been made from practically all conceivable materials, including wood, bone, tortoise shell, ivory, horn, rubber, gutta perche, celluloid, steel, aluminum and later of plastic. In addition they were often highly polished, cut, carved, engraved, inlaid with silver, gold, or ivory. Even photographs were transferred to the handles. On many of the plainer types of handles, evidence still remains of the customs and pride of ownership exhibited by the owner, in carving his initials or name and date on the handle.

Straight razors in the United States today are practically a thing of the past except at barber shops, where for the most part, they are used on a very limited basis (for shaving and trimming the neck and sideburns after a haircut). The barber schools no longer teach the art of shaving a man's face, with a straight razor. The old "Double Duck" razor of the late 19th century is a *dead duck* today. The social changes that have occurred since the safety razor was introduced, have marked the straight razor for obscurity, unless the current generation of bearded youth revives its use. In either event, straight razors are destined to become collectible items, in the same way as the decorated shaving mug.

Less than a decade ago, if you collected razors, you found choice used razors for about fifty cents. Today the price will average from $2 to $4 or $6, with some costing as much as $10-$15 and even higher for the fancier, more eye-appealing ones.

The hobby of collecting straight razors is perhaps one of the most overlooked areas of antiques. These relics of the past can still be found almost everywhere, at fairly modest prices. A small select collection makes a very rewarding and excellent display for any shaving mug collector and requires very little space for exhibiting them. An old oval-type picture frame with curved glass makes an ideal "display rack", to hang on the wall, and costs only a few dollars.

The following list is intended as an aid in quick identification of many popular brand names found engraved on the blades of straight razors. It is only a partial list of perhaps thousands of varieties which were commonplace in the United States as late as the 1920's. It should be noted too that some razors also had the manufacturer's name and country of origin engraved on the blade. Others contained the name of the distributor, retailer or dealer. Many barber supply companies and hardware dealers had their own names engraved on the blade.

Razors

—A—

Acme
Ace
Admiral
(Three Admirals)
Adoration Hand Forged
Anchor
Antiseptic
Antoni Tadross
Arc Magnetic
Army & Navy
Autocrat

—B—

Barbers Best
Barbers Pet
Barbers Friend
Barbers Use
Barbers Gem
Barbers Boss
Barbers Special
Barbers Prince
Barbers Rattler
Bengal
Best
Bismarck
Blue Steel
Boss

—C—

Celebrated
(The) Champion of Liberty
Classic
Clover Brand
Colonial
Congress Razor
Comfort
Copper King

—D—

Damascus
Damascus Steel
Deluxe
Diamond

Diamond Edge
Diamond Spear
Diamond Steel
Diamond Zenith
Dubl Duck

—E—

Eagle
Electric
Encore
Era
Extra
Excelsior

—F—

Falconette
Favorite
Figaro
Fred 'k Reynolds
FWE Special

—G—

Gold Seal
(The) Great Bertholci Statute
Guaranteed

—H—

Hamburg Ring
Hammer
Henry Martin
Hollow Ground
Holy Cross

—I—

Ideal
Imperial Society
Improved Razor King
Improved Eagle Razor

—J—

(G.) Johnson's Star and Hammer
Justrite

—K—

King Bee
Keen Kutter
King Midas
Koeller Gun-Metal

—M—

Magnetic Steel
Marcella
Matchless
Master Barber
Master Razor
Monte Carlo

—N—

Never Dull
Never Nip
Next
Non - XLL
Nev-A-Home

—O—

Original Pipe Razor

—P—

Pearl
Peaso Solinger
Peerless
Phoenix
Pipe
Pleezall
Price $2.00
Pyramid Brand

—R—

Real Sweden Pattern
Red Devil
Regal
Reliable
Reliance
Reynolds
Rogers
Rooster

133

Royal Blue

—S—

Saturday
Saturday Night
Silver Steel
Special
S & M
Speed
Speedwell
Sterling
Shumate Trade Mark
Shur Edge
Surprise
Success

—T—

Tally-Ho (Old Fox)
Top Flight
Try Me
Troika
Tree Brand

—U—

U.S.M.C.
U.S.A.
U.S.N.

—V—

Victor
Vienna Shaver

—W—

Wade & Butcher
Warrented
Wedge
West Point
White Eagle
Whisker King
Wiss
Wizard
Winner
Wyeth Trade Mark Warranted

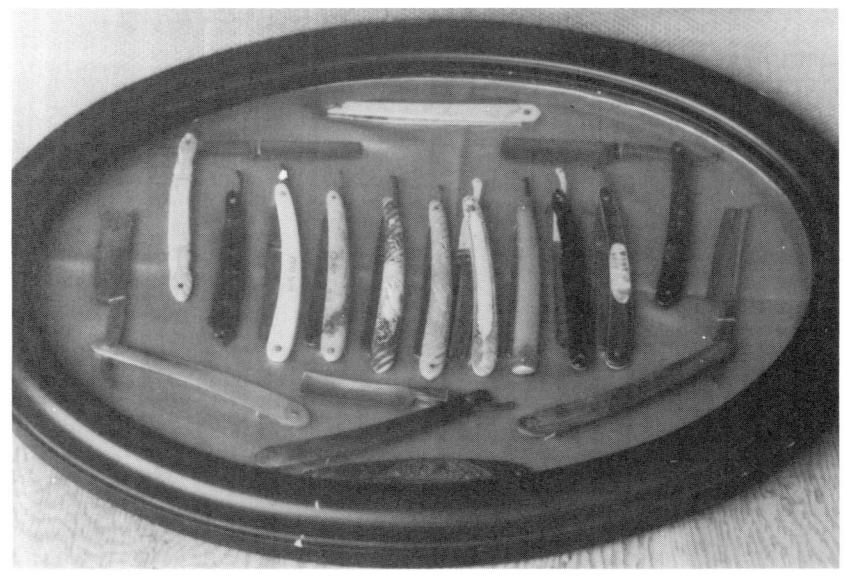

Author's collection.

Section 17
Barber Bottles

Barber shop *"stand bottles"* in use during the shaving mug era were once as plentiful as were the decorated mugs in most of America's barber shops. Their prominence in the barber shops was secondary only to the personalized decorated mugs.

Many shops displayed these *stand bottles* in the same mug cases, alongside the mugs. Just as all barber shops were not the same size or physically arranged the same (with respect to furnishings), so were the mug cases and racks different. Some were "combination toilet goods and mug cases", with shelving to accomodate the taller bottles. Some were open — others had glass doors. Some were arranged for the storage of the bottles at the top or bottom of the case. Other variations in shelving arrangements were also commonplace.

Variations in glass barber bottles (stand bottles) were as numerous as the glass blowers' imaginations of how bottles should be shaped and the many colors and shades of glass, which was mostly imported from Europe, much of it from Bohemia.

In classifying antique Barber bottles one of the basic things to remember is that there were different terminologies used by the barbers in the various sections of the country, which in many instances had the same general meaning.

As an example, the term *Stand Bottles* was generally used to denote a "stand" or "set" of bottles kept on the barber's "stand (workstand), or "cabinet shelf" or "work bench". However, in and near Boston, Massachusetts these bottles were called *"Bench Bottles"*.

In the different barber supply catalogs they were called by both names, and in some catalogs they were simply referred to as *"Bottles"*, *"Glassware"* or *"Glass Bottles"*. This was the general generic classification. And from these we get literally scores of names of sub-classifications in the bottles.

From the time (1896) when the barber supply business was scarcely known to the public until 1906 when it employed millions of capital, gave agreeable employment to thousands of men, and was recognized the world over as a leading and energetic industry, this booming industry, in its race with competition, constantly added new names and new types of bottles to the list. Most of them were European imports from the glass factories of Bohemia, Italy and France. This fast pace for imports continued until the beginning of World War I, when because of the war, imported items slowed to a standstill.

Barber bottles. *Collection of Mr. James Matthews.*

Among the sub-classes of the barbers' bottles of that period, to mention only a few were: (Actual wording of the listings as continued in catalogs.)

1. Decorated Opal Bottles
2. Imported Bohemia Bottles
3. Venetian or Spiral Bottles
4. Peach Blow Bottles
5. Venetian Polka Dot Bottles
6. Pineapple Bottles (sometimes listed as Hobnail Bottles and other variations.)
7. Engraved Ruby Bottles
8. Melon Shaped Bottles
9. New Opalescent Bottles
10. Cut Glass Bottles
11. French Cut Glass Bottles
12. Marbled Bottles
13. Painted Toilet Bottles
14. Fancy Globe Bottles
15. Octagon Recess Bottles
16. Square Recess Bottles
17. Shield Recess Bottles
18. Clear Glass Bottles (various shapes)
19. Glass Label Bottles (Lithographed)
20. Honeycomb Bottles
21. Flint Bottles

Originally a "stand of bottles" consisted of four bottles in the early barber shops, but as the popularity of the barber shop grew, so grew the number of tools and accessories of the trade — a compliment to the early supply salesmen, whose aspirations were for every "boss barber" to carry a stock equal to that of a drug store, so that instead of "$5, $10 and $20 orders for sundries" the orders would "amount into the hundreds for sundries with single establishments". (This was the exhortation by E. E. Koken at one of the early Koken company sales meetings.) "Then all of our salesmen will practically be wholesale salemen and the barber himself will supply the retail demand and do much of the business now done by the retail druggist. Think of the already large line of articles we handle and of the possibilities by addition and by creation and invention of new things for the barber, for the hair dresser and the manicurist."

As these thoughts were injected into the mainstream of the barbering profession by the barber supply salesmen, who a few years before had been looked down upon by the salesmen of better-known lines of merchandise such as dry goods, drugs, breweries, etc., a new era

Author's collection.

Water bowl, shaving paper vase and barber bottles. *Collection of Mr. James Matthews.*

developed, and with it came innovations and additional supplies and products for the retail trade.

There were now six bottles to a "stand of bottles". Witch hazel and Tonic were added. A "Water" bottle was likewise added, making seven bottles.

For some regions of the country these changes came rapidly — for others in the then remote areas they came more slowly. But for all, there was a choice of selecting the kinds of bottles that appealed to a particular shop owner or his clientele.

In practically each of the above twenty-odd sub-classes, it was possible to buy at least a small "stand" in the various assorted popular colors of the day — or with the names of each (contents) hand-painted, together with the usual popular floral or scenic designs of the day. The hand-painted bottles were usually decorated by the barber supply firms who decorated the barber-shop type shaving mugs, while the colored glass bottles were European imports.

The *personalized* barbershop stand bottles however belong to a class all their own. Such bottles, *personalized* with the owner's name, are much more difficult to find than even the most expensive occupation shaving mug. The reason for this fact is not known, but research indicates they were used only in certain localities, and the custom was never widespread as in the case of personalized shaving mugs. Local

Pair of personalized barber's bottles.
Pennsylvania Farm Museum of Landis Valley. (Museum photo)

customs varied greatly, and in at least one town in the old Territory of Oklahoma the local barbershop used *"personalized towels"* for certain regular customers. These *personalized towels* each had the name or initials of the owner embroidered on the towel, and were kept separate from the ordinary face towels used on transient or irregular customers. The shop was the first barber shop in Comanche, Oklahoma, where L. M. Zigler worked as a shoeshine boy.

These personalized bottles were, however, decorated by the same Barber Supply Company artists who decorated the shaving mugs, as indicated in early photographs of decorating rooms of the old firms. The writer has never run across a complete set of bottles and shaving mug (to match) which were personalized with the same owner name and decoration, although it is quite reasonabe to assume that some private collections do contain such one-of-a-kind rarities.

Decorations of these stand bottles were personalized with the owner's name and sometimes his favorite decoration, such as a fraternal emblem or scene, as in the two opaque white glass Hair Tonic and Bay Rum bottles pictured, with the owner's name "B. F. Decker" and the fraternal emblem of the Redmen prominently displayed on the side. (These bottles are 10⅜ inches high and 3⅜ inches dia., blown pressed glass with metal caps. All decorations were hand-painted, Circa 1880.)

Five personalized barber's bottles, circa 1880; clear glass; blown pressed; metal caps; applied glass labels painted in reverse with portrait of woman, name of male owner of bottle, and type of bottle contents. *Pennsylvania Farm Museum of Landis Valley. (Museum photo)*

Left:
Rare pair of handpainted "personalized" barber bottles bearing owner's name. *Author's Collection. Right:* Early Toilet Water bottles handpainted at the Koken Barber Supply Company bear the firm name molded in the bottom. *Collection of Mrs. Joan Webb.*

    The pair of bottles personalized with the name "J. Stevenson" and the wording "Bay Rum" and "Tonic" are among the author's collection and are hand-painted Bristol glass, bearing an early mark of the Whitehall Tatum Company of Millville, N. J., on the bottom.

    One of the most unique and among today's rarest types of personalized bottles was the *glass label bottle* as shown in the picture of five such Bay Rum bottles. These clear, glass-blown, pressed glass bottles with pewter or Brittania metal screw-caps were decorated and personalized with applied (glued) lithographed colored portraits of notable stage actresses of the period. Covering the printed label on each bottle was a thin layer of clear glass, contoured to fit the bottle, and glued onto the bottle. On the back side of this thin glass layer was *reverse-painted* (in gold) the owner's name at the top and the words "Bay Rum" at the bottom. Circa 1880. (Apothecary jars and bottles bearing reverse-painted gold labels of applied glass were in general use from the early 1870's.)

These bottles are 10½ inches high and 3⅜ inches diameter. They are identical in shape to the "Superior" brand of Bay Rum, Hair Oil and Seafoam bottled goods pictured in one of Koken's early catalogs, which were sold in both the 4-oz. and 8 oz. sizes. These "Superior" brand bottles however, had plain printed labels glued onto the bottles (without a thin glass covering the labels.)

Also pictured are two "tree bark" stand bottles, circa 1870-1880. These bottles are 7¼ inches high (includes cap) and 2¼ inches diameter. One is a cologne bottle and the other is Bay Rum. The bottles are glass, covered with a papier-mache', molded to represent a tree trunk with sawed-off limbs, branches and leaves. The sawed-off limbs are in reality, small wooden limbs that have been implanted into the papier-mache'. The tree trunk bark is so realistic, it seems apparent that when made, real tree bark was impressed into the papier-mache' to make it appear so genuine. The true brown coloring completes its realistic appearance, and some branches and leaves are colored green.

The ladies' portraits are examples of early chromolith printing on paper and are glued onto the glass bottles, then covered with a thin layer of contoured clear glass that had been "reverse-painted" with both white paint and gold, outlining the portraits. The wording "cologne" and "Bay Rum" is also reverse-painted on the back side of the thin contoured glass. The lettering is similarly done in gold and shaded with black and red paint, the glass then glued over the portrait, onto the bottle, in the "cut-out" of the tree bark. This type barber bottle is very rare and would enhance any collection, because of its many aesthetic qualities, in addition to its generic classification of being a glass label barber bottle.

Rare Tree Bark Barber's bottles. *Author's collection.*

Top (l to r) : Handpainted honey-amber bottle, Hobnail clear opalescent, Bristol-type with handpainted cherub design (Bohemia). *Second row:* Pair of ametheyst-cut-to-clear bottles. *Author's collection.*

Most dealers and collectors will recognize the "Hobnail" barber bottle pictured above, but not all of them are aware that this type bottle was listed as a *"Pineapple Bottle"* in the old Barber Supply catalogs. Small "Pineapple" water bowls and powder bowls were also made in this style and listed in the catalogs. The Pineapple bottles and bowls were made in clear, blue, amber and rose colored glass, with the rose color being the most expensive. (40¢ each for the blue or amber Pineapple Bottle and 50¢ each for the rose colored bottle. The price variance was similar with respect to the colored Pineapple Bowls.)

A 16-ounce "Fancy Globe Bottle", with silverplated tube, made in amber, blue and rose with a neck ribbon of "crystal" sold for 85¢. A French Cut-Glass Bottle (14-oz. size) with silver-plated tube was priced at $1.00. A Cut-Glass Polka Dot Bottle was 85¢, and a Painted Toilet Bottle was available in a small 16-ounce size for $1, or the large size (24-oz.) for $1.50.

Glass Powder Stands were also listed and sold to the barber for 10¢ to 60¢. These were 4 to 6 inches high and some resemble a champagne glass or an ice cream dish (with a pedestal base). They usually came in two sizes — large or small.

Imported Bohemian Bottles.

No. 151.

Flashed Ruby Peach Blow, having gold veins under the flashing. Very rich.
Price, each $1 00

No. 189.

Peach Blow Bottle, in beautifully blended rose color.
Price, each $1 00

No. 190.

Imported Bohemian Glass variegated colors, with gold filaments. Very rich.
Price, each $1 25

No. 228.
CUT GLASS STAND BOTTLE
Each $1.15

No. 191.

WHITE BOTTLE.
Pink Top, Gold Ornamentation, Green-Lettering.

No. 192.

PEA GREEN BOTTLE.
Colored Flowered Decoration, Gold Lettering.

No. 193.

WHITE BOTTLE.
Colored Flowered Decoration, Black Lettering.

These Bottles come in sets of three, each style is lettered only as shown above. Single bottles will be sold, but the lettering cannot be varied. They contain 12 ounces and are about 10 inches high.

Price, per set of three as shown $1 75
   " per single bottle 65
Bowls to match any of the above, each 55
The bottles are furnished with White Metal Stoppers.

No. 187.

ENGRAVED RUBY BOTTLE.
Bay Rum, Sea Foam and Cologne.
Price, each $0 60

No. 194.

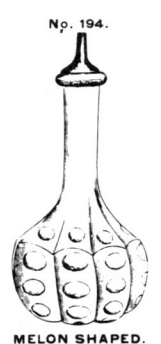

MELON SHAPED.
Contains 11 ounces.
Opalescent, Ruby, Blue and White.
Price, each $0 50

No. 195.

MELON SHAPED.
Contains 11 ounces.
Amber, Green and Blue.
Price, each $0 40

No. 152.

NEW SQUARE STYLE.
Three Colors—Ruby, Blue and Smoke.
Price, set of 3 bottles, $1 50
Price, each 50

Stand Bottles.

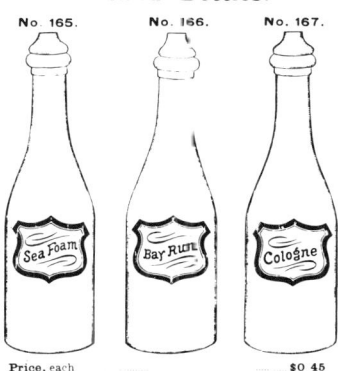

Price, each $0 45
" per set of 3 Bottles 1 25

Decorated Opal Bottles.

Price, per set of 3 Bottles $1 75
Price each 60
Extra Bottles, Sea Foam, etc., each 60

VENETIAN OR SPIRAL.
Price per set of 3 bottles, 12 oz $1 80
Price, 12 oz ....each 60

PEACH BLOW BOTTLE.
Rose and Green.
Each $0 75

PINEAPPLE BOTTLE.
Holds about 1 oz. With britannia tube.
Blue or amber .... each 40c
Rose .... " 50c

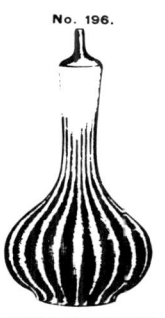

NEW OPALESCENT.
Ruby, Blue and Smoke.
Price each with Stopper 50c

Section 18
Display Cases, Wall Cases, Mug Cases

Wall cases, mug cases and various other types of Display cases were listed in the old Barber supply company catalogs. They were designed and intended to help the "barber merchant idea" of enabling the barber to display a variety of choice articles for the toilet which he might sell to his customers. These catalogs encouraged barbers to become "merchants as well as artists", as practiced in all the larger European cities and thus add to their income without additional labor.

Other smaller show cases included cigar cases (lifting top) and combination counter and show case, etc. Most of them had beveled French Plate Top glass, with double strength glass on the sides.

Among the designs of 1896 for mug cases is found the description extolling the virtues of the newer design of having the mug compartments divided by narrow vertical strips (wood) which are "substantially fastened to each shelf" Constructed in this manner, the compartments are "more easily cleaned and better ventilated than the old-fashioned pigeon holes."

This reference is to the "old fashioned" black walnut or oak (antique finish), carved or engraved "cabinet mug case of 1890 which had white china knob drawers, small white china plates (with gilt border and blue numerals). The old-fashioned type resembles a large section from the Post Office Mailboxes — without the glass windows. In fact, without having seen it pictured in an old catalog, it would be difficult to convince even a mug collector of its authenticity. This type of mug case may be a "sleeper" in a few of the antique shops, and well worth watching for.

One 1890 catalog pictures an elaborately carved and veneered mug case made of black walnut or cherry, which has an "8-day time clock" in the top and which has a "sliding writing shelf". The case held 72 mugs, had glass doors and was complete with solid brass trimmings.

At one time this merchandising idea was prevalent in most shops in all our large cities, but like many other things was changed in the process of time. As the decorated mugs began to disappear from the old-time barber shops, so began the exodus of the cases that contained them. And along with the old cases went the method of merchandising, until today when there hardly exists a shop that encourages the idea of merchandising men's toilet items.

Today only a handful of progressive-thinking shop owners make any effort along these lines.

MUG CASES

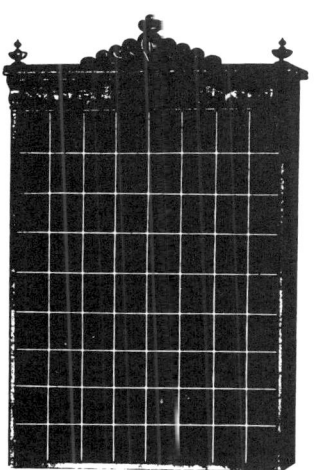

Mug Case.
Made of Oak, golden finish
No. 613—With 20 spaces .... each, $4.75
No. 613—With 35 spaces .... each, 6.00
No. 613—With 49 spaces .... each, 9.00
No. 613—With 72 spaces .... each, 12.50

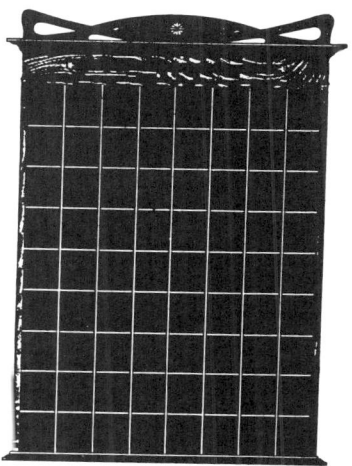

Mug Case.
Art Nouveaux design. Quarter-sawn oak, golden finish.
No. 620—With 35 spaces .... each, $9.00
No. 620—With 49 spaces .... each, 12.00
No. 620—With 72 spaces .... each, 15.00

COMBINATION CASE, No. 680. FOR MUGS AND TOILET GOODS
Made of quarter-sawed oak, golden finish. The shelves for displaying perfumery and toilet goods are covered by glass doors, fitted with good locks. Height, 4 feet 10 inches; width, 5 feet 6 inches.
Price $22.25

MUG CASES
Made of oak, golden finish.
No. 433. 35 holes, 3 ft. 6 in. wide; 3 ft. 11 in. high...... $7.80
No. 434. 48 holes, 3 ft. 11 in. wide; 4 ft. 6 in. high...... 9.35
No. 435. 56 holes, 3 ft. 11 in. wide; 5 ft. 2 in. high...... 10.65

Wall Case.

This Wall Case is set on nickel plated brackets. It is made of choice quarter-sawn Oak, golden finish. It is intended to help the Barber Merchant Idea, enabling the latter to display a variety of choice articles for the toilet which he may sell to his customers. The barbers should encourage the idea of becoming merchants as well as artists, as it is practiced in all the larger cities of Europe, and thus add to their income without additional labor. Extreme height, 65 in.; width over all, 43 in.

No. 654 ....each $20.00

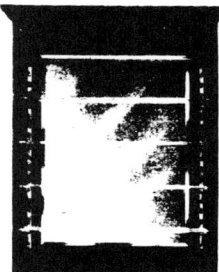

MUG RACK, No. 686

Made of quarter-sawed oak, golden finish. Beveled French-plate mirror, size 24 x 30. Nickel-plated standards and adjustable brackets. Five plate-glass shelves, 6 x 28 inches, with polished edges on all sides. Width of fixture, 3 feet; height, 3 feet 6 inches.
Price $21.00

MUG RACK, No. 688
Same as No. 686, but white-enameled.
Price $21.00

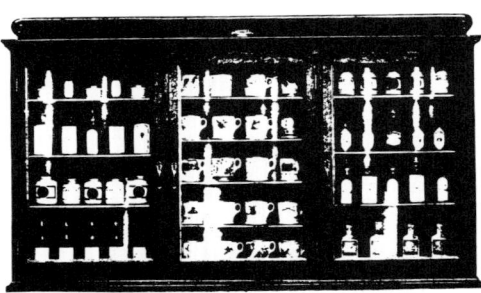

COMBINATION TOILET GOODS AND MUG CASE, No. 682

Made of quarter-sawed oak, golden finish. Fitted with glass doors, with locks and brass hinges. Polished plate-glass shelves throughout. An ornamental top-piece is fastened to the fixture, permitting the top to be used as a shelf. An up-to-date and practical piece of furniture for the modern shop. Length of the case, 5 feet 8 inches. Height, 3 feet 4 inches.

Price $27.00

MUG CASE, No. 635
Made of quarter-sawed oak, golden finish. Holds 72 mugs. Height, 7 feet 9 inches; width, 4 feet 1 inch.
Price $32.00
No. 636. Same mug case, with glass doors. Price.........$39.00

MUG CASE, No. 644
Made of quarter-sawed oak, golden finish. Holds 100 mugs. Height, 8 feet 6 inches; width, 5 feet 2 inches. Price.....$45.00
No. 645. Same mug case, with glass doors. Price.........$53.00

BARBER MERCHANT DISPLAY CASES.

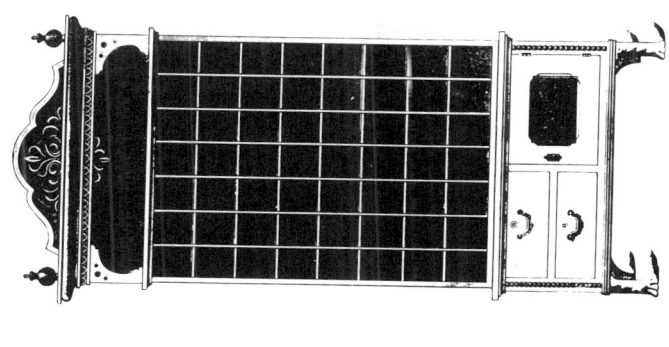

MUG CASE, No. 638

Made of quarter-sawed oak, golden finish. Holds 72 mugs. Doors fitted with glass panels and locks. Copper-oxidized finished metal legs. Height, 7 feet 10 inches; width, 4 feet 3 inches. Price $38.00
No. 639. Same mug case, with glass doors. Price $43.00

Made of choice Quarter-sawn Oak, Golden Finish. Nickel Plated Front Legs. A fine piece of Furniture.

	Height	Width	Price
No. 619 With 42 Spaces	7 ft. 8 in.	3 ft. 10½ in.	$28.50
No. 619 With 56 Spaces	8 ft. 2 in.	3 ft. 10½ in.	32.00
No. 619 With 72 Spaces	8 ft. 10 in.	4 ft. 1 in.	36.00
No. 619 With 100 Spaces	9 ft. 6 in.	4 ft. 3 in.	44.00

With or without Glass Doors
Made of Best Quarter-sawn Oak, Golden finish.

	Height	Width	Plain	With Doors
No. 616 With 72 Spaces	8 ft. 10½ in.	4 ft. 1½ in.	$37.50	$44.50
No. 616 With 108 Spaces	9 ft. 6 in.	5 ft. 1 in.	45.00	54.00

An extra charge will be made for matching combination cases.

MUG CASES.

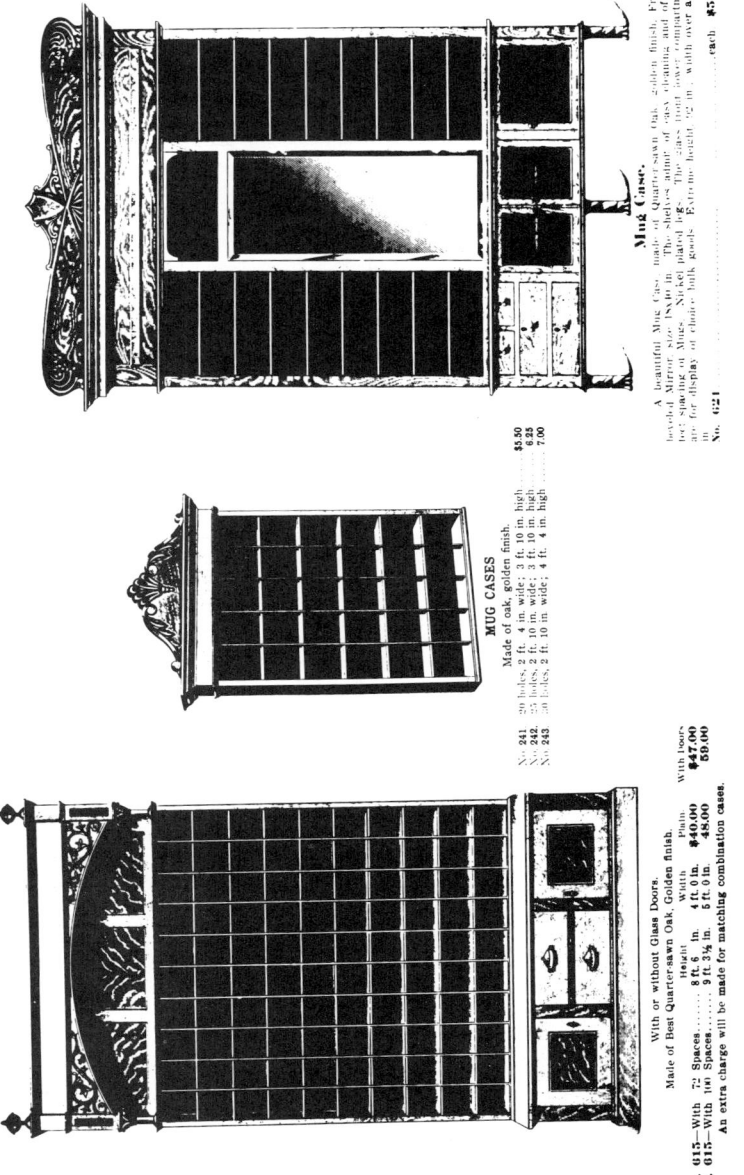

MUG CASES
Made of oak, golden finish.

No. 241 20 holes, 2 ft. 4 in. wide; 3 ft. 10 in. high $5.50
No. 242 25 holes, 2 ft. 10 in. wide; 3 ft. 10 in. high 6.25
No. 243 30 holes, 2 ft. 10 in. wide; 4 ft. 4 in. high 7.00

Mug Case.

A beautiful Mug Case, made of Quarter-sawn Oak, golden finish. French beveled Mirror size No. in. The shelves unfurl of glass, cleaning and of pet best Spanish Mug Stand. Nickel plated legs. The glass front lower compartments are for display of choice bulk goods. Extreme height 72 in. width over all 45 in. each $55.00
No. 624

With or without Glass Doors.
Made of Best Quarter-sawn Oak, Golden finish.

	Height	Width	Plain	With Doors
No. 615—With 72 Spaces	8 ft. 0 in.	4 ft. 0 in.	$40.00	$47.00
No. 615—With 100 Spaces	9 ft. 3¼ in.	5 ft. 0 in.	48.00	59.00

An extra charge will be made for matching combination cases.

Section 19
Barbership Pottery & Glassware

Pictured are original and exclusive designs in pottery. Towel urns and matching vases in beautiful rich shades and tones of color on finely detailed patterns and embossed floral designs were plentifully portrayed in color in the old catalogs. Judging from the color pictures some of this pottery would be classed as "art pottery" by today's collectors.

One of the more unusual styles or shapes was the large towel urn that set on the floor as a receptacle for used towels was cylindrical-shaped, with a hole on one side near the top (to be used as a handle). On the opposite side was a large cut-out opening which extended from the top rim downward about 1/3 or 1/4 of the height of the urn. These larger urns sold for $2 to $3.25 each. Matching smaller pottery vases ranged in price from 55¢ to $1.25 each.

"Art Pottery Urns" cost from $4.50 to $6.00. Some were square, some bulbous and others cylindrical. A few were square with concave sides and cutouts on 2 sides for handles. Matching Art Pottery vases cost from 45¢ to $1.50.

TOWEL URNS

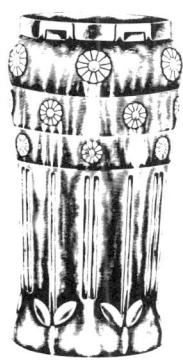  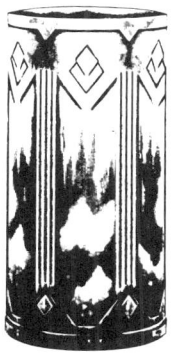

Shaving Paper Vases

Imported glassware (much of it Bohemiam) was also illustrated in many colors and many varieties of glass. They were usually very ornate in design and decoration with lots of gold decoration. These items included, in addition to the better known "barber bottles" such pieces of glassware as glass bowls, pomade jars, talcom sifters, shaving paper vases, and antiseptic jars. Many pieces had gilt tops, and some had nickel plated tops. Many of these items today are completely unknown to collectors, and even to many dealers, and can be occasionally purchased at a reasonably modest price, in comparison to the prices usually paid for decorated shaving mugs. However, I have seen some pieces among collections of art glass, and the fact that some of the old catalogs lists their glassware as "Art Glassware — Imported and Domestic" lends credence to that fact, although today's standard definitions may vary in some degree.

Section 20
Fakes and Reproductions

This is probably the most important chapter in the book, at least for the new collectors or the dealers who know little about antique shaving mugs. It is intended to assist in recognizing shaving mugs which are not genuine antiques. If after reading this chapter you are able to "spot" just one such fake or reporduction, which you otherwise may have purchased, then you will have profited from reading this book.

Unfortunately fakes and so-called reporductions (as well as duplicates, imitations, facsimiles, copies and replicas) do exist in shaving mugs, just as they exist in most other categories of antiques. It matters not whether you are a collector or a dealer, for if you cannot recognize an authentic article, you could be victimized.

So let us approach the subject in an intelligent manner and consider the many aspects, in order to properly reason with the situations that may arise. Although the definitions of the two words "fakes" and "reproductions" have different literal meanings in the strict sense of the words, both are undesirable in the realm of collecting. The word "reproduction" literally means to re-introduce (without implying any deceit).

A typical example of a "reproduction" of a shaving mug would be to use the *original* mold; thus it would be *exactly* like the original shaving mug. It would be a duplicate or an imitation of the original genuine antique article.

The word "fake" is a common slang expression implying both deceit and fraud. A typical example would be a "copy — as nearly like the original as the copyist can make it." It would be a facsimile — like the original in appearance. Remember, a fake by any other name is still a fake.

New shaving mugs are frequently manufactured as "replicas" of the past, and have been for years, which were not originally intended as "fakes" for any fradulent purposes. But somehow they find their way into the antique market, and so we must contend with them.

Assume for example, that you purchased a so-called "reproduction" or a "new" shaving mug (known by the seller as a reproduction or a new one), without being told that it was a reproduction. Then both deceit and fraud were present or implied in the transaction. So, although the words "reproduction" and "fake" have different generical meanings, they can likewise have the same meanings under certain circumstances. In other words, when a reproduction or a new mug is sold as a genuine antique, it then becomes a *fake* to the purchaser, when he later finds it out. This is true regardless of whether or not it was willfully or wittingly sold as a genuine antique shaving mug.

Consequently it behooves the dealers who sell shaving mugs to acquire some degree of knowledge concerning the reproductions, lest they should unwittingly sell them for genuine articles. There is a greater probability of a "fake" being sold as a genuine antique, than there is for a genuine antique shaving mug to be sold as a fake.

It is doubtful that all fakes will ever completely disappear, but if enough collectors and dealers recognize them for what they really are, then it will become less profitable for them to continue to exist.

Mis-Nomer

Then there is the "mug mis-nomer" or incorrect designation — oftentimes concerning a so-called "occupational" shaving mug. With the increased interest and activity in antiques, and particularly in shaving mugs, it seems that mis-nomers are becoming more and more frequent at antique shows, in antique shops and consequently among uninformed collectors.

A mis-nomer can easily become a fake or a fraud to an unsuspecting buyer. A typical example is the decorated shaving mug, which has the hand-painted dwsign lf draped curtains and floral dewrorations. The writer has seen this particular type mug called an "occupation" on many different occasions. This particular mug or one very similar to it, has been described as an "undertaker's mug", an "interior decorator's mug", a "florist's mug", a "theatrical or actor's mug," — to mention a few. To be absolutely truthful, this mug is pictured in many of the old barber supply catalogs, and is listed therein simply as a *"decorated"* or *"fancy decorated" mug*.

It is interesting and even hilarious on occasions to re-call some of the comments or sales talk concerning some so-called occupationals, at various locations around the country. Some over-zealous dealers will tell you what they think you want to hear and assume that you're some kind of a gullible, four-legged, long-eared animal, judging by some of the stories they dream up about shaving mugs. One dealer in a small resort town, proudly showed the writer, among her tables of fine cut glass and art glass, a few shaving mugs, one of which she proudly proclaimed a "genuine Washer Woman occupational", which was a heavy looking coffee mug with a decal under glaze, that had a cake of soap in it, and an old brush. The only thing about it that was old was the brush.

If you will acquaint yourself with the pictures of the mugs from the old catalog pages and remember some of the outstanding characteristics in design of some of them, then you will have some insurance against being "taken in" with a tall tale.

In the past few years there has been a tremendous demand for nearly all antiques, by people to "decorate" their homes and by serious collectors alike. The increased number of shaving mug buffs is in direct proportion to the popularity of all antiques.

The better quality old shaving mugs are, and have been for some time, difficult to locate, and in many instances rather expensive. So, with the supply becoming short and the demand steadily increasing, it naturally follows for the price to rise. Then when the prices rise to a certain point — where it seems profitable to make an easy buck with fakes — there are always some people who will take advantage of the situation. This condition exists today with respect to shaving mugs.

It will prove worthwhile for the serious collector to pay an occasional visit to a few barber supply firms, retail stores, drug stores, etc., to see for himself what the new mugs look like, because although they are now new, some of them will find their way into the hands of unscrupulous persons who in turn pawn them off as genuine old ones. And, you can be sure that after they have changed owners a few times the prices have doubled and re-doubled from the usual cost of $2 to $4 at the first retail outlet.

Most of the "new" mugs are decorated with decals and may have gold stripes or bands at the top and/or base. Some of these are pictured in this chapter. Others may be seen at some of the retail outlets. Just remember, if you see a *replica* of a mustache cup with a decal representing a bygone era, that same decal or part of it may also have been used on "new" shaving mugs. (this has been noted with reference to some now being imported from Japan.)

Fake Decal-Type Mugs

Perhaps the easiest mug to be faked is the plain decal-type mug without gold bands. Only three steps (if you have a plain blank mug, or one that has gold stripes or bands only) are required. The 3 steps are: (1) applying the decal to a genuine old mug (this is often done rather than using a new plain mug); (2) applying the slip or glaze, and (3) re-firing it in the kiln. This is fairly simple to do and would require much less time than china or porcelain-painting, where the mug detailed painting requires a person quite skilled in the art, and perhaps fired and re-fired several times in the kiln. But if you think for

Left: Genuine coffee mug, circa 1962-?. *Right:* Genuine old shaving mug ("Excelsior", pat. 1870) with the same Colt decal.

Left: Old white opaque glass shaving mug with new decal. *Right:* Current Japanese import, circa 1965-?

a minute there aren't some people who do this, look at the example illustrated in this chapter, of the faked decal-mug alongside the coffee cup or mug with the identical decal (except for the omission of the words "The Colt Peacemaker". Here is a classic example. One basic fact to remember is that the so-called "occupations" were always hand-painted, no matter how fine the detail work in the painting. Decals were NOT used for decorating occupation-type (Trades) shaving mugs.

There are several ways to detect a fake decal — shaving mug. The most obvious, of course, is to recognize the decal as a new decal. (Having seen a coffee cup with the "Colt Peacemaker" decal on it, I recognized the decal when I saw it on the mug pictured here even though the mug itself was a genuine old patented mug.

Examine the gold stripes or bands. If the gold has been "touched up", it will probably show under a magnifying glass, or maybe without a magnifier. If it has been touched up and re-fired, you should also be able to tell, in most cases. Seldom does the gold appear of uniform color, in comparing the old gold with the touched-up areas. (there are different qualities of gold, and the gold changes shades of appearance, when covered with a glaze and fired in a kiln.)

Look for worn areas of gold that are completely covered with a new glaze. Remember, if a shaving mug was used much, the places of wear are usually the handle, the top rim and the bottom rim or base, These are the first places to look, in your examination of a mug. Quite often the person who did the "gold touch-up" work was careless or amateurish, and you can detect it. Gold striping or gold banding an old mug, to make it appear genuine, is apparently very difficult to do, judging by the results I've seen on some fakes, particularly on the one pictured here. Another item worthy of mention about this particular mug is simply that originally decal decorations (including gold bands and stripe) were apparently never used on this type of mug. I've seen perhaps more than a hundred mugs of this variety (note shape of handle) with separate soap compartment and drain holes. Customarily this type mug was decorated with hand-painted flowers, or flowers and butterflies or birds. Never have I seen another one with gold bands.

There are other places on the mug to look for normal wear. If you want to know where they are, pick up one of your mugs in your hand and hold it tightly, just as you would if you were mixing lather in it with a brush.

Now about the bottom of the mug. Nearly all old mugs that were used much will have wear marks on the bottom and bottom rim edge.

Sometimes a new glaze can be seen, covering the bottom of the mug, and also covering the wear of perhaps 50 years. You may also note smudge marks of gold, carelessly left there by a non-professional mug decorator. The edges of gold stripes or bands are also a good place to examine for irregular new gold lines which do not cover up all the old gold of the professional decorator. Or the gold may have the appearance near the base of the mug to have "run" or "puddled".

The new mug pictured showing an "Oldsmobile Runabout 1903" was purchased from a local retail store in 1965. It and many other similar mugs were also available through some Barber Supply Companies. This one cost $2. It is a heavy mug, but the quality of china is not the best. The handle is shaped distinctively different than the old Barber Shop mugs. on the bottom there is a gold mark (under glaze) around the wording "Milbern Hand Decorated U.S.A." "Hand-decorated" does not necessarily mean "hand-painted", because the car and wording under the car is a decal. I don't believe many collectok would be fooled into buying one exactly like this. But if the same decal (less the wording of the car name and date) was cleverly used on a genuine old "blank" mug with perhaps the original gold banding or striping, and then re-fired, it could likely deceive many people.

Other similar new mugs I've seen are of different old-time automobiles. Some are scenes relating to old-time firemen, policemen and certain other trades.

I was offered an old mug (with original gold stripes) and a new decal of an old car. The decal had been "touched up" by hand-painting, which disguised its appearance, but not enough for the $35 asking price of the mug.

An old silverplated horse-radish tankard made by Pairpoint of New Bedford, Mass., minus the lid with hinge near the top of the handle, could easily pass for an old shaving mug. It has a glass liner of white opaque glass. The mark on the bottom is the letter "P" inside a diamond.

One "Character type" shaving mug currently being reproduced is the *"Fish Head"* mug. The reproduction has been seen at various antique shows. It is a solid dark green color with a high gloss. A solid brown color mug of this type has also been seen. So there may likewise be various other color shades and/or decorations of this mug.

New English Imports

Among the newest of English imports are a variety of scuttle shaving mugs marked "Lord Nelson Pottery — England". Also seen are

Two top rows: New English imports (decals of old photos and ads). Circa 1971.
Lower Row: Genuine old mug on left, beside a Japanese reproduction, Circa 1969, (two colors — dark brown, dark green).

Top: Old milk glass mustard jar (without top), sometimes thought to be a "two-handled shaving mug". *Middle row: (Left)* Genuine coffee mug, circa 1950. *(Right)* New shaving mug, circa 1960, mold-marked "USA". *Bottom row:* Three fakes or reproductions, circa 1960.

Current reproduction scuttle mug, marked "Old Foley Staffordshire", very authentic looking. Sells retail for less than $10.

Two of many assorted types of Currier and Ives reproductions shaving mugs and mustache mugs. Current selling for less than $3 each.

Buggy decal, circa 1960.   Racehorse decal circa 1970.

Expert quality and workmanship examples of authentic-looking new shaving mugs, decal-decorated, bold bands .and "name" on reverse side, made in California by Liscott Studio. All such replicas are marked "Liscott" and the year of manufacture on the bottom. Sold as gift mugs.

Left: Excellent quality painting of barber scene. Circa 1969.

Lower left: Glass mug on left has been "reproduced" in recent years (in various colors). *Lower right:* Old clear glass Historical campaign novelty item (top missing). Sometimes sold as a shaving mug. *Lower right:* Old Spice coffee mugs (replicas of shave mugs), an advertising offer of 1970. Set of 4 for $3.50.

large bulbous scuttle shaving mugs which have one drain hole in the top soap compartment. The entire mug is literally covered with scenic decal decorations. The base is impressed (under glaze) with either *James Kent, Ltd. — England* or *Staffordshire England*. In addition they bear a variety of stamped marks reading "Old (or Olde) Foley", "James Kent, Ltd.", "Staffordshire, England" or "Ye Olde Foley Ware". And there are undoubtedly additional similar markings.

These mugs quality-wise are worth the current $3 or $4 price tag, but a beginner collector should be careful not to pay an *antique price* for a new mug.

Japanese Mugs Flooding the Market

The Japanese are very clever artisans at "copying" or reproducing anything. Following World War II, while high feelings of animosity in America were still prevalent, and most Americans wouldn't buy even a ten cent toy which had been made in Japan — the Japanese overcame this obstacle to a large degree through the cleverness of changing the *name* of a Japanese city to "U.S.A.". Thus an item made in that city bore the words "Made in USA", and with a separate, small paper label also attached, which read "Japan" or the name or initials of the manufacturer and the word "Japan". This ruse apparently proved profitable for the Japanese, because it is still being used, with variations, and Japan today is among the top industrial powers of the world.

In addition, other clever variations are being used. As an example, in shaving mugs, mustache cups, coffee cups, beer steins, and other Japanese porcelain export items of today, you will find the word "Brandenburg" above an *Anchor* mark, stamped under the glaze. In addition, each item also has a small paper label with the word "Japan" on it. The shaving mugs and mustache cups are excellent reproductions of genuine old items, and they even look *German*, as the name *Brandenburg* implys. And when that small paper label becomes detached (as it usually does), the re-sale value somehow sky-rockets. Several such incidents around the country have been reported to the author by collectors, and in one instance the selling price was $75. (Note: These mugs normally sell for $2 to $3 each as a newly-imported item, of the year 1970.)

Another mark found under the glaze on Japanese imported shaving mugs is the words "ARNART — 5th AVE." (and with a small paper label of "Japan". The implication here is also obvious. With the paper label lost, I'm sure there are people who would assume that the wording under glazing alludes to an American made item, and not know the mug is even new, much less a Japanese import.

There is currently on the market a novelty package manufactured and distributed by the "Mohawk Company" for $6.95. It contains a badger shaving brush and a mug. On the cellophane-topped box is printed the words "Brush n Mug Set by Mohawk".

The mug is bulbous-shaped and bears a decal of a "Civil War Drum" under which is a banner with the wording describing it. It is authentic-looking except for the fact that the mug is not a shaving mug, but is a mustache cup, for it has the partition across the inside top which keeps the mustache out of the cup.

The container has no other identifying marks as to the manufacturer's address, although the mug does have a "Royal Porcelain" mark on the bottom. (This is evidently another Japanese-made item, although the one I saw at a local retail outlet has no paper label attached.)

Japanese import. Circa 1960-?

Others have the mark "Royal Crown — Imperial" under a crown mark, all under glaze, and with a paper label with the word "ARNART".

Mugs such as the one pictured with a barber pole decal were made at least twelve years ago and maybe a little earlier. They are currently being revived again by the Japanese.

Lefton China shaving mugs are all new. There are quite a variety of these, with various marks and with a variety of decals. One has a decal Fireman insignia-design with a banner proclaiming "Fire Helmet — Fire Axe — Fire Trumpet — About 1877", and with a man's name in small letters across the front of the helmet. These same decorations are also found on mustache cups now being imported. They can be bought for about $3, so don't pay more. They are very plentiful.

Another mark (Japanese) is "LEFTON CHINA — Handpainted" with a small crown design, or simply "Lefton China" as seen on the new decal-decorated "Jockey Hitching Post — About 1881" banner mug. The decoration reminds you of the early American-type horse hitching post.

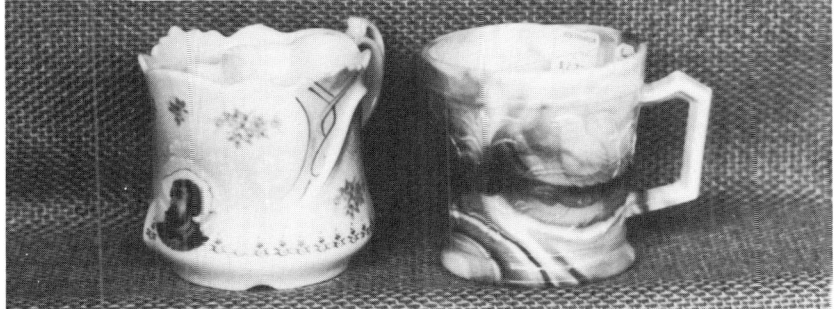

Left: Japanese "Brandenburg" marked import. Circa 1970-? *Right:* New glass mug (singing bird)

American "reproductions" marked "U S A" on bottom.

Another Japanese mark seen on the bottom of mugs is "ROYAL CROWN" and a number such as "2804". This mark will be found on many mugs, including one which has a banner proclaiming a "Conestoga" wagon, and another fireman's insignia design — bright red helmet and hose nozzle design.

Silk Screen Mugs — Japanese Imports

Current Japanese-made "occupation-type" shaving mugs in at least six different designs are available in some areas of the country. These heavy-porcelain type mugs are shaped like many of the old blank mugs imported from France and Germany before 1891. And the quality of composition and high gloss are remarkably good, compared with the genuine old mugs. The decorations of designs could easily deceive many people because they appear to be hand-painted, which is a main characteristic of the genuine old occupation on trade design shaving mug. However, the opinions of several experts in the packaging field and the printing industry are that these designs are "printed" on the mugs by the silk screen printing process.

Their introduction to this country was at first to a few large American cutlery chain stores and later through antique reproduction outlet firms in several eastern cities. After more than two years, they are now available at many small outlets in the country. They have a "Viking" label. See reproduction of this label with accompanying pictures.

Silk screen printing is a method widely used today in specialized commercial printing and art reproduction work. Many of the colorful metal business signs you see are products of the silk screen artisan.

New Japanese shaving mugs. Circa 1970-?

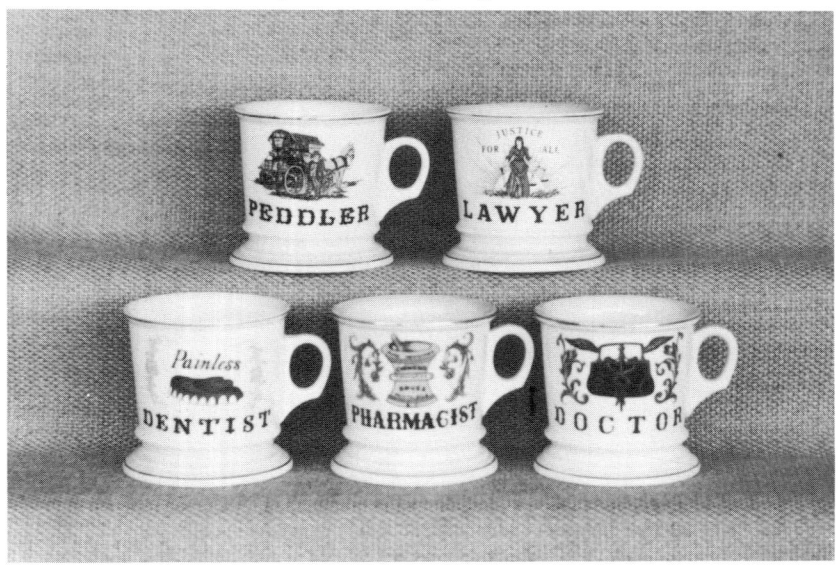

The process involves writing on silk by first coating the silk screen with wax and then cutting away portions of the wax, thus exposing the silk threads. The screen is then used as a stencil, with the ink pigment being forced through the silk threads onto the surface to form the design. This step is repeated with different silk screens (or stencilling) and different colors of ink to make a multi-colored print.

Many items of glass and porcelain decorated with silk screen designs, have been imported in recent years, but these are the first shaving mugs to my knowledge that were made by this process and bearing the occupational-type designs.

And because of their quality, both in composition, workmanship and eye appeal they may become collector's items of the future. They are both colorful and cheap — a combination eagerly sought by collectors and dealers alike. Future demand will determine the selling price, but my prediction is that as soon as they become unavailable through the regular retail marketing stores and are no longer imported to this country, the asking price will scarce you.

Here's the list of these "new" mugs.

1. Pharmacist
2. Doctor
3. Dentist

2. Lawyer
5. Fireman
6. Painters

There also is presently on the market a new double compartment shaving mug similar to the old "Wild Root" mug which was made by the Buffalo China company in the early 1920's. The new mug is believed to be a current or recent Japanese import, as reported by a fellow collector, who recently saw a shelf full of them in one antique shop. Each had a red mark on the bottom which had been defaced or obliterated to the extent it was impossible to clearly read the mark. The quality of china was comparable to the genuine old mugs, and they had a variety of scenic and floral decorations on the sides, which are believed to be silk screen process printing, which are quite authentic in appearance.

SPORTSMAN BRAND — The Golden Duck Shaving Mug

From 1953 through 1955 the Sportsman Division of The Lambert Company, currently the Warner-Lambert Pharmacuetical Company of Morris Plains, N. J., made its mark in the men's shaving soap business and also in the world of collecting antique-type shaving mugs. The idea for packing one of the firm's products (shaving soap) in a shaving mug was not new (for this was done by other firms many years ago — but in plain glass mugs and in wooden bowls), but the "package" itself, a hand-painted, china shaving mug, styled after the genuine articles of the past, representing the old *trade designs* so popular during the shaving mug era, was unique and in itself a large undertaking.

The idea for a series of such mugs as a sales promotion, originated in 1951 with Mr. John Hudson Moore, President of the Sportsman Division of the company. He was a frequent visitor to De Zembler's barber shop in Rockefeller Plaza which at that time contained one of the most extensive collections of shaving mugs and barber basins in the world.

Mr. Moore conferred with Mr. Don O'Brien (Warner-Lambert's package design expert) and with Mr. Nelson Lebo, President of Nelson Lebo, ceramic manufacturers of Trenton, N. J., to select the right cup shape, size, etc. Mr. O'Brien previously did fairly extensive research on the subject with De Zembler's and in the New York Public Library, in order to perfect the most representative cup of the era that the mug was designed to recall.

The first series covered a list of twelve male occupations as listed below:

Autoist		Farmer
Broker		Horseman
Sea Captain		Ice Man
Doctor		Lawyer
Engineer		Policeman
Fireman	*1953 Edition*	Salesman

The initial production of these mugs was a huge undertaking. The pottery was made by Cook Ceramic Manufacturing Company, which went out of business about 1960. To provide the initial quantity for the anticipated large-scale nationwide sales volume, actual production began in 1951, with the firm Tatler, Inc., decorating the mugs. The Nelson Lebo Company purchased the Tatler firm in 1953 and took over the task of decorating. These mugs were sold on the retail market from 1953 through 1955.

Reproduction of original 12 x 18 inch color brochure picturing twelve mugs from the Sportsman collection of "Old Style Shaving Mugs". *Author's Collection.*

According to the Warner-Lambert Company "the principal outlets were leading department stores and a selection of some 5,000 quality drugstores throughout the United States. The occupation mugs sold for $4.95."

"Each mug was hand painted (NO decals were used); each of the occupation mugs was decorated with a ring of 14 kt. gold, and each mug kiln-fired twice."

The trademark of the Sportsman Division of the firm was a flying duck. This mark, together with the word *"Sportsman"*, was the original *incised* mark put on the bottom of the mugs. However, in the firing process, the tin white glaze flows more than other glazes and some trademarks were hard to read. So a rubber stamp label was added. This accounts for the fact that some mugs are marked on the bottom both ways, and later versions were marked with a rubber stamp label only. Some have even turned up without marks; these are believed to have been tampered with at a later time to obliterate the mark, although it is possible for some to have been decorated and shipped without the stamp. Occasionally one will be found with only a slight depression (part of the incised mark which filled-in with the tin white glaze when it was fired).

The advertising, timed to precede Fathers' Day and Christmas, when the mugs enjoyed a brisk sale, was placed in Town and Country magazine, The New Yorker, and Esquire, according to company records.

Later, *personalized* versions of these and other mugs was produced, which a customer could order with his own name emblazoned in gold lettering. The *personalized* mugs sold for $6.96 each.

A grand total of 375,000 of the Sportsman mugs were made and sold during the period 1953-1955. Tatler, Inc. decorated 250,000 and the Nelson Lebo Company painted 125,000, after purchasing the former company. Records are not available as to the quantity that were personalized.

The company reports that "special display racks of antique wormy chestnut were also prepared by Mr. O'Brien in conjunction with a supplier, and these proved so attractive that they were in many cases purchased by retail customers to display their mugs at home."

In addition to the twelve mugs listed, other trades later represented on these mugs were The Bartender, The Lamplighter, The Musician, The Pharmacist, The Dentist, The Oilman, Father, Rancher, Butcher, Barber and the barber shop Quartet.

Left: Author's Collection. Right: Collection of Mrs. Omega Belle O'Connor.

Some mugs are painted in a solid color on the back side of the mug (where the handle is located) and there are several variations. The gold ornamentation on each side of the main picture will also vary from one mug to the other, depending on the trade represented. The porcelain is of consistent good quality, but the size will vary slightly, as will the thickness of the different mugs.

Some of the mugs have a certain distinguishing characteristic, a slight bulge on the inside of the mug, where the handle was attached (when it was pressed to the mug). This does not detract from the overall appearance of the mug, but is a noticeable trait on some mugs — probably some of the earlier models. This deficiency was corrected in later issues when mugs were of a considerable more thickness and the bulge was eliminated. By thickening the mug, additional strength was added, but this changed slightly the contour of the base of the mug, and refined its overall appearance.

The color of the porcelain of most of the mugs would be described as "egg shell white" (slightly less than pure white), yet some of the varieties (the thicker ones) are more white in appearance. This was due to the glaze used and the heat in firing the mugs.

Most of these mugs, although less than 20 years old, show a remarkable quality for reasonable likeness to the quality of hand-painting found on the genuine old mugs. These Sportsman mugs were *NOT* exact copies of the antique shaving mugs and were not intended to be exact copies, but rather they were designed to depict certain trades of the bygone era.

The Difference

One main difference, for a quick identification of these first Sportsman mugs is, in addition to the "Sportsman" name incised on the bottom of the mug, or the rubber stamp label, is the word *"The"* which appears in gold on the fact of the mug, such as "The Farmer", "The Dentist", "The Policeman", etc. All Sportsman mugs used the old English style of lettering, in identifying the trades for today's generation. (The genuine *old* shaving mugs, likewise used the Old English style of lettering, but sometimes used Script, block lettering or other styles. And the old barber supply company decorators never used the word *"The"* before a trade name. In those days, the hand painted design was sufficient to depict the trade or occupation, for even the whiskerless youth of the day could recognize a farmer plowing a field, or a dentist pulling a tooth. But these newer mugs were produced to appeal to a new generation with a flair for the past.

The *marks* on the mug will show different variations of the following sketches; the duck is sometimes outlined in gold; the word "Sportsman" will be found in a script style, raised or indented from the mold itself, other wording may be either in gold or as part of the mold.

Collection of Mrs. Omega Belle O'Connor.

Although the mugs were produced literally by the hundreds of thousands and sold all over the country, they are unique additions to the family of shaving mugs. They are however often mistakenly advertised and sold as genuine old ones, and the price sometimes reaches the $80 - $100 range. The current average fair market value, among knowledgeable collectors and dealers, is a much more modest figure, depending on the areas of the country. Except for the genuine old shaving mugs, these mugs are the most collectible of all the newer mugs.

Decoy Shaving Bowl

During the same period the Sportsman line also included a "Decoy Shaving Bowl" as pictured in an advertisement in the December 19, 1953 issue of The New Yorker magazine (page 77). Made of glass in a clear or marigold color, shaped like a duck or duck decoy, with the inside of the bill painted gold or yellowish, and with a clear glass bottom, it contained shaving soap and sold for $3.50 each. (Some were made in clear glass.) Soap refills were obtainable for $1.00. This attractive collectible is not marked in any manner and is seldom recognized but for its shape and size. See photo. The bowl is in two pieces, with the top half of the *duck* as a cover for the lower bowl. The thickness varies from about 1/4 to 3/16 inches. Height 4½ inches to the top of the head. Length 5¾ inches. Width 4⅞ inches.

These glass duck decoys will possibly become sought after, when it is realized what they were made for and that they have been discontinued for several years.

Author's collection.

Double — Triple Values

If you are a collector of shaving mugs and related items, in a general classification way, you probably have found it increasingly difficult to enhance your collection with certain types of mugs or items, and wondered why. Why for example, certain milk glass shaving mugs are difficult to locate. Why pewter mugs, earthenware mugs, tin mugs, etc., (to mention only a few), are all so hard to find. And why the price is so high when you do find something in these and certain other categories.

Perhaps you realize who your real competition is for these items and perhaps you don't. Competition or demand for certain items cause prices to rise. And you have competition, whether you know it yet or not.

For example, let's consider a plain milk glass shaving mug. Your competition for such a mug would be, in addition to other shaving mug collectors, people who collect milk glass. And, believe me, there are lots of them.

Now, let's consider a milk glass shaving mug which has a "cameo likeness' of President Garfield or Garfield and his wife on opposite sides of the mug. This type of mug would be in the "multi-value" category. Your competition for this mug would be tremendous. Not only are you competing against shaving mug collectors for such a mug, but against collectors of milk glass, collectors of Historical Glass or Historical items, and collectors of Political items as well.

Another multi-value mug recently seen in an Oklahoma collection was a custard glass shaving mug with an advertising message appearing on it — "Complimentary of_____, " and in addition, it had the wording "Indian Territory" on it, indicating a period of time before Oklahoma became a state. (Such an item would be a "collectible" in four different categories — mugs, custard glass, advertising and Indian Territory items.)

And, too, you may also be competing against some museum as well. So if you do find such an item, take these things into consideration, before you pass it up.

As a collector, the only thing in your favor, would be that the shop owner who had it, was not aware of its potential multi-value. As a shop owner, you must rely on your past experience in such matters if you want to sell it at the highest margin of profit, consistent with good or fair business practices. Many a shop owner has sold such a piece of merchandise for a mere pittance of what it was really worth.

Any way you look at it, the person with the "knowledge" has the advantage.

Another competitive area among the general classification of shaving mugs are the Lenox shaving mugs. I suspect that there are many collectors of fine Lenox wares around the country. Thus the Lenox shaving mug would be a "double-value" mug.

Tin shaving mugs likewise fall into a double value category, if they are of the Civil War era. There are people who collect Civil War items, and the chances are good that they can easily recognize a Civil War Tin shaving cup from just an ordinary tin cup when they see one. Old photographic mugs (with the picture of the owner in Confederate uniform) could also be of double or triple value.

Redware and other earthenware pottery type shaving basins and shaving mugs, particularly sgraffito designs, are rarely discovered or bought by the shaving mug collector, because of the heavy demand among collectors of primitives and museums.

Pewter shaving mugs and barbers basins are more rare than much of the Art Glass because for many years the museums have been searching for these items, among the big collections of pewter. And most of these pieces have been in collections for years, and are seldom seen on the market for sale.

If you're fortunate enough to own a shaving mug with the name of a known circus performer, then consider yourself lucky that the mug isn't among a collection of "circus items" Or a mug that has circus wagons painted on the side, for here again, your competitor is the collector of circus items.

What this all amounts to, to you as a collector and to you as a dealer, is simply this. There are collectors (accumulators) and then there are collectors who are specialists. My thoughts along this line are that if you have a hobby collecting something that is worthwhile, then it is also worthwhile to take the time to find out all you can about it. If you don't do this, then you are cheating yourself. Cheating yourself out of the fullest enjoyment of your hobby, because your rewards of collecting will be in direct proportion to your knowledge of the subject. As a dealer, you're cheating yourself from the proper profit you should make from your original investment, by not knowing the true value or values of an item.

The paragraphs above are only a few of the multi-value items you might expect, if you collect shaving mugs and related items. P. T. Barnum is supposed to have once said there was a sucker born every minute. Just be sure he wasn't talking about you.

Barber Shop in the Street of Shops — *"Courtesy of The Henry Ford Museum, Dearborn, Michigan."*

Collection of Mrs. Oma Anderson.

PART II
Section 1

EVOLUTION OF THE KOKEN BARBER SUPPLY COMPANY

Author's Note: Historians record for future generations the deeds of great men and events in their lives that shape their destiny and the destiny of those around them. It is the considered opinion of the author, after collecting the facts brought out in the following story of the Koken Barber Supply Company, and after reading and studying many speeches made by E. E. Koken, that he was a great man, in every sense of the word. Much of this supportive information deals not with the main purpose of this book, and has therefore been omitted.

He was a true leader in his chosen profession, and he would have been a true leader in any profession because his qualities of leadership would have been transferrable to any job he might have undertaken. His imaginative concepts of new ideas which were useful for the betterment of man, even in his own particular field of endeavor, were an outstanding characteristic, but he was quick to recognize and applaud the efforts and ideas of those who worked for him — to give credit where credit was due. He was always interested in those things that would make for the betterment of mankind and willingly and gladly lent himself to their advancement.

After his death, the Koken Barber Supply Company in 1910, sent to many of Mr. Koken's old friends a booklet containing his photograph and several addresses that he had made on different occasions to those that were associated with him as heads of departments and salesmen. His intuitive admonitions to each faithful employee are carefully woven as an integral part of each speech. That he was a great leader, thinker, speaker and builder of better things for our society are quite evident.

Other speeches the author was privileged to read, such as "The True Object of the Association — Its Scope and the Spirit of Membership", read before the National Convention of Barber Supply Dealers in New York City, September 19, 1906, characterize the real E. E. Koken.

This story then is written first as a tribute to his memory, second as a reference guide for future historians, and last but not least, as the Hub of the Wheel from which evolved the many antiques of today concerning shaving mugs, barber chairs, and scores of other barbering "collectibles" attributed to this early industrialist.

————RBP

OUR FACTORY—Erected January 3d, 1893.

LOCATED ON THE NORTH-EAST CORNER SIDNEY STREET AND OHIO AVENUE.
Average frontage of grounds, 241 feet; depth, 125 feet. Average frontage of main building, 77 feet; depth, 125 feet.

Ernest E. Koken 1855-1907

The evolution of the Koken Barber Supply Company, which had its humble beginning (a one man, one-room shop) in 1874, spans nearly 100 years of business activities through its present-day counterpart, Koken Companies, Inc.

The business "prospered from its very inception," relates Mr. Hugo H. Davis, who worked for the firm for over fifty years and served from 1959 to 1969 as its President.

In the early years it was a one-man operation, conceived by the aspirations of a young American and nurtured in hard work by that young man in his twenties, with a business acuity seldom paralleled either a century ago or in today's business world. This was the firm established by ERNEST EDWARD KOKEN.

Ernest Edward Koken's father, Theodore Werner William Koken was a German by birth and educated in Germany, where he received a diploma from the University of Bonn. In 1838 he made his first trip to the United States from Germany, when he sailed as a passenger from Brenerhaven to Vera Cruz, Mexico, aboard a 90-foot schooner brig, the "Weser".

He was the only passenger accompanying the Captain, a helmsman, a carpenter, a cook, a steward and three sailors. He boarded the ship on April 24, 1838 and did not reach the harbor of Vera Cruz until June 18th. However, they were "fired upon by a French schooner and not able to land, as the French-Mexican war was on." They had to turn about and go to New Orleans, where they landed.

Theodore Koken kept a diary of that voyage, according to his granddaughter, Mrs. Olive K. Yackey, and he tried to learn the Spanish language with the Captain, whom his diary relates was "unable to retain the words with ease, and thus my progress is continually being retarded."

It is not known what type of work he was engaged in during the thirteen years he remained in the United States. Before returning to Germany in 1851, he had become a United States citizen on October 6, 1845, had married and had three small sons, William Theodore, Charles and Frank.

His youngest son, Ernest Edward Koken (founder of Koken Barber Supply Company), was born four years later in 1855 in Aerzen, Germany, (a suburb of the beautiful city of Hildesheim) during which time the elder Koken was a co-partner of Schilling-Koken Cedar Cigar Box Factory. This business failed after Schilling's health gave way and he mis-appropriated some of the funds of the business and it became bankrupt. It was after this disappointment that Theodore Koken returned to the United States with his family in 1858 or 1859. This time he brought with him an oil portrait of his great-grandfather, John Charles Koken, who also had been a man of letters and an Evangelical Minister.

Settling in St. Louis, Missouri, he was employed by the "Westlicke Post", a German newspaper. His health failed and he died in 1871. Shortly thereafter young Ernest Edward Koken had to leave school and help his brothers support his mother. He was only sixteen at that time.

Nearly forty years later, in late 1909 or the winter of 1910, after E. E. Koken's death, his close friend A. B Greene, a commercial artist eulogized phases of his life — the simple story of his early years — which E. E. Koken was not too proud to tell — of his boyhood poverty and the needs of his family, "how he looked out into a big and to him a new world with a longing and a mastering ambition to *do* something and to *be* something useful and helpful."

Mr. Green wrote "with what vigor he tackled his first humble job, and with his first realization of his ability to climb upward, his faculties were buckled down to the problem that was growing more and more realistic." His early aspirations were recalled — of his thirst for knowledge — his mental striving by night work over his books, and as he gleaned little by little and his boyish faculties broadened came the youthful speculation as to what his future was to be.

E. E. Koken's First Job

Young Ernest's first job was an apprentice in an instrument and optical workers shop in St. Louis. In this shop "he probably first struck a congenial and educating lead, there his soul began to expand, and like the prophet of old he 'saw visions' of all the wonder that was to be."

This meticulous type of work prepared him for his first venture into business for himself. In 1874, when he was twenty years of age, young Koken, an amateur artist, began "taking orders for decorated shaving mugs, by going from shop to shop (barber shop) for orders."

Decorating the mugs and doing with a remarkable ability, the old fashioned glass drug labels with lettering in gold and colors, led him to think along artistic lines, and with a small boy, his only assistant, up two flights of dirty stairs in an old fashioned building, he worked industriously full time. Then the idea came of branching out just a little — adding an article or two which he might sell at a profit to anyone. It happened to be the — BARBERS! He bought a couple of barber chairs which he sold at a profit. Then another article was added, and — the BARBER again! This grew quickly into a small business which seemed encouraging, then "if I only had the *means* to increase" — was the racking thought that kept his brain sleepless many a night.

"The Divinity that shapes our ends" was leading him, and soon he had a partner, Mr. Boppert, who could furnish some funds. Before long (1881) they were *making* Barbers' chairs and in an humble store not far from the present location was to be found most of the goods then used by barbers.

Koken's First Patented Barber Chair

Koken's first patent Reclining Chair (Patented October 25, 1881) was made of black walnut with cane seat and back, nickle plated trimmings and was plush on the arms and headrest. It sold for $30 in 1888. Another model (No. 2) upholstered in Tapestry Brussels Carpet, with gilt engraving and bronzed trimmings sold for $25. These were the forerunners of many more ornately adorned and more expensive models yet to be built, such as the "CONGRESS" series of revolving and reclining chairs which had several improved qualities, including the improved footrest. Next he invented the Koken Hydraulic Barber Chair, received a patent on it and sailed ahead toward a most successful and rewarding business career.

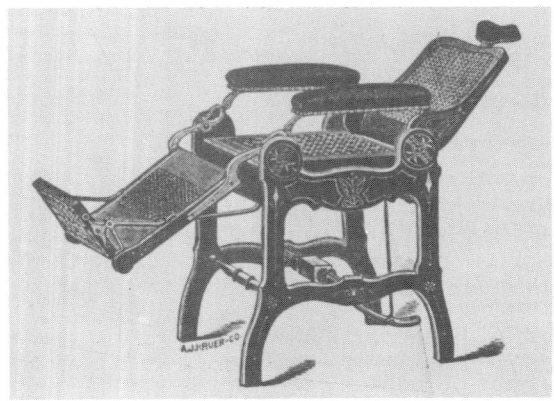

Koken's Patent Reclining Chair
(Patented Oct. 25, 1881)
Black Walnut. Nickel-plated trimmings. Cane seat and back.

In recounting the worries of those early days which were discussed between Ernest Koken and his old friend, A. B. Greene wrote — "the days that were so fearfully counted till — the *notes* became due and the harassing experiences of collecting in the forenoon what might be obtained to meet the bill or note that had to be paid before the closing hour."

"Many of you know nothing of those days of struggle — you have seen only the effulgence of the brighter sun that was forced to shine and grow brighter by the integrity — the indomitable will — the Grant like but beautifully human and conscientious labors of a man who was a *man* in its highest meaning.

"Then, by the grace of this same Divinity still shaping the course of our friend, comes into the plan of operation *another* — and who in all the world could have made as wise and perfect a selection — the *rim* on the *Hub* of the wheel, reverse it if you please, but still there is no wheel without both. The gentleman. . .Mr. George Sutherland, partner.

"In the mental make up of Mr. Koken were many natural endowments. There was — and I speak of it first — an inborn talent in the Artistic line, uncultivated and permitted only in a partial way to crop out in the occasional uses he made of it. Although owing to the business cares of his later career this talent was applied largely to mechanical and constructive work. We all know how well he did it and with what careful, methodical procedure, the *German* heredity handed down possible from his grandparents. Yet while we speak of this mechanical side of the subject, there was another and to me a more wonderful phase — the Aesthetic side. I have often been surprised at his descrenment of the truly meritorious features in works of Art and at his detection of the weak spots. His hand has produced some evidences of this uncultivated talent which do him great credit.

"He had a *mathematical* faculty which considering his limited schooling, was to me marvelous. His knowledge of Chemistry, picked up along the way was another evidence of this versatility and wonderful ability to get to the bottom of anything that attracted his attention.

"In physical and mental science he was able to hold his own with highly cultured gentlemen whose study the subjects were specialties. I have sat with him at the lunch table and heard him ask questions of expert electricians present and amaze them with his knowledge of electrical and other principles and theories, and always with that modest yet absolute command of the subject that interested me.

"If there was ever a problem came up between us, — any subject which could not at once be answered and settled satisfactorily, the next day — no matter how much of the night it took — he was pre-

Koken's mammoth exhibit at the 1904 Louisiana Purchase Exposition, St. Louis, Mo. Exhibit was 25-feet in height with 8-foot carved cedar barber poles atop each corner. Giant barber chair in center and regular size chair atop the arches.

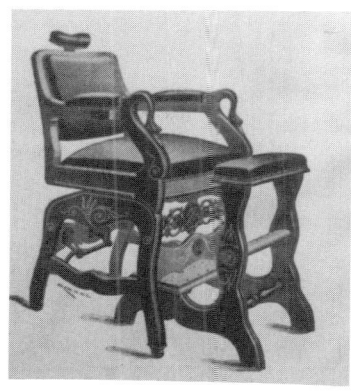

Koken's Adjustable Barber's Chair No. 11, from 1892 catalog. Solid oak or walnut, covered in Tapestry Brussels Carpet ($23) or in Mohair Plush ($27). Adjustable by rear pedal.

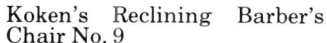

Koken's Reclining Barber's Chair No. 9

Koken's Patent Reclining Chair No. 2, patented October 25, 1881, upholstered in Tapestry Brussels Carpet with gift engraving and bronzed trimmings ($25). Pedal adjustable (any position).

Koken's Star No. 4 Elevating Chair, featured in 1892 catalog.

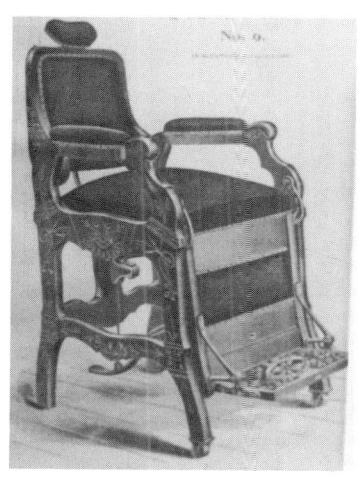

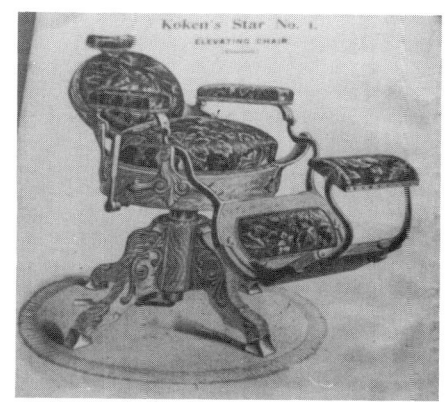

pared to settle it thoroughly and correctly. Books to him were mines from which he was constantly digging treasures.

"There was also that charitable, unselfish trait, too seldom found in man. His heart was as big as his fellows' needs. His hand over responded to what seemed true giving. His heart bled with sympathy for the suffering one and his help, always wordless, was given in the spirit of the Master's teaching.

"Analyzing him in my silent hours of retrospection, I ever find new and constantly recurring evidences of qualities that make the memory of his living a tribute to his many merits.". . .quoting from Mr. Green.

Mr. Oliver T. Johnson, who was born in 1881 (the year the firm name was changed to Koken & Boppert) was a nephew of Ernest Koken. His father was Mrs. Ernest Koken's brother. The Johnsons and the Kokens lived in their identical, single-family, two-story homes, separated by their side-yards, where as children, Oliver Johnson and his Koken cousins played.

Mr. Johnson, who at age 89 (in 1970), recalling vividly the early days of his childhood, relates the Koken house had "two finished rooms in the basement, as well as a cellar-like room under open joists, inside exposed foundation walls, and with no floor save the bare earth, through which seeped several inches of water during the Spring, spreading through the basement."

"In the far corner of the cellar stood a wood-turning lathe, operated by a foot treadle and served with a high stool. On the lathe, at each end, stood a plain, old-fashioned kitchen coal-oil lamp. Over the water stretched a wooden causeway from the stool, across and beyond the cellar to the staircase leading upstairs.

"Thus it was at night, in that cellar corner in water and darkness, that Mr. Koken at the lathe, turned out the wooden patterns, already designed and draughted by him on other nights at a flat dining table up in a first-floor room. Thus did that modest man, with his own hands, turn his dreams into facts."

That cellar drama, which Mr. Johnson witnessed only once, as a small boy, (it being night with water all around) made a deep and lasting impression on his mind, for it has remained in his memory for the better part of a century.

Mr. Johnson, who at age 89 is still active as an attorney in St. Louis, served the Koken Barbers Supply Company as that firm's attorney from 1905 through 1918. During this time attempts were made to unionize the company. There was even a nationwide boycott, which did not hurt the Koken company, because its heart, the patented hydraulic barber chair, was above and beyond competition. That chair was the child of the Ernest Edward Koken mind. Mr. Koken at that time was paying his employees more than the union's scales, and he would not submit to union representatives entering the plant and to union labels appearing on the products of the company. According to Mr. Johnson, a union leader suggested that if he were quietly "taken care of", he would have the boycott lifted. Mr. Koken denounced him as a traitor to those trusting him, and ordered him out of the Koken office.

Mr. Johnson further recalls that the Koch Barber Supply firm in Chicago, was the largest competitor to the Koken firm — but did NOT have the chair. It approached Mr. Koken on combining the companies and driving others out of business. Mr. Koken answered that he had no ambition to drive other men out of business.

The business ability and high principle of Mr. Koken asserted themselves while he was curator of the estates of several minor children of his deceased brother. Those assets he had invested in stock of a large trust company, which, in time, ran into financial straits. A committee of bankers and depositors, he being one, succeeding in phasing out the peril. The leading banker in St. Louis said "Mr. Koken, where have you been in this town all these years? You should have been out in front, for St. Louis needs men like you." Mr. Koken had declared to me (reports Mr. Johnson, his attorney) that his brother's children would lose nothing — as he would step into their financial shoes, although he in no wise had been negligent as a curator. But the trust company was rescued.

His sure-fire technical competence asserted itself when he was on a Federal Court jury in a personal injury case, arising from a falling beam. It had been tied up under the roof temporarily — the plantiff claimed negligently because only one knot had been used. Eleven jurors thought so too, but not Mr. Koken. They denounced him and he asked that some book on knots be sent into the jury room. With permission of all counsel, the Court did so, and the stand of Mr. Koken was justified.

Ernest Koken's many business activities during the thirty-four years following his hydraulic barber chair invention, were crowned with success, and had he not been stricken with coronary thrombosis and died at age 54, the world may have known another automobile family. For, after his death, his son Walter found on his desk at home, an unfinished draft on his drawing board of a gasoline engine that may have been a competitor of the Ford engine.

Mrs. Koken and their two daughters, Ellen and Olive, had just arrived in Italy for a tour of Europe when they received a cablegram telling of the death of their husband and father. They had begged him to go with them on the trip, but he had said he did not have time because he was busy on some project. Had it not been for his untimely death, many of us today might be driving a *Koken* instead of a Ford or a Chrysler.

Although personal decorated shaving mugs had made a sporadic appearance in the United States even before the Civil War, in barber shops of the larger cities, their peak in popularity was not reached until Ernest E. Koken was well established in business.

Every Phase of Barbering

His foresight in expanding the business to include every phase of the barbering profession could easily be termed the company's salvation, for as time changes all things, so did it change man's habits of shaving. According to Mr. H. H. Davis, former President of Koken and the company's oldest employee, "we ceased to produce decorated shaving mugs along about 1922 or 1923. At that time the safety razor made such inroads into the shaving business that barbers bascially lost interest in shaving, and our mug decorating business reached the vanishing point. In the early twenties we decided to abandon it."

Mr. Davis further relates that the company "purchased the blank china mugs originally from European sources, but in the latter part of the shaving mug business the mugs were purchased from pottery companies in Ohio."

"...Little Grains of Sand..."

The degree of success achieved in business during the lifetime of Ernest Koken is evidenced by the pictures of the early Koken offices and factory buildings, found in the old company catalog of 1908. These buildings appear at the beginning of this story, and are a reduction from a large full-page layout of the 1908 catalog, loaned by Mr. Davis for featuring in this book, on the eve of the company's Centennial Anniversary. Note the handwriting concerning "Little drops of water, and little grains of sand," etc., and the initials "E.E.K." in the drawing of young Koken at work decorating shaving mugs in his first business in 1874. Note also the size of the different factories and the dates — lower left was the factory in 1881; center left, 1883; center right 1892, and the large factory titled "The Present Factory" was in reference to the year of 1908.

In 1881 Mr. Koken took a partner, and the company became "Koken and Boppert". The firm name changed back to "E. E. Koken, in 1886" on account of the death of Mr. Boppert. The concern became "Koken Barbers' Supply Company, Inc., February 4, 1889." At the present it is a Missouri corporation, formed in 1938.

Value of Advertising

One of Mr. Koken's business attributes was his recognition of the value of advertising. Even in his early catalogs, which the writer was provileged to see and to use, the name "Koken" is emblazoned on many of the mugs pictured. Names of employees were likewise shown on mugs in the catalogs.

In addition to the founder, E. E. Koken, there were: W. F. Koken, his son, who at one time was President of the company and the last of the Koken family to be active in the firm (until his death in 1937); there was also Charles E. Koken, the elder Koken's brother, who was at one time in charge of the preparation of toilet articles; Wm. T. Koken, a nephew, and officer of Banner Iron Works; Roy T. Koken, a nephew and principal executive of Scharff-Koken Paper Box Company; Oliver T. Johnson, a cousin of W. F. Koken and T. W. Van Shoiak, a brother-in-law of W. F. Koken, who was Sales Manager.

Other Kokenites

Other names listed on the mug pictures in the old catalogs were salesmen for the company — Ed Tritschler, E. E. Pairo, W. S. Williams, J. M. Byrne; W. L. McKim (sales correspondent) and Jack Heade (clerk), were likewise shown, as was Curt Grimm, the last foreman of Koken's shaving mug or art department, together with R. F. Wendel, mug decorator and razor grinder for the company. Richard (Dick) J. Cloonan was the shipping clerk. George F. Rogers did designing work at the plant, and was also known to have been a salesman, according to Mr. Oliver T. Johnson, the oldest living former employee of the company.

Mr. Johnson also relates that "In the earliest days a man named Bleeck, an old-time German mechanic, would walk to a lumber yard and carry back lumber enough to do a single job, at which he was about the only man. His industry and fidelity placed him high in the plant throughout many years, and Mr. Koken held him high." Then there was "Andrew Johnson — a city salesman, for whom barbers from all over the country asked for as soon as they came into the store — calling him 'Andy'".

TONIQUE — The Liquid HEADREST

Perhaps the one single bit of advertising for which the company is best remembered (by present-day shaving mug enthusiasts) is the type employed for selling "TONIQUE — The Liquid Headrest". This product was sold by the company, and during a sales campaign, the emblem-slogan was painted on shaving mugs, which were given to shops ordering the "Tonique". Company records do not indicate how many of these mugs were made, but is reported to have been a special "sales promotion" lasting about a year. Few of these mugs are known to exist today.

A second advertising idea of the period 1881-1885 was "Turkish Pomade for the Hair", packaged "as represented in a substantial shaving mug, which may be used for shaving after the pomade is removed". These mugs bore a prominent label in the shape of a shield, proclaiming "Koken & Boppert Sole Proprietors, St. Louis". Today these mugs are likewise rare collectors' items.

Private Mailing Cards Used

Another business method utilized was to mail out post cards to clients and prospective clients, advising them of the expected arrival date and name of the company salesman or representative. This postcard was a sort of "private mailing card" with one side for the address, stamp and short message. On the reverse was a picture of "A Corner of the China Decorating Department of the largest plant on earth, making greatest number of Barber's chairs and fixtures, owned by Koken Barbers' Supply Co., St. Louis."

700 Carloads of Barber Chairs

An old issue of *Ready Mirror* (Dec. 18, 1914, pp. 219) from the archives of the Missouri Historical Society in St. Louis, supports the claim of manufacturing prowess, in reporting that "700 carloads of barber chairs, or 9,600 were sold last year, and that the hides of 14,400 animals were used in making strops during the same length of time."

KOKEN'S CATALOG

A leader in the industry for nearly a century, Koken's catalog of 1968 contains only fine furniture which the firm manufacturers. All styles and color combinations of barber and beauty equipment are richly displayed by color-process printing, keyed to today's modern moods. Even the Barber Poles are streamlined with either stainless steel or red plastic domes, and not over thirty-three inches high.

Gone are the large elaborately carved and painted wooden poles and the richly ornate chairs of the Victorian era. Also missing are the items of art glass pottery, stand bottles, hand-painted shaving mugs, and hundreds of other small items. The only hint of yesteryear in the entire catalog is the "Gaslight Barber Chair" with wood panels of oak or walnut and its companion "Gaslight Mirror Case" which features a touch of Victorian elegance with the convenience of modern design.

Also missing is the subtle humor so evident in the old catalogs with some of the names painted on the old shavings mugs, corresponding to the painting on the mugs such as: a bouquet of red clover, bearing the name "R. Clover"; a mug painted with shades of green, with the name "C. Green"; a bouquet of roses, with the name "M. C. Rose". Others included a handsome painting of a bird dog, with the owner's name shown as (you guessed it) "A Pointer"; a secret society type mug (fraternal) with a Woodmen emblem — a tree stump, above the name "W. W. Stump".

Popular Toiletry Items

Listed among Koken's more popular toiletry items were: Witch Hazel Cologne, Cream of Almonds, Violet Toilet Water, Rosaline Toilet Lotion, Dandruff Cure, Lilac Toilet Water, Cactus Shampoo Liquor and Tonique De Luxe. A full page color ad appeared in one old catalog, advertising that "The Royal Qualities of Our Two Finest Brands Are Concentrated in This Tonic (Tonique De Luxe).

Then there was Koken's Antiseptilene, an antiseptic face lotion which was available in two odors — lilac and violet.

"The Inimitable *Hairfertilizer"*, an old fashioned Hair Restorative, was pictured and priced at $3 per dozen 6-oz. bottles.

All these toiletry items, packaged in labeled bottles, are much sought after as collector items today, among bottle collectors. And, there is a good possibility that more than one of these items was advertised on *"give-away"* shaving mugs. One full page catalog ad of Koken's PURITY Shaving Soap features a shaving mug with the portrait of a lady wearing a white puritan-type bonnet and holding a bouquet of lilies. It is not known if mugs advertising this product were actually made (resembling the mug in this full-page ad), but it is certainly worth remembering, in case you happen across one.

Even the top grain leather cover of the old type catalog is missing, but in today's constantly changing economy and highly specialized and competitive markets, the firm has kept pace. Today's business, like today's catalog, is done in an entirely different manner than when shaving mugs were in vogue, or were considered a necessity. Today everything is sold strictly *wholesale* and is sold only to dealers, who in turn, call upon the trade. It's a world of specialty and specialized operations, and Koken's specialty is *manufacturing* barber furniture.

H. H. Davis — From Office Boy To President

More than half a century ago Hugo H. Davis, at age fourteen, went to work as an office boy for The Koken Company in St. Louis, Mo., when the firm was already the largest of its kind in the world, supplying virtually everything required in the barbering line. The founder of the company, E. E. Koken, had started the business by decorating shaving mugs, and by this time (forty-odd years later) still boasted the "largest mug decorating department in the world".

This was the environment which surrounded young Hugo in 1917, when he earned $4 a week, but it was somehow "different from most jobs", and he was impressed with many things about the company. First of all, he liked his job because he could "ride his bicycle to work each day". And he was impressed with the "chances for advancement" which the firm offered, even though there were between 250 and 300 employees at that time.

Born during the "Golden Age of the Shaving Mug", in 1902, he went to work for Koken about the time the "safety razor was beginning to change men's habits of shaving, and the barber shop shave was to become a lost art.

But "the early 1920's was really the Golden Age for the Barber Business", Mr. Davis explains, because Irene Castle, the sensationally popular ballroom dancer who became the toast of two continents, wore "bobbed hair". Her bobbed hair style became as popular among the women in America as did her dancing. Practically overnight women flocked to the barber shops everywhere — "to get their hair bobbed like Irene Castle, and every barber shop had to put in extra chairs to take care of the sudden business boom".

From Barber Shop to Beauty Shop

The barber shop, which had always been strictly man's domain, was soon to become the mecca for the hair-style conscious American woman. And it was the women who complained about the "old overstuffed, plain-Jane type barber chairs". The Koken Company was quick to respond in providing the new porcelain chromed models to satisfy even the most discriminating woman customer. This was before the days that beauty parlors per se' had achieved their national prominence or status, but it led to another "Golden Age" for barbershops. And from this "came the Beauty Shops", relates Mr. Davis. The women had started a new era in the barber supply business at a time when the clamor for decorated shaving mugs had become only a whisper of the past and near the time of the demise of Koken's Shaving Mug Department.

The young office boy who "rode his bicycle to work" and was impressed with "the chances for advancement" in the company, was destined to impress others and to make his mark in the business world. Mr. H. H. Davis, who started out in business in knee pants on his bicycle, has held every major position with the company, having worked in the Order Department, the Purchasing Department and the Cost Department. He has been the Purchasing Agent, the Expediter, in charge of the Chicago Branch Office, salesman, District Manager, Vice President and President.

Departments in 1917

Recalling the different departments of the company in 1917, he states "there were twenty-six in those days, and that included even a stable with two horses for city salesmen". Other departments were:

Mug Decorating Department
Razor Grinding Department
Razor Strop Manufacturing Department
Tannery
Laboratory for tonics, creams, talcs, etc.
Shoe Polish Department
Tool and Die Works
Machine Shop
Sheetmetal Department
Foundry
Plating and Polishing Department
Wood Carving Department
Cabinet Making Department
Mill
Upholstering Department
Marble Cutting and Polishing Department

Finishing Department (Painting)
Assembly of Wood Work
Assembly of Barber Chairs
Supply Department for Accessories (razors, shears, neck dusters, towels, soap, and all sundry items used in barber shops)
Dry Kilns for lumber
Receiving
Shipping
Porcelain Enameling, ie., furnaces
Sand Blasting Department

In recalling the history of the company, he points out that the firm was "over-extended in the late 20's and early 30's, and the depression ruined the firm. Bankruptcy was declared in 1937, and in 1938 the firm was re-organized as a Missouri corporation".

One of the important policy changes in the early 1920's was that the firm changed from "direct selling to barbers — to selling through barber supply dealers".

Since the first Koken chair was made, nearly a hundred years ago, the firm has introduced many models to keep abreast of the changing times, and in 1964, with a view toward the future, Koken began production of a different kind of chair — a far cry from the old barber chairs of the past. This time it was an orthondontist chair — brightly colored and chromed to appeal to today's generation of children, it is designed somewhat like an astronaut's chair in a space ship, and helps relieve the apprehensions of children who are having their teeth straightened.

Thus the cycle of evolution is completed — from the chair originally used by early barber-surgeons and the barber-dentists of old — to a chair for the barber trade only — back to a chair for the surgeon or dentist.

In commenting on the barbering profession, Mr. Davis says the barber today is suffering because of the hippie-trend to long, dirty hair for boys and men and the long stretches between hair cuts. There is an attempt to establish men's hair styling shops and perhaps "5 to 7% of the barbers now do hair styling at from $7 to $15 a throw". However they are in the minority, so most barbers are on short rations.

He believes that eventually the Barber and the Beauty Shop will be a single business — where both men and women will go for hair services. Women love to go to men stylists, and a good-looking lady-barber can probably induce any male patron to get more than just a simple hair cut.

CURT GRIMM
Shaving Mug Designer-Artist

In 1864 when Curt Wilhelm Grimm was born in Germany, his parents never fancied that he would some day come to America or that he would become the prince of designers and china decorators for the largest business of its kind in the United States and the world.

Young Curt Grimm began his apprenticeship training as a china decorator and worker in enamels at the age of sixteen, under the guidance of his older brother, Hans Wilhelm Grimm, who was a china decorator in one of Germany's porcelain manufacturing plants.

He learned to work with enamels in Germany during the period of time that little was known about this industry in America. About 1892 Niedringhaus Enameling and Stamping Company of St. Louis, Missouri had a large contract for making enameled street signs, but needed competent men who were knowledgeable in working with enamels in order to complete the contract. The Niedringhaus Company sent to Germany to hire men who had this knowledge and experience. This prompted young Grimm to accept a job with that company and move to the United States. He brought his own formulas for enamel with him to this country.

After several years in America he had met other German immigrants, and among them was Ernest E. Koken, who by this time had been in the business of decorating shaving mugs for some 20 years and whose firm had prospered from its very inception, to the extent of having become the largest manufacturing and wholesaling firm of barber chairs in the world. A mutual admiration and close association was formed, and in 1895 Curt Grimm joined the large Koken Company.

A New Barber Chair Idea

Up until this time barber chairs were mostly made of either all wood construction or a combination of cast iron frame with carved wood panels for decoration. Curt Grimm gave Mr. Koken his formula for the white enamel and in return was given some company stock and a lifetime job with the company. Thus began the era of the more modern looking, white enamel or porcelainized-type barber chairs, as well as Mr. Grimm's lifetime career of china painter, or decorator-designer of handsomely adorned shaving mugs.

The white enamel barber chair idea caught on quickly and soon became a standard for the "up-to-date barber shops" all over the country. This standard is still a familiar sight for today's generation, although the more modern and expensive chairs of recent years are

Koken Mug Decorating Department in 1898. Seated to left of stove — Curt Grimm. Standing to left — A decorator named Schmitt. Man seated at back table (in center) is Robert Wendel. Other two men seated and man standing at right are unidentified. *(Photo — permission by Dr. Justin Grimm.)*

slowly changing the ideas of how a barber shop and barber chair should look, especially in the more elite barber shops and hair styling shops of today, and among the new generation.

The knowledge of working with enamels and his early training as a china decorator soon led Curt Grimm to the work for which he is perhaps best known and best remembered — that of painting and designing shaving mug decorations.

For his knowledge and proficiency in the art of china painting, he was rewarded by being made the foreman of Koken's Art Department, or China Decorating Department, a position he held until 1925, at which time the decorated shaving mug business became practically a thing of the past, and he retired from the company.

Designer-Decorator For Thirty Years

The 30 years that spanned his career as designer-decorator for Koken was during the real hey-day of the decorated shaving mugs in the United States. Mr. Grimm perhaps designed more individual mug decorations than any other person, and he was the last foreman and china decorator employed by the Koken Company.

Most of the mugs pictured in the old Koken catalogs from the years 1895 till 1925 were examples of his design and handiwork, although he is not known to have ever signed his name or made his mark on a mug or stand bottle that he had decorated. The quality of his craftsmanship was his "mark". (According to his son, most of Curt Grimm's painting was done "freehand", for he "very seldom used a stenciled outline" as was done by many other china painters employed by the company.)

His designs for mug decorations which became most popular and for which the demand became greater, were made into copper plates, from which many tissue-paper templates or embossings were made. These embossed tissues were made by pressing the tissues against the plates, thus embossing the tissues with tiny pinholes.

The tissue was then placed against the side of a blank mug and patted lightly with a small bag of charcoal dust or powder. When the tissue was removed, an outline of tiny charcoal dots remained, as guides for painting the main design. (The tissues were expendable because new embossings could readily be made from the original plates.

With the use of these tissue-templates, even the less experienced artisans could produce paintings on china mugs which were for all practical purposes, of similar and consistent quality in design, if not in craftsmanship.

The plain blank porcelain mugs were imported from European countries in great quantities from about 1865 until World War I. The better grade mugs came from France, Germany and Austria, with smaller quantities coming from other countries. Marks from factories in these countries are evident on mugs imported after 1890.

Painting and Baking Process

The process employed generally was first to paint the first color or colors onto the mug. The mugs thus painted were then baked in the ovens (kilns) to temper or hold their colors. After a gradual cooling process which usually lasted overnight, the mugs were painted with additional colors and details. They were then baked again. Thus the "stock designed" mugs were completed except for adding the owner's names. They were then placed in sorted bins in the decorating rooms, awaiting orders that required only the painting of the name in gold, and the gold bands or stripes. (Some mugs with very simple decoration were completed with one painting and one firing of the kiln; an example of this would be a mug with only the name, or the name and some small amount of decorating.)

The baking process after each successive painting application was at reduced temperatures, to prevent colors from running together or fusing to an undesireable result, and to harden the decoration and make it more durable.

The last decorations applied were the gold decorations — gold bands and stripes and the name of the new owner. The mug was once again baked in the oven, and after cooling, the gold was polished. Mr. Grimm's son, recalling the early days when his father worked at the Koken Company, relates that "A mug would require 2-3 firings." One job he was permitted to do for his father was to "*brush the gold.*"

Gold Polished with "Glass Brush"

"When a mug came out of the kiln, the lines and any other gold paint was brown in color, and had to be polished with a glass brush. This brush was about the size of a fountain pen in diameter and length. It was made of strands of glass fibres bound together. In the process of brushing, the brown pigment was removed and the gold color appeared," he also recalls. (This left scratches in the gold, which if over-exposed to the brushing process, would mar the gold decoration. Many collectors and dealers alike, are under the impression that a mug which shows scratches in the gold is a fake, or has been scratched to make the mug look old, by showing wear. This is not necessarily true. It is true, though, that if the brushing process is over-done, it weakens the durability of the gold. This is why some mugs show the gold so badly worn, because the protective layer of glaze of the firing process has been somewhat destroyed.)

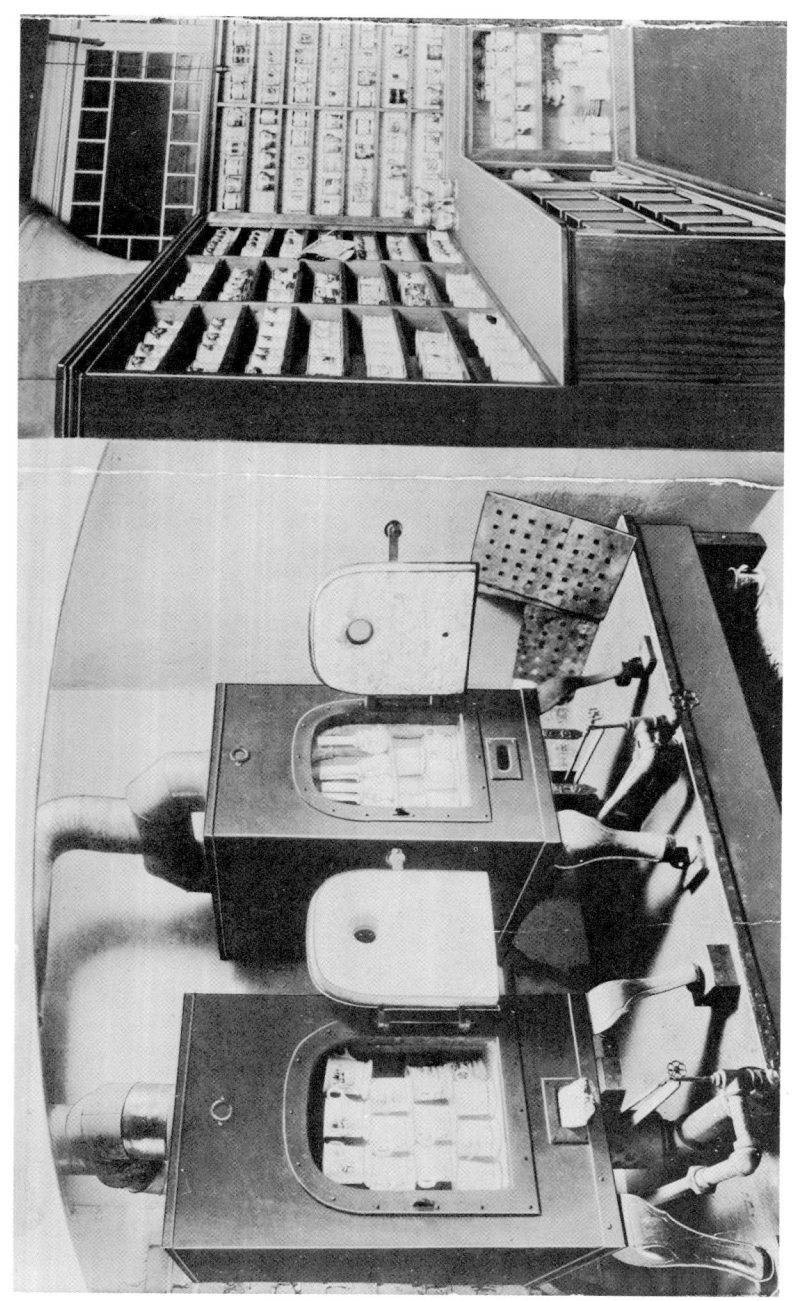

Other half of photo showing mug storage shelves and ovens used to "fire" the mugs and bottles after hand-painted decorations. *(Photo permission by Dr. Justin Grimm.)*

Half of wide-angle photo showing Koken Mug Decorating Department about 1915. Seated at desk near clock — unidentified employee. Curt Grimm at table in foreground. Back table (left to right) — Edgar H. Wendel and his father, Robert F. Wendel. *(Photo permission by Dr. Justin Grimm.)*

The pictures on the two preceeding pages are in reality one old photograph, which has become wrinkled and torn in half from age. It was made for the Koken Company in 1915, at which time Koken was the largest barber supply company in the world.

The oven on the left holds mugs to be fired or baked. The lower three tiers of mugs were Koken "advertising shaving mugs", which were given to barber shop owners who ordered "Tonique De Luxe — the Liquid Headrest." (See inset picture of one of these mugs and a companion clear glass Tonique bottle (patented) of unusual shape and design, which had a gold and grey colored lithograph label, covered with a thin layer of glass (glass label). The glass labels which were applied to Koken stand bottles and to shaving mugs "were all manufactured by a local St. Louis firm which has long since gone out of business and whose specialty was making labels for apothecary bottles", explains Mr. Hugo H. Davis, who worked with the Koken Company for over 50 years.

The first ovens used at Koken were heated by firing coke, a hard, brittle by-product of coal, which was a clean-burning fuel (being mostly carbon) and which burns with an intense heat and is smokeless.

In later years oil ovens were used, and finally the ovens were converted to natural gas when it became accessible and competitive in price.

Tools of the Trade

The tools of the trade of mug decorating were few, but the techniques employed were generally the same. The work tables in the Art Department were always crowded with mugs in various stages of painting. The artist usually worked a full 8-hour day, 6 days a week. He rested or steadied his arm and hand holding the brush, on a small box atop the work table. He held the mug in the other hand, resting it on the table top. (See photos).

Besides a few brushes of different sizes and textures, and a few bottles of paint, the artist had little else to work with except his ingenuity and a rag to use in wiping off his mistakes and to clean his brushes. "Very fine camel hair brushes were used in applying the gold. A turntable was used to make the lines and bands that would encircle the mug, yet always done with a very fine brush", relates the son of the last foreman of Koken's Art Department. And, of course, there was the "Glass brush".

THE WENDELS...Two Generations of Mug Decorators

In the winter of 1969-70 the most interesting development in connection with the writing of this book, suddenly came to light when I discovered the last of the old-time Barber Supply Company mug decorators was not only still living, but that he was a second-generation artisan in this unique trade.

It all happened this way: Through my correspondence with Mr. Hugo H. Davis, then President of the present Koken firm, I learned the name of Koken's last foreman of the Decorating Department — Curt Grimm. Mr. Davis, who has been associated with the firm for over half a century, remembers well the shaving mug era, in its heyday, and he remembers the mug decorating department and when it was finally closed down. He also remembers Curt Grimm.

Through Mr. Davis I learned the whereabouts of Mr. Grimm's son, and I promptly wrote to him for information about his father. One of my questions was if he knew the names of any of the other mug decorators who worked with his father. The only name he knew was "Robert Wendel", but he gave me a lead as to where Robert Wendel's son may be located.

With this encouragement, I wrote several letters and after having most of them returned "undelivered" by the postman, I gave up in vain, seeking other sources of information.

Later, when I was surprised to learn that Mr. Ernest E. Koken's daughter was still living, I began corresponding with her. And it was through her efforts that I was able to obtain the current address of Edgar Wendel, the son of Robert Wendel.

Encouraged once more, I again wrote to Edgar Wendel. This time my efforts were not in vain, for within two weeks I not only received a reply, but old photographs as well. My big surprise however, came when I read the letter and the names identifying the men pictured in the old photograph, at work decorating mugs for the Koken Barber Supply Company.

Here was all I had hoped for — and then some! Edgar H. Wendel had also been a mug decorator for the Koken Company, when his father Robert F. Wendel was foreman of that department. And before my very eyes was all the proof I could ask for. In the one picture were three older men and one young man of seventeen — all busily engaged in their work of decorating the mugs and bottles. The tables and shelves were full of examples of their handicraft. Literally hundreds and hundreds of them.

Finding that young man in the old photo (now nearly 80 years old), was by far a bigger thrill for me than finding a rare, one-of-a-kind decorated mug for my collection, for it opened for me new avenues of information about the most important part of this book.

Here was perhaps the first and only chance I'd ever have to get the answers to many questions I had often pondered over — in connection with the true practices, customs, etc., in this lost art. And, to think that he worked at Koken's — the particular barber supply company that I had decided to feature in this book.

My dream of an exclusive interview — one never to be duplicated — which I once had as a young man of nineteen, when I worked in Washington, D. C. for the Associated Press — was about to be fulfilled. My subsequent correspondence and later visit to meet Mr. Wendel, was crowned with success, since it is very doubtful that there is still to be found yet another "old-timer" who decorated shaving mugs.

Robert Wendel — 44 Years With Koken

Mr. Wendel told me that his father, Robert Wendel, was born in Suhl, Germany, where he learned "china painting in one of the trade schools and worked for a short time at this trade." When he was eighteen years old, he came to America, leaving his family and friends.

His first "steady job" in America was with the Koken Barber Supply Company in St. Louis, where he went to work as a decorator of shaving mugs and barber bottles. This was in 1887, and he worked a total of 44 years at Kokens, many of them as foreman of the Mug Decorating Department. The last five years he spent as foreman of the Grinding Department, until he retired in 1931.

Edgar Wendel — Second Generation Mug Decorator

He raised two sons, and his oldest son Edgar, who was artistically inclined, started at an early age to learn his father's trade, by drawing and painting — with the expert assistance, advice and admonitions from his father — the master decorator for the Koken Company. Under the critical eye and expert guidance of his father, young Edgar had mastered much of the art of china painting at an early age, when as a lad of seventeen, he was hired by Mr. Koken. Now there was a father and son team of decorators working at Kokens. This would not have been a rare thing in the old country (Germany), where china painters were plentiful, but it was novel in America.

BOTTLES BY THE THOUSANDS

When asked if he remembered the very first item he painted at the Koken Company, Mr. Wendel quickly replied that it was a "Tonique DeLuxe" bottle — a free, give-away bottle, which he "painted by the hundreds."

Although he only worked at Koken's as a china decorator for a little over four years, he remembers many of the old trade customs and practices. He painted literally "thousands of bottles in a year". But Tonique De Luxe was "their famous Hair Tonic," and was a product they "pushed" by advertising. "We even painted mugs advertising Tonique DeLuxe, and gave a free mug which had a Tonique slogan painted on it, with each order for the hair tonic", he relates. (This would indicate that although many mugs were painted, advertising Tonique DeLuxe, the quantity of bottles far outnumbered the Tonique shaving mugs.

In order to estimate the volume of production at the plant, I asked Mr. Wendel how many mugs he personally painted in a day. His reply was that he "painted an average of ten mugs a day." (So, with a little simple arithmetic, it is easy to figure the thousands that were turned out each year by just four china painters. And four decorators were considered a minimum number at Koken's, for at times there were as many as eight or nine.).

"China decorators were scarce in those days", relates Mr. Wendel. "And good ones even scarcer. We painted mugs for other barber supply companies too, such as the August Kern Company of St. Louis and the Heimerdinger Company of Louisville, Ky., and many others in the smaller towns."

Photographic Mugs Most Unusual

"Photo mugs were the most unusual type mugs I remember", he says. "These mugs had the photo burnt right into the mugs," Mr. Wendel continues, and he believes the Koken Company to have been the first company to make the "photographic mugs". At the time he worked as china decorator for Koken, his father, Robert Wendel, was foreman of the Mug Decorating Department. He still remembers his father "first mixing his own photo material with paint on the glass plates of the camera, then using the large camera to take close-ups of the portraits furnished by the customer", then "developing the picture on the side of the mugs", after which the mug was decorated with either floral vignettes or designs around the portrait, and the owner's name painted below the portrait, either in gold on in black. On a few mugs, the date was also painted on. Mugs of this variety were made at Koken's as late as 1917.

View of the 1917 Koken Mug Decorating Room. Left to right — Edgar Wendel, Curt Grimm, Mr. Schmitt, Robert Wendell. Storage shelves contain hundreds of decorated mugs — awaiting orders, when the gold names will be painted on and then fired in the ovens. *(Photo — Author's Collection.)*

Tombstone Photo Plaques

A most interesting sidelight in connection with this process, was that his father also used a similar process to make "photo plaques which were set in tombstones at the cemetery". These plaques were portraits or pictures "developed and burned on oval china plaques, which were set in tombstones — to last forever", he relates. Some of these may still be seen in certain old cemeteries around the country. The custom is believed to have ended about 1919 or 1920.

"We used the best quality of gold paint on all our mugs", Mr. Wendel continued. "When we would get the order, we sketched the design on the mug and then filled in with paint. Curt Grimm did all the lettering, especially the gold names and the gold bands. He would save all the rags (used to clean the brushes and wipe off a mistake in painting) till the end of the year, when we would burn them to retrieve the gold nugget — which we sold and split among us. About $20 in all."

Among the most popular mugs in 1915, or rather those most ordered, were the ones with the fraternal emblem decorations — specifically the "Masonic, Knights of Columbus, and I.O.O.F."

Facts or Fiction — Record Set Straight

This one-time mug decorator dispels the popular belief today that all mugs decorated in barber supply company decorating rooms were "completely hand-painted", for he says that "some of the cheaper mugs were decorated with decals or transfers." (This practice was not prevalent from the beginning, but was started only toward the end of the golden era of shaving mugs — about 1918 or 1919. He also remembers that occasionally the decal mugs were "touched up" — to "liven up their appearance." To his knowledge and recollection though, none of the china painters at Koken's ever used any type of secret mark or signature to identify their own particular china painting.

Much fuss is made today over what some people call "left-handed" shaving mugs. It may be of interest to some, that according to the recollections of Mr. Wendel, the position of the painting on the mug itself, had absolutely nothing to do with a mug being a "left-handed" or a "right-handed" mug. Mr. Wendel, now nearly eighty years of age, says he had never seen a "left-handed shaving mug".

Neither were so-called "ladies shaving mugs" (a term common today) ever made for milady up to the time he worked at Koken's. This characterization is perhaps a description evolved in recent years by ever-zealous enthusiasts.

In an effort to further separate fact from fiction, Mr. Wendel was asked about "miniature shaving mugs". To dispel the idea of miniature shaving mugs having been made as "salesmen's samples", the old-timer's reply to the question was a terse "no", followed by the statement that Koken "had a beautiful colored catalog, showing in detail and listing literally hundreds of different decorated mugs." And, they "mailed these catalogs everywhere", he says.

Razor Grinding Department

Although for many years Koken maintained the largest razor grinding department in America, the firm imported all razors from one of the world's major steel producers in Germany. Mr. Wendel reports that only a few razors were made from the "blank wedges of steel" at Kokens (probably experiments in razor manufacture). All engraving on the blades and tangs of the razors likewise was done in the German factory, the reason being a matter of company pride in the foreign trademark. (During this time in history the imported steel razors were considered of superior quality to these manufactured in the United States.) Koken did however, grind new edges on razors and replace broken handles, etc.

Two pages from the "1924 Golden Anniversary" Koken supply catalog.

PART II
Section 2

BARBER SUPPLY COMPANIES
MARKS ON MUGS

This list of Barber Supply Companies has been compiled from the names appearing on the bottom of antique shaving mugs among collections all over the country. The names are listed as seen on the mugs, either by the author or as reported by different collectors in their own personal collections.

For fifty years, prior to the early 1920's, Barber Supply Companies were not only manufacturers but distributors and dealers of all equipment and supplies used in the barbering trade. They sold direct to the barbers. Thus in a sense the barbers were *dealers* (on a limited basis). If you wanted to buy a personalized, hand-painted shaving mug or a razor, you placed your order with your barber.

In the early 1920's barber supply *dealers* were established in the smaller cities and towns all over the nation to serve specific territories or areas. At that time the original large manufacturing dealers, such as Koken, Koch, etc., quit selling direct to the barbers and sold only to the established dealers. These dealers were likewise known as *barber supply companies*. This was about the time of the demise of the shaving mug decorating department at Koken's.

The custom of marking or stamping the bottom of the mugs with the name of the manufacturing supply company then changed, for many of them were stamped with the name of the newly-established dealers.

Thus a point of information to remember is that the name of a barber supply company on a mug does not necessarily mean that it was decorated at that particular company. Actually mug decorations were accomplished only by a few of the larger firms such as Koken, Koch, or a few china decorating firms. According to Mr. H. H. Davis, Koken was the last of the firms to quit decorating mugs, and Koken's last employed mug decorator was Curt Grimm, who retired in 1925, about two years following the closing of the mug decorating department.

EARLY BARBER SUPPLY COMPANIES

—A—

Alpha
Apotheker Bros, Barber Supply, N.Y.
Geo W. Archer & Company, Rochester, N.Y.
Herry Arnd & Bro., China Decorators, St. Louis

—B—

Eugene Berninghaus (Cincinnati, Ohio)
Ross W. Flack
Boston Barber Supply
Buckeye Barber Supply, Baywick, Ohio
Buerger Bros. Barber Supplies (Denver, Colo.)

—C—

C. B. C. & Co.
C. B. S. Co.
Central Supply Co. (Brooklyn, N.Y.

—D—

Denison Barber Supply Co., Denison, Texas
Andrew Domedion, Buffalo, N.Y.
Fred Dolle, Decorator, Chicago, Ill.

—E—

East St. Louis B.S. Co.
P. Eiseman

—F—

G. H. Fralick Barber's Supplies (Wichita

—G—

Louis M. Geckle & Son
Gunkel B. S. Co., St. Louis

—H—

A. Halverson (Okla. City)
Hecker Bros. Decorators, Kansas City, Mo.
Heckle Bros. (Kansas City)
R. H. Hegener B. Supplies, Minneapolis,
Herold Bros. (Cleveland, Ohio)
W. C. Heimerdinger (Louisville, Ky.)
Hytes B. S. Co., Topeka, Kansas

—K—

John A. Kennedy & Co., Barber Supplies & Furniture (Boston, Mass.)
August Kern (St. Louis)
Gust Knecht Mfg. Co., Chicago
Theo A. Kochs (Chicago)
Koken Company (St. Louis)
Alfred J. Krank (St. Paul, Minn.)
Kraut & Dohnal
E. H. Kuster Co. (St. Joseph, Mo.)

—L—

J. J. Lang & Co.

—M—

Maher & Grosh Cutlery Co. (Toledo, Ohio)
Melchior Bros., Decorators (Chicago & Omaha)
E. J. Mooney

—N—

Neville (Quincey, Ill.)
T. Noonan & Co. Barber Supplies, Boston,

—R—

Ransom & Randolph Co., Toledo, Ohio
Regold Bros. B. S. Cleveland, Ohio
A. Riedel
John Rieder & Co., B. S., Des Moines, Iowa
M. Riethmueller, St. Louis, Mo.
J. Ritter Barber Supplies (Philadelphia)

—S—

St. Louis Electric Grinding Co.
The Schweitzer Barbers' supply House, Altoona,
C. A. Smith Barber Supplies, Phila.
Spokane Barber Supply Co, Spokane
Lewis Stenger B. S. Co., Portland
B. Stuebner's Sons, Artistic China Decorators, 822 Broadway, Brooklyn, N. Y.
Smith Bros. (Boston)
G. R. Springer B. S. (Kansas City)

—T—

G. G. Thomas Co. (Decorators), Ottumwa, Iowa
Tripoli B. S. C.

—U—

A. L. Undelund, Decorator (Omaha)

—V—

Decorated by J. R. Voldan

—W—

Robert F. Walter & Sons, Peoria, Ill.
C. Weischel Co. B. S., Dallas
C. H. Weyer (St. Joe, Mo.)
Waco B. S. Co. (Waco, Texas)
Geo. E. Wagner & Co. (St. Joe, Mo.)

Barber Supply Company Marks

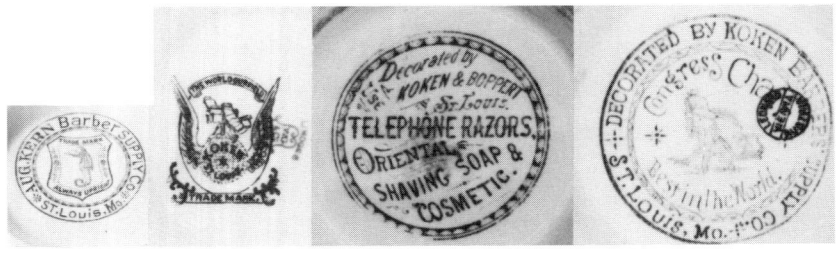

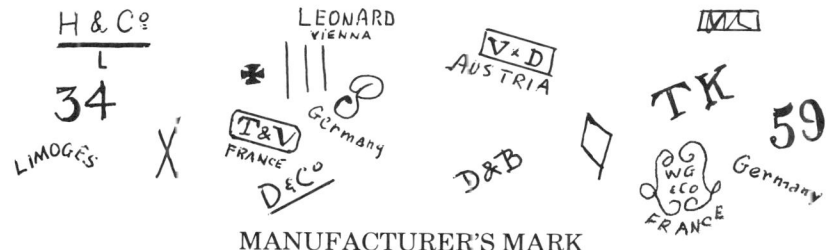

MANUFACTURER'S MARK

The uninformed or uninitiated person, whether he is a collector, dealer, or both, often places too much importance on the manufacturer's "mark" on the bottom of shaving mugs. Have you ever tried to identify the different marks appearing on the bottom of shaving mugs? If you have, then you know how perplexing it can be. In a collection of 300 or 400 shaving mugs which may contain 30 or 40 marks, you'll be lucky to find a half dozen of the marks listed in the several "mark" books available to you.

Most experts on porcelain marks will tell you that the least reliable but easiest way to identify porcelain is by the mark. They will also tell you that marks are often forged and changed. The books on marks generally list the better-known marks, and judging by the number of marks we are unable to identify, we deduce that there must surely have been literally thousands of marks never listed.

During the early period of importing blank shaving mugs (and also certain varieties of decorated mugs) to the United States from Europe (about 1870 to 1891), there was no law requiring marks of the country-of-origin. After 1891, however, the import laws (McKinley Tariff Act of 1891) were more stringent, and imported shaving mugs began to be "marked" with the country of origin and other identifying marks, usually numbers, i.e., "Germany 141" or "Germany Three Crown 242", etc. Sometimes the word "Germany" was *impressed* into the bottom of the mug.

It is impossible to trace the origin of a mug marked "Germany 141", or some other such number, today. But it is generally assumed that the "141" indicates the code for a particular German factory, or a particular design on mugs. If there is a book showing all the marks such as the above, I have failed to locate it. Some people say the "141" (or other such number) refers to the pattern or design, but here again, no actual proof has been found.

Many marks from Germany, Austria, Bavaria, and even many of the French marks will not be found in any book of marks, presumably because of their late date.

PART II
SECTION 3

BARBER SUPPLY COMPANIES DECORATED SHAVING MUGS

All the old barber supply catalogs followed the same or similar format in listing shaving mugs, and the prices quoted therein were always prices to "barbers only". The mugs sometimes were divided into two categories, the first being "Decorated Shaving Mugs — List of mugs with Fancy Decoration", and the second being "Trade Designs and Society Emblems". Each category contained a full page of listings. Some old catalogs simply listed "Price List of Decorated Shaving Mugs," and all mugs were listed therein. Most catalogs were about 9 inches x 12 inches in size. The mugs were listed by number (for use when ordering), and the trade designs and society emblems mugs were also listed alphabetically (for customer convenience). Some of the Fancy Decorated mugs were illustrated on separate pages and this fact was noted in the list, alongside the appropriate number. In addition, the mugs were offered in two sizes — "Medium" and "Large". Most catalogs also contained the notation "Please be careful always to state whether medium or large mugs are wanted. If no size is stated, medium-sized mugs will be sent."

All prices quoted in the catalogs were for complete mugs (to barbers only), with name and decoration or design. In addition, extra charges were made for "additional decoration", such as autograph or facsimiles of owners' handwriting — an extra charge of 20¢. Or there was an extra charge of 20¢ for 2-letter monograms and 30¢ extra for 3-letter monograms. Ten cents extra was charged for "black and gold letters". Also 10¢ for "script, Roman or block letters." The "mugs with fancy decoration" were generally less expensive than the "trade designs and society emblems." Regardless of the particular type of mug listed — the "medium" size mug was 10¢ cheaper than the "large" one, with identical decoration.

Forty cents (price to barbers) for a medium mug was the cheapest one listed which was personalized by the owner's name, with a "stroke below and stripes in gold." Fifty cents would buy a "medium mug" with a "gold wreath around owner's name."

In the medium-price range the cost was from 80¢ to a dollar, with the more expensive "fancy decoration mugs" costing as much as some of the "trade designs and society emblems" mugs.

Listed among the "fancy decoration" mugs were some mugs which were even more expensive than many of the "trades and society emblems". These were listed as "Extra Fancy" and were priced higher. Among these were mugs which showed animals, birds, butterflys and flowers, scenery, landscape, children, marine scenes, sportsman designs, humorous designs, jockey designs and hunting or fishing scenes. The prices on these types ranged from $1 to $3. (One old catalong even lists butterflys and birds decoration as a trade design mug.)

TRADE DESIGNS AND SOCIETY EMBLEMS

The cheaper mugs in this category sold from 70¢ to a dollar, and included mugs with paintings of the following: society emblems, society monograms, trade tools, musical instruments, coffin and casket, chicken, dog, fish, flag of any nation, hand and pen, hands clasped, hat and cap, horse, horseshoe, lantern, milk can, painter's palette painter's brush, and others.

The higher-priced mugs listed were those that showed *action* by the subject depicted on the mug, such as a man driving a sulky or team of horses, a man driving an automobile, a man killing a steer, a plasterer at work, a painter at work, etc.

PLAIN OR NUMBERED

Also listed, but sold by the dozen, were "Plain" or "Numbered" mugs, in both the medium and large sizes. The price varied according to whether the mugs were "gold striped" or "gold banded", on top or on both top and bottom

Plain mugs cost from $1.75 a dozen (medium) to $3.35 (prices varied with gold decoration) and from $2.40 to $4.10 a dozen for large mugs.

Numbered mugs (gilt or gold numbers) were $3.50 to $4.60 a dozen for medium, and $4.50 to $5.60 a dozen for large mugs.

Many companies advertised in their catalogs "We can make any mug shown in other catalogs or mug sheets at the prices quoted therein", a point which evidenced the high competitive spirit that existed for the shaving mug trade during that era.

Old World Style Lettering

Long before the era of name-decorated shaving mugs in the United States, the "Old English" style of type was commonplace and was widely used in most forms of printing, such as business announcements, letterheads etc.

Type styles from the 8th Century Vatican through the 15th and 16th Centuries German and Gothic had many similarities with the Old English type. Consequently the adaptation of the Old English lettering for use in name decoration on American decorated shaving mugs was a natural transformation or development by first or second generation European immigrants who were the china-decorators of most of the old mugs. Some of these professionals were even brought to the United States especially for this purpose.

This probably accounts for the fact that not all "Old English" lettering is *pure*, but may be a mixture of the different styles, which are so similar.

Many such letters, especially the *capital letters*, were most difficult to read or distinguish, which fact eventually led to the use of script, Roman or block lettering in the printing trades and ultimately in much of the decorating of shaving mugs, for which an extra charge was usually made by the decorator. (Today Old English style types are almost exclusively limited to ecclesiastical or other forms of formal printing.)

ALPHABETICAL LIST OF MUGS

This list of shaving mugs, alphabetically arranged for convenience, is a consolidation of mugs listed in Barber Supply catalogs from 1890 until 1915, and includes trade designs (occupation designs), secret societies (fraternal) designs, sports designs and other popular designs (handpainted by Barber Supply Company decorators or china painters) as originally listed in the old catalogs. This period of time is considered representative of the period when decorated shaving mugs were at their peak in popularity.

Because this list was compiled from various catalogs, some listings will be similar by descriptive terms and some will be cross-indexed, while others may not. Prices shown are original prices, and may vary considerably, due no doubt to the difference in the years of manufacture and the various firms who decorated the mugs.

Originally mugs were ordered through the local barber, who customarily added a small mark-up for his own profit.

This list is by no means complete, for it is impossible to assemble a complete list or pictures of all the varieties produced by so many different firms over so long a time, due to the fact that most of the barber supply companies are today non-existent, or complete and accurate records were not kept this long after the period of shaving mug popularity among the male population of the nation. Frequently mugs turn up that are "one-of-a-kind", decoration-wise, having been decorated according to the whims of the owner. These will not necessarily be found in any old catalog, but the quality and craftsmanship of the painted decoration will be easily recognized by the collector. This is what makes the hobby so interesting. There were enough varieties of mugs made to fit even the most discriminating of specialized collectors' desires.

Consolidated List of Occupational Types, Fraternals, etc — (All shaving mugs handpainted by decorators employed by Barber Supply Companies.)

—A—

1. Accordian .95
2. American Legion of Honor 1.00
3. Anchor .35
4. Anvil and Hammer .25
5. Anvil, Hammer and Tongs .80
6. A. O. H. (Hibernian) .95
7. A. O. U. W. (United Workmen) .90
8. A. P. A. Emblem 1.00
9. Arc Light .85
10. Architect Emblem .50
11. Auctioneer's Emblem .85
12. Autograph or Facsimile of Owner's handwriting .75
13. Automobile 1.35

—B—

14. Baggage Master, Truck and Car 1.45
15. Baker Shop 1.45
16. Baker at Work in front of oven 1.35
17. Baker's Emblem (two lions and pretzel) 1.10
18. Bakerwagon, horse and driver 1.10
19. Band Instruments .90
20. Barber Shop 1.25
21. Barber Tools, razor and shears .75
22. Barn Yard .90
23. Bartender 1.40
24. Baseball and Bats .70
25. Baseball Player 1.35
26. Basket Maker 1.35
27. Basket Maker at Work 1.40
28. Basket of Eggs .50
29. Basket of Peaches 1.20
30. Bass Fiddle 1.05
31. Bass Violin .50
32. Bear 1.20
33. Beer Brewers Emblem 1.20
34. Beer Barrel .50
35. Beer Barrel, bottle and glasses 1.30
36. Beer Glass .65
37. Beer Wagon, horses and driver 1.30
38. Ben Hur (T. B. H.) 1.00
39. Bicycle 1.05
40. Bicycle and rider 1.30
41. Bill Poster posting bills 1.40
42. Billiard Table, balls and cues 1.05
43. Billiard Players at table 1.50
44. Bird, any kind .50
45. Blacksmith at anvil 1.30
46. Blacksmith shoeing horse 1.20
47. Boat, Shoe and Gaitor .95
48. Boilermaker at work 1.30
49. B. of L. F. (Fireman's Monogram) .95
50. B. of L. F. Emblem 1.00
51. B. of L. E., Engineer's Monogram .95
52. B. of R.R.C. emblem, Conductors 1.00
53. B. of R.R.T., Trainmen Emblem .95
54. Book 1.00
55. Book in Hand 1.20
56. Bookbinders at work 1.40
57. Bookbinders' Emblem 1.20
58. Bookkeeper at desk 1.30
59. Boot .35
60. Boot and Shoe .80
61. Boot and Shoe, Fine 1.10
62. Bottle blower at work 1.40
63. Bowling Alley 1.40
64. B.P.O.E. (Order of Elks) .95
65. Brass Horn or Cornet 1.05
66. Brewer's Emblem 1.20
67. Bridge Span 1.40
68. Bridge (steel) 1.20
69. Bricklayer at work 1.10
70. Bricklayer's Emblem, Trowel, and Square .75
71. Brush Maker's Emblem 1.20
72. Brush Maker's Store 1.00
73. Buggy .75
74. Buggy and Horse 1.00

215

#	Item	Price
75.	Buggy Maker's Emblem	1.40
76.	Buggy Trimmer's Emblem	1.20
77.	Buggy without horses	1.10
78.	Buggy, 2 horses and driver	1.30
79.	Bull	1.10
80.	Bull's head and tools	.50
81.	Bunch of Grapes	.95
82.	Butcher Shop	1.30
83.	Butcher Dressing a Steer	1.60
84.	Butcher Dressing a Hog	1.40
85.	Butcher Slaughtering a Steer	1.60
86.	Butcher Standing by Steer	1.40
87.	Butcher Chopping Meat	1.45
88.	Butcher Store	1.45
89.	Bucher's design (bullhead)	.90
90.	Butcher's design (bull's head and tools)	.90
91.	Butcher's Emblem (knife, saw, cleaver and steel)	.25
92.	Butcher Killing Steer	1.30

—C—

#	Item	Price
93.	Caboose	1.10
94.	Calf	1.20
95.	Caliper in Hand	1.20
96.	Calipers & Hammer (machinists' emblem)	.95
97.	Camera	1.00
98.	Camera with stand	1.00
99.	Cannon on Gun Carriage	1.30
100.	Card in Hand	1.00
101.	Cards (hand holding playing cards)	1.00
102.	Carpenter at work	1.30
103.	Carpenter's Emblem	.90
104.	Carpenter Tools, saw, planner and square	.95
105.	Carriage	.75
106.	Carriage with horses, driver	1.00
107.	Chicken	1.00
108.	Chair Maker at Work	1.40
109.	China Dealer's Store	1.60
110.	Cigar Box	.85
111.	Cigar Bunch	.75
112.	Cigar	.60
113.	Cigar Store	1.30
114.	Cigar Maker's Emblem	.80
115.	Clarionet	.85
116.	Clerk at Desk	1.30
117.	Clothing Store and clerk	1.30
118.	Clothing Store	1.50
119.	Clock	1.05
120.	Coach	1.20
121.	Coach and horses	1.60
122.	Coal Cart	1.00
123.	Coal Cart, horse and driver	1.10
124.	Coal Miner with Tools	1.40
125.	Coal Miner's Tools	1.10
126.	Coal Miner at work	1.00
127.	Coal Pick and Scoop	.35
128.	Coat of Arms of any state	1.20
129.	Cobbler	1.40
130.	Coffin or Casket	.85
131.	Commission Merchant (3 barrels, Pork, Whiskey & Flour)	1.40
132.	Compass, Square & Three Links	1.00
133.	Conductor's Punch	.90
134.	Confectioner's Emblem	.50
135.	Confectioner's Store	1.60
136.	Confectioner's Pyramid	1.00
137.	Confectioner's Design	1.10
138.	Confederate Flag	1.00
139.	Cooper at work	.75
140.	Cooper making Barrel	1.10
141.	Cornet	.85
142.	Cotton Field with Darkey Picking Cotton	1.60
143.	Cow	.75
144.	Cowboy (riding)	1.60
145.	Cowboy lassoing steer	1.50
146.	Cylinder Printing Press, large	1.80
147.	Cylinder Printing Press, Small	1.45

—D—

#	Item	Price
148.	Deer	1.25
149.	Deer's Head	1.00
150.	Deer running and scenery	1.25
151.	Dentist Drawing Teeth	1.30
152.	Dentists' Emblem (set of teeth)	.85
153.	Dog	.90
154.	Doctor Attending Patient	1.35
155.	Donkey	1.25
156.	Dray and horses	1.40
157.	Dog and Safe	1.00
158.	Dray	.75
159.	Dray, two horses and driver	1.30
160.	Drove of cattle	1.45
161.	Druggists' Mortar & Pestle	.35
162.	Druggist Working	1.50
163.	Drug Store	1.30
164.	Druid Emblem	.95
165.	Drum	.85
166.	Dry Goods Emblem	.90
167.	Dry Goods Store and clerk	1.30
168.	Dynamo	1.40

—E—

169. Eagle		1.05
170. Eagle and Banner		1.25
171. Eagle and two flags		1.25
172. Eagle, Shield and flags		1.25
173. Electric Street Car		1.25
174. Electric Car and Trolley		1.35
175. Electric Crane		1.30
176. Encampment (I.O.O.F.)		1.00
177. Engine, Stationary		1.25
178. Engine (Steam)		1.20
179. Encampment Emblem		1.00
180. Epworth League		1.00
181. Express Wagon		1.25
182. Express Wagon, two horses		1.50
183. Express Wagon, horse and driver		1.50
184. Eye and three links (I.O.O.F.)		.85

—F—

185. Farmer Plowing Field		1.25
186. Farmer Plowing with Two Horses		1.25
187. Fire Engine (Steam) A		1.45
188. Fire Engine with two horses		1.00
189. Fire Engine (steam) with horses		1.30
190. Fireman's Emblem		1.20
191. Fireman's Hat		.85
192. Fish		.75
193. Fisherman		1.75
194. Fisherman and scenery		1.35
195. Fishing Tackle		.90
196. Fish Stand and Salesman		1.65
197. Flag of any nation		.85
198. Flags, two of any nation		1.10
199. Flag, Sword and Cannon		1.20
200. Flint Glass Gaffer		1.60
201. Flint Glass Blower at Work		1.60
202. Flint Glass Worker		1.60
203. Flint Glass Worker at Press		1.60
204. Flour and Feed Emblem		.95
205. Flour and Feed Store		1.00
206. Flour Dealer's Store		1.45
207. Flute		.95
208. F. O. E. (Order of Eagles)		.95
209. Foresters (I. O. F.)		1.10
210. Foresters Emblem (Independent Order)		.50
211. Foresters (F.O.A.) with flags		1.10
212. Foresters (Catholic)		.95
213. Foresters Emblem (Ancient Order)		1.00
214. Freight Elevator		1.00
215. Freight Car		1.10
216. Freight Propeller		1.40
217. Fruit Stand		1.30
218. Furniture Design (sofa and chairs)		1.30
219. Furniture Store		1.50

—G—

220. Gambrinus, Glass in Hand		1.20
221. Gambrinus and Keg		1.20
222. Gas Engine		1.35
223. Gas Fitter's Emblem		1.40
224. Gas Fitter Tools		1.40
225. German Flag		1.20
226. Good Templars		1.10
227. Grain Elevator		1.00
228. Grand Army Republic (emblem)		1.00
229. Grocery Store		1.30
230. Grocery Store and clerk		1.45
231. Grocery Wagon and horses		1.30
232. Grocery Wagon with one horse		1.40
233. Grocers Wagon, horse and driver		1.25
234. Guitar		.90
235. Gunning Skiff		1.40
236. Gun Store		1.65
237. Gunsmith		1.60
238. Gunsmith and Customer		1.60

—H—

239. Hand and Pen		.65
240. Hand Car		1.10
241. Hand Printing Press		1.20
242. Hand Holding Card		.50
243. Hands Clasped		.85
244. Hardware Store		1.30
245. Hare		.80
246. Hare or Rabbit		.50
247. Harnessmaker at work		1.30
248. Harp		.85
249. Harp and shamrock		.95
250. Hat and Cap		.75
251. Hat in Hand		.85
252. Hatchet		.80
253. Hats on Pedestal		.50
254. Hatter at work		.40
255. Hearse, Horses and Driver		1.30
256. Hod		.35
257. Hod Carrier Carrying Brick		1.40
258. Hoe		.50
259. Hog		.90
260. Hog's Head, Knife and Steel		1.25
261. Hook and Ladder, Truck only		1.40
262. Hook and Ladder, Two Horses		1.70

263.	Hook and Ladder Truck, horses and driver	1.00
264.	Horn	1.05
265.	Horse	.90
266.	Horse Head	.90
267.	Horse Cart	1.10
268.	Horse and Wagon	1.40
269.	Horse Racer on Horseback	1.40
270.	Horse Racer in Sulky	1.50
271.	Horse Shoe	.70
272.	Horse Shoe (Good Luck)	.25
273.	Horseshoer at Work	1.50
274.	Horse (One or Two) and Vehicle	1.00
275.	Horse Trainer Training Horse	1.40
276.	Hose Carriage, twmhorses, fine	1.70
277.	Hose carriage, horses and driver	1.30
278.	Hose Cart, horses and driver	1.25
279.	Hose Cart	.75
280.	Hostler	1.45
281.	Hotel Register	1.20
282.	Hunter with two dogs	1.40
283.	Hunter shooting ducks	1.25
284.	Hunter Under Tree	1.25
285.	Hunter, Dog and Rabbit	1.35
286.	Hydrant, Hose	.80

—I—

287.	I.B.E.W. (Intl. Brotherhood Electrical Workers	.95
288.	Ice Wagon	1.20
289.	Ice Wagon, horses and driver	1.35
290.	Incandescent Lamp	.85
291.	Indian Smoking Pipe	1.25
292.	I.O. of A.M.	1.00
293.	I.O.G.T. (Templars)	1.10
294.	I.O.O.F. Encampment	1.00
295.	I.O.O.F. (three links)	.65
296.	I.O.R.M. (Indian Head)	1.10
297.	I.O.R.M. (Redmen's Encampment)	.95
298.	Irish Flag	1.20
299.	Irish Flag with Shamrock	1.25
300.	Iron Moulder at Work	1.30
301.	Iron Moulder of N.A.	1.10
302.	Iron Puddler at Work	1.50
303.	Iron Safe	1.10
304.	I.O.F. (Foresters)	1.00

—J—

305.	Jeweler's Store	1.65
306.	Jeweler Design	1.10
307.	Jockey's Emblem (cap & Whip)	.85
308.	Jockey Driving Horse	1.00
309.	Jockey Riding Horse	1.00
310.	Jr. O.U.A.M. (American Mechanics, without flags)	1.00
311.	Jr. O.U.A.M. (American Mechanics, with flags)	1.20
312.	Jug	.35
313.	Justice of the Peace	1.40
314.	Justice (scales)	1.65

—K—

315.	Keg of Beer	.50
316.	Keystone (Masonic) Emblem	.75
317.	Knight Templar Emblem	1.00
318.	Knight Templar (cross and crown)	.95
319.	Knight Templar (double eagle)	1.25
320.	Knight Templar (mounted)	1.25
321.	Knights of Golden Eagle	1.10
322.	Knights of Golden Eagle Emblem	.50
323.	Knights of Columbus	1.10
324.	Knights of Columbus Emblem	1.00
325.	Knights of Honor Emblem	.50
326.	Knights of Labor Emblem	.50
327.	Knights and Ladies of Honor Emblem	1.00
328.	Knights of Maccabee	.95
329.	Knights of Pythias	.85
330.	Knights of Pythias (Uniform Rank)	.95
331.	Knights of St. John	1.10
332.	Knights of Malta	.95

—L—

333.	Lager Beer Wagon	1.60
334.	Lager Beer Wagon, Horses and Driver	1.00
335.	Lantern	.90
336.	League of American Wheelman Emblem	.75
337.	Ledger	.90
338.	Leopard	1.10
339.	Letter Carrier in Uniform	1.10
340.	Lion	1.25
341.	Liquor Dealer Testing Wine	1.40
342.	Livery Stable	1.35
343.	Loaf of Bread	.75
344.	Locomotive and Train of Cars	1.50
345.	Locomotive and Tender	1.20
346.	Lumberman's Rule	.35
347.	Lumberman's Scale	.75
348.	Lumber Yard	1.30
349.	Lyon	1.10
350.	Lyre	.90

—M—

351.	Machinist at Lathe	1.50
352.	Machinist Calipers	.85
353.	Mail Pouch	.90
354.	Mail Wagon	1.20
355.	Mail Wagon, horse and driver	1.40
356.	Malt Shovel	.75
357.	Maltese Cross (Mason c)	.90
358.	Man on Horseback	1.00
359.	Man Shearing Sheep	1.50
360.	Mantle Grate and Front	1.40
361.	Marble Cutter	1.35
362.	Marble Cutter at Work	1.40
363.	Masonic, three great lights, special design	1.10
364.	Masonic (square and compass)	.85
365.	Masonic Keystone Emblem	.75
366.	Mattress Maker at Work	1.40
367.	Mechanic's Emblem (hand and hammer)	.70
368.	Mechanic's Emblem, compass, square, arm and hammer	1.00-
369.	Milk Can	.75
370.	Milk Wagon, horse and driver	1.30
371.	Mill Stone	.35
372.	Miller Dressing Burr	1.00
373.	Miller's Roller	1.00
374.	Miller's Emblem	1.40
375.	Miller Sharpening Mill Stone	1.40
376.	Miller's Design, Two Picks, Crop	.50
377.	Milk Wagon and horses	1.25
378.	Merchant Tailor Design	.75
379.	Merchant Tailor Establishment, 6 figures	2.50
380.	Miner's Design, two picks crossed	.35
381.	Miner's Equipment	1.00
382.	Miner with Pick and Shovel	1.20
383.	Miner's Hat with Lamp	.90
384.	Miner's Hat, Pick, Lamp and Shovel	1.00
385.	Miner with Pick on Shoulder	1.25
386.	Modern Woodmen	.85
397.	Modern Woodmen Emblem	.95
388.	Monogram only	.85
389.	Moose Emblem	1.00
390.	Moulder at Work	1.00
391.	Moulder's Emblem	.50
392.	Mule	1.25
393.	Music Store Design	.75
394.	Musician, with any instrument	1.60
395.	Mystic Chain	.95
396.	Mystic Shrine	1.10

—N—

397.	Nailer at Work	1.65
398.	Notion Dealer's Store	1.60

—O—

399.	Ocean Steamer	1.30
400.	Oil Dealer	1.20
401.	Oil Derrick	.95
402.	Oil Derrick and Scenery	1.30
403.	Odd Fellows (Three Links) Emblem	.60
404.	O. K. T.	.50
405.	Omnibus with Horses	1.50
406.	Omnibus, horses and driver	1.30
407.	One Hand	1.00
408.	Orangemen's Emblem	1.20
409.	Order of Iron Hall	.75
410.	Order of Owls	.75
411.	Order of Tonti	.80
412.	Organ, Parlor	1.00
413.	O. R. C. (Conductors)	1.00
414.	O. R. T. (Telegraphers)	1.00
415.	Ow	.70
416.	Ox	.50
417.	Oyster or Oyster Basket	.90
418.	O. of I. A.	1.00

—P—

419.	Padlock	.80
420.	Par or Organ	1.20
421.	Painter at Work (house painter)	1.30
422.	Paint Pot and brush	.75
423.	Passenger Car	1.10
424.	Passenger Coach	1.10
425.	Passenger Elevator	1.00
426.	Paperhanger at Work	1.30
427.	Painter's Palette	.75
428.	Patriotic Order Sons of America	.90
429.	Piano or Organ	1.30
430.	Piano Player	1.65
431.	Piano, upright, square or grand	1.20
432.	Pick & Shovel	.75
433.	Pistol or Revolver	.75
434.	Peacock	.95
435.	Pen in Hand	1.00
436.	Pennsylvania Coat of Arms	1.10
437.	Photographic Mug, gold decoration	3.00

438. Photographer Posing a Lady	1.30
439. Photographer at Camera	1.45
440. Photographer's Instrument	1.00
441. Plumber at Work	1.40
442. Plumber's Emblem (furnace)	.90
443. Plasterer's Trowel and Hock	.75
444. Plow	.90
445. Policeman in Uniform	1.00
446. Propeller	.75
447. Propeller (steam)	1.30
448. Printer at Case	1.30
449. Printer's Stick	.25
450. Printer's stick in hand	.65
451. Printer Setting Type	1.40
452. Plasterer at Wrok	1.40
453. Portable Engine	1.50
454. Porter Carrying Trunk	1.45
455. Power Printing Press	1.50
456. Pretzel Baker's Emblem	1.20

—R—

457. Rabbit	.60
458. Race Horse Head	1.20
459. Razor and Shears	.80
460. Real Estate Office	1.30
461. Redmen's Emblem	.95
462. Redmen's Encampment Emblem	1.00
463. Restaurant	1.30
464. Restaurant and Bar	1.60
465. Royal Arcanum	1.00
466. Royal Arch (Keystone)	.75
467. Royal League	1.00
468. Royal League Emblem	.75
469. Rooster	1.00
470. Roller Skate	.75

—S—

471. Saddle	.95
472. Saddler at Work	1.40
473. Saddler's Emblem	1.00
474. Safety Bicycle	.75
475. Sailor with Cannon, Flag	1.65
476. Salesman	1.30
477. Saloon (bartender and Customers)	1.00
478. Saloon Keeper's design (Saloon)	1.30
479. Saloon No. 1., Bartender and Customer	1.00
480. Saloon No. 2., Fancy, Bartender and four customers	2.00
481. Saloon, new design	1.30

482. Satchel	.90
483. Saw Mill	1.80
484. Sawyer Working	1.45
485. Schooner (sailing)	1.30
486. Scotch Thistle	.85
487. Scroll Sawyer at Work	1.40
488. Scull Boat	1.00
489. Scull Boat and Sculler	1.40
490. Set of Teeth	1.00
491. Sewing Machine	.95
492. Sheriff, Criminal and Jail	1.65
493. Sheriff with Felon	1.80
494. Sheaf of Wheat	.90
495. Shingles (bunch)	.85
496. Sheep or Sheep's Head	.50
497. Ship Sailing	1.45
498. Shirt and Collar	.80
499. Shoe Store	1.60
500. Shoemaker at Work	1.30
501. Shoe Store and Clerk	1.20
502. Shriner	1.60
503. Signpainter at work	1.40
504. Skull and Crossbones	.65
505. Sledge in Hand	1.20
506. Soldier and Flag	1.10
507. Soldier with Lady	1.20
508. Sons of Herman	.65
509. Sons of St. George	.65
510. Sons of Veterans	1.00
511. S.M.A.A. (Switchmen)	.95
512. Sons of Temperance	1.25
513. Sofa	.40
514. Sofa and Chair	1.20
515. Stage Coach, 4 or 6 horses	1.50
516. Star and Crescent	.50
517. Stationary Engine	1.10
518. Stationery Store	1.60
519. State Coat of Arms	1.50
520. Steamboat	1.30
521. Steamboat with Sails	1.40
522. Steam Hammer	1.40
523. Steam Passenger Boat	1.50
524. Steam Propeller	1.40
525. Steam Ship Sailing	1.40
526. Steel Hammer	.75
527. Steer's Head, Knife & Steel	1.25
528. Stone Cutter at Work	1.35
529. Stove	1.25
530. Stork	1.00
531. Street Car, horse	1.50
532. Street Car, Horses, Driver & Conductor	1.50
533. Sulky, Driver and Horse	1.50

534. Surveyor with Instrument	1.40	
535. Surveyor's Transit	1.35	
536. Switchman's Emblem	.75	
537. Sr. O.U.A.M. (American Mechanics)	1.10	
538. Switch Engine	1.50	
539. Sportsman and Dog	1.25	

—T—

540. Tailor Cutting	1.20
541. Tailor at Work	1.30
542. Tailor's Shears	.75
543. Tailor Behind Counter, Cutting	1.40
544. Tailor Measuring Coat	1.20
545. Tailor Holding Coat	1.20
546. Tanner's Emblem	.80
547. Telegraph Key	.80
548. Telegraph Key and Hand	1.00
549. Telegraph Operator	1.30
540. Telegraph Instrument	1.25
551. Telephone	.80
552. Ten Pin Alley	.75
553. Ten Pin Playing	1.60
554. Tea Store Desig	1.00
555. Tiger	1.25
556. Tinner's Emblem	.95
557. Tinner's Emblem, Shears and Solder Iron	.50
558. Tinner at Work	1.25
559. Tinner's Furnace and Iron	.80
560. Tinsmith at Work	1.10
561. Tinsmith's Furnace, Ion and Shears	.80
562. Tinsmith's Emblem	.85
563. Tinsmith's Iron and Torch	.85
564. Tobacconist Store	1.60
565. Tool Grinder	1.20
566. Tool Grinder at Work	1.30
567. Tow Boat	1.40
568. Toy Store	1.60
569. Toy Shop	1.50
570. T.P.A. (Travelers' Prot. A.)	.95
571. Trotting Horse	1.25
572. Trotting Horse and Wagon	1.40

573. Trowel and Hammer	.70
574. Truck Wagon	1.40
575. Truck Wagon, two horses	1.60
576. Trunk	.80
577. Tug Boat	1.00
578. Temple of Honor Emblem	1.25
579. Three Links	.10

—U—

580. U.C.T. (U. Com. Travelers)	1.10
581. Umbrella, Open	.90
582. Uniform Rank, Knights of Pythias	.95
583. United States Flag	.70
584. United States Coat of Arms	1.20
585. U. S. Flags (crossed)	.50
586. United Mine Workers of America	1.00

—V—

587. Violin and Bow	.85
588. Violin Player	1.30

—W—

589. Wagon, one or two horses and driver	1.00
590. Watch	.70
591. Watch and Chain	1.00
592. Windmill	1.30
593. Window Glass Blower	1.60
594. Whiskey Barrel	1.00
595. Wheelwright	1.45
596. Wood Turner at Work	1.40
596. Workmen's Emblem	.95
597. W.O.W. (Stump)	.85
598. W.O.W. (Woodmen of the World — Leaf)	1.00

—Y—

599. Yacht, Sailing	1.30
600. Yeoman Emblem	.90

This list was compiled from hand-painted design mugs known to exist among various collections. Many of these are considered unusual one-of-a-kind or limited trade types and have not been found listed or pictured in any barber supply catalogs.

—A—

Airplane
Airplane & RR Locomotive
Ambulance Wagon
Artist working
Auctioneer at work
Auto Mechanic at work
Auto Radiator Repairman
Auto Tire
Axe Manufacturer

—B—

Banker —Coin or Teller at window
Barber Pole
Bee Keeper — hive
Binnacle
Boarding House
Bottling Machine & Capper
Broom Manufacturer
Buggy Top Maker

—C—

Carbon Arc Movie Projector
Cheese Maker
Cheese Wagon
Cigarette Salesman
Cloth Sponger — Wagon
College Fraternity
Compass
Confectioners Wagon and store
Cotton Gin
Cut Glass cutter at work

—D—

Deep Sea Diver
Diamond Cutter
Diner and/or Restaurant

—E—

Electrician at work

—F—

Federal Marshall — baige & handcuffs
Ferry Boat
Fire Insurance — Burning Building
Floor Tile Layer working
Florist — store or window
Fighting Cocks and Handlers
Funeral Procession (undertaker)

—G—

Gambler — dice, card players, roulette wheel
Gas Meter Inventer
Golfer
Gramaphone
Greenhouse

—H—

Hide Splitter
Horn Comb Manufacturer
House Mover — house being moved
Huckster & pushcart

—I—

Ice Cream Parlor
Ice Cream Peddlar (wagon or pushcart)
Insurance Salesman

—K—

Knitting Machine

—L—

Lantern Slide Projector
Lawyer and jury
Linotype Machine
Liquor Wagon
Lobster

—M—

Magician (Rabbit in hat)
Marble Quarry
Moving Van Wagon
Mustard Wagon

—N—

Newsboy
Neopolitan Ice Cream Inventor

—O—

Optician & Optometrist
Opera Singers
Orchestra Conductor
Oyster Bar

—P—

Peddlar & Wagon
 (fruit and/or vegetables)
Picture Frame Dealer
Police Wagon (Black Maria)
Playwright
Priest

—Q—

Quartet Singers

—R—

RR Control Tower
RR Crossing Watchman
RR Flat Car Builder
RR Pile Driver & crew
RR Mail & Baggage car (RMS)
RR Steam Shovel
RR Wreckmaster (train wreck)
RR Roundhouse (Locomotive Turntable)
Roofer working
Rope Maker at work

—S—

Scull and crew boat racers
Schoolteacher and pupils
Sheep Shearer (shears)
Short Order Cook
Shipfitter
Soda Fountain
Ships Chandler Wagon
Shoe Shine Boy

Slot Machine
Stained Glass Window Maker
Stonecutter (Gravestone) at work
Stone Pavement Layer working
Stepladder
Steeplejack

—T—

Trolley Wire Repair Wagon
Tanner at work
Taxidermist working
Taffy Puller Working
Telephone Lineman Wagon
Tea & Coffee Wagon
Tea Importer
Tobacco grower (leaf)

—U—

Upholsterer working

—V—

Vet Surgeon (horse on operating table)

—W—

Watch Maker
Western Sheriff
Wood Carver working
Wrecking Company — crane & crew
Wine Maker
Water Well Driller working
Watermelon
Wine Taster

Author's collection.

PART III
Section 1
Barbering Equipment, Supplies and Furniture

Art Congress.

The cut represents the chair in antique oak. The "quarter-saw" lights are plainly to be seen. In addition to the rich carving, this chair is handsomely ornamented with oxidized cast brass corner plates. The tried and approved machinery of the "reliable Congress" is used.
It is needless to say that the finish and upholstering are first class.

We are now covering the Improved Foot Rest with new style Iron Plate Copper oxidized; as shown on Star No. 2 Chair, page 8.

Price, covered in Finest Plush or Leather, any color	$60 00
" " in Embossed Leather	65 00
" Made of Genuine Mahogany Wood, add	10 00

Kept in stock in Oak and Walnut.

Koken's Star No. 2.
ELEVATING CHAIR.
Patented.

SOMETHING NEW in style of frame as well as machinery, without exception this is as fine and complete a chair as was ever offered to the tonsorial profession. For fuller description of mechanism see description of Star No. 1, on pages 12 and 13.

Improved Foot Rest covered with New Style Iron Plate as shown in cut.

Price, upholstered with finest Plush or Leather, any color	$50 00
" " Embossed Leather	55 00
" Made of Genuine Mahogany, add	10 00
Summer Seat, extra	3 00

Kept in stock in Oak and Walnut

Koken's Congress Chair.

BEST IN THE WORLD.

Patented.

INCLINED POSITION.

With a record of 8 years in the market, its reputation to-day is ahead of anything offered by other manufacturers.

Improved Foot Rest covered with Iron Plate, as shown on Star No. 2 Chair, page 8.

Price, covered in Finest Plush or Leather, any color, with improved foot rest	$45 00
" Foot Rest only	5 00
" Summer Seat, extra	3 00

Kept in stock in Walnut, Oak and Cherry.

TWO-BOWL CENTER WASHSTAND, No. 365

No. 502. SHINING STAND

No. 549. SHOESHINING STAND

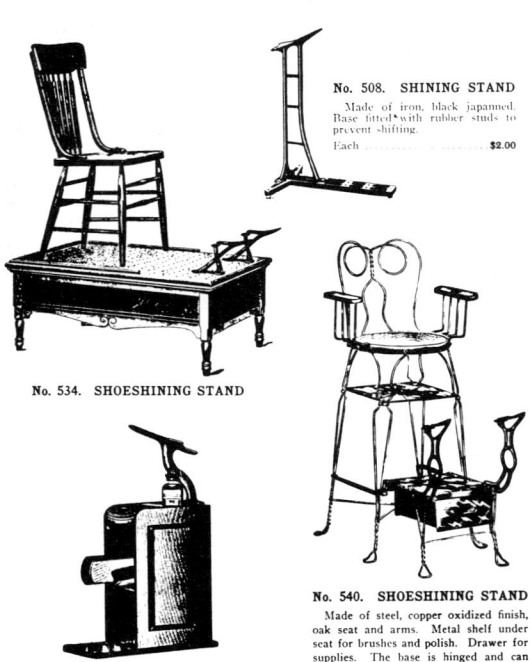

No. 508. SHINING STAND
Made of iron, black japanned. Base fitted with rubber studs to prevent shifting.
Each $2.00

No. 534. SHOESHINING STAND

No. 550. SHINING STAND

No. 540. SHOESHINING STAND
Made of steel, copper oxidized finish, oak seat and arms. Metal shelf under seat for brushes and polish. Drawer for supplies. The base is hinged and can easily be put under the chair.
Each $9.50

No. 691. SHOESHINING STAND

No. 503. SHINING STAND
Made of steel, copper oxidized finish. Polished oak seat, oxidized foot-rest. Tray under seat.
Each $3.50

No. 460. SETTEE

No. 418. SETTEE

No. 77. CHILD'S
HAIR-CUTTING CHAIR
Made of steel, copper-oxidized finish. Polished oak seat.
Extra strong frame.
Price $5.40

No. 613. WAITING CHAIR

No. 40.
FOLDING BARBERS' CHAIR
Made of oak, antique finish. Upholstered with velour. This portable chair is used by traveling barbers and by soldiers in camp.
Price $13.50

WAITING CHAIRS

No. 111. FOLDING CHILD'S SEAT

No. 627. WAITING CHAIR

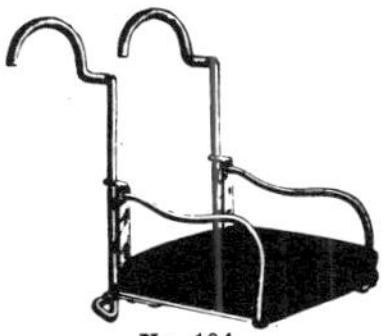

No. 104.
ADJUSTABLE CHILD'S SEAT

No. 507. REVOLVING SHAMPOOING STOOL

No. 505. SHAMPOOING STOOL

No. 100. CHILD'S SEAT

No. 648. WAITING CHAIR

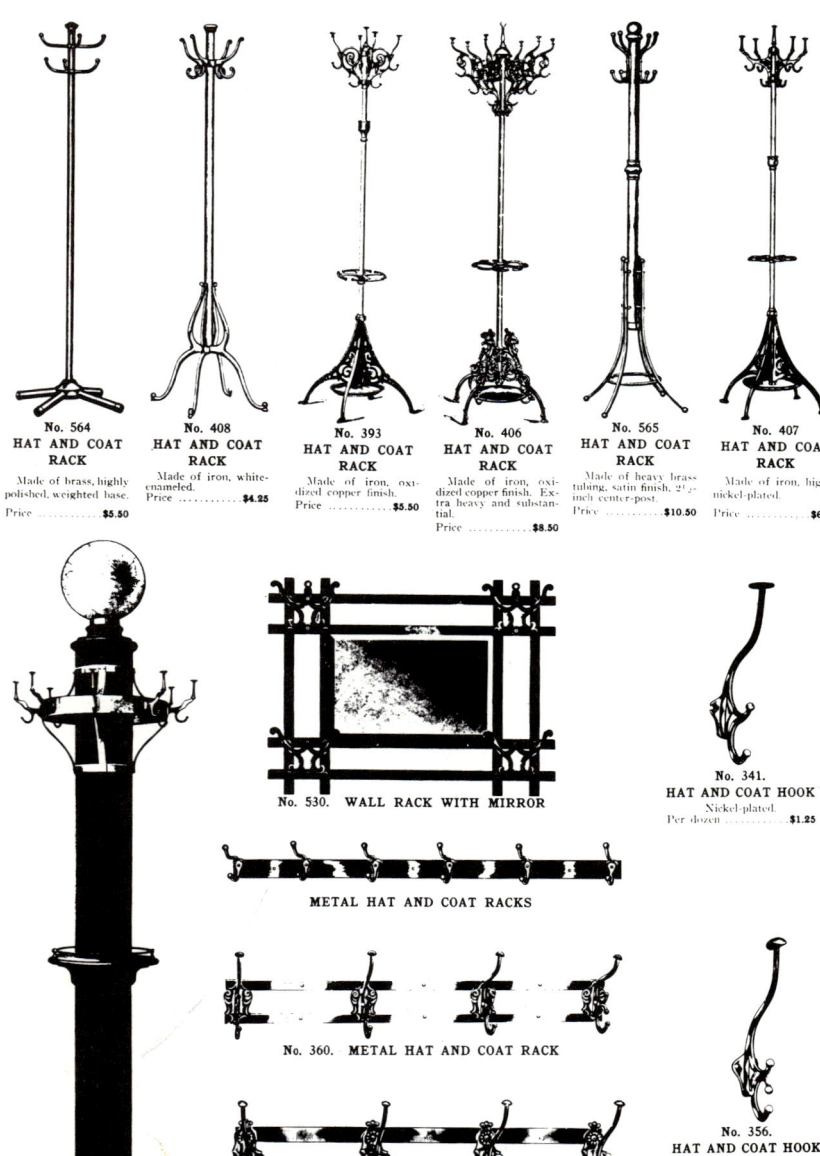

PORTABLE WORKCABINET, No. 258

PORTABLE WASHSTAND, No. 217

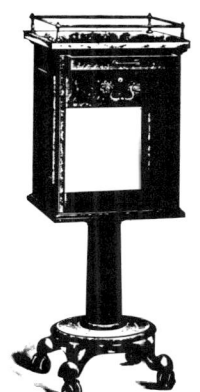
PORTABLE WORKCABINET, No. 229

ONE-BOWL WALL WASHSTAND, No. 261

ONE-BOWL CENTER WASHSTAND, No. 263

WORKSTAND, No. 227

WORKSTAND, No. 226
Made of oak, golden finish. Height, 3 feet.
Price $4.25

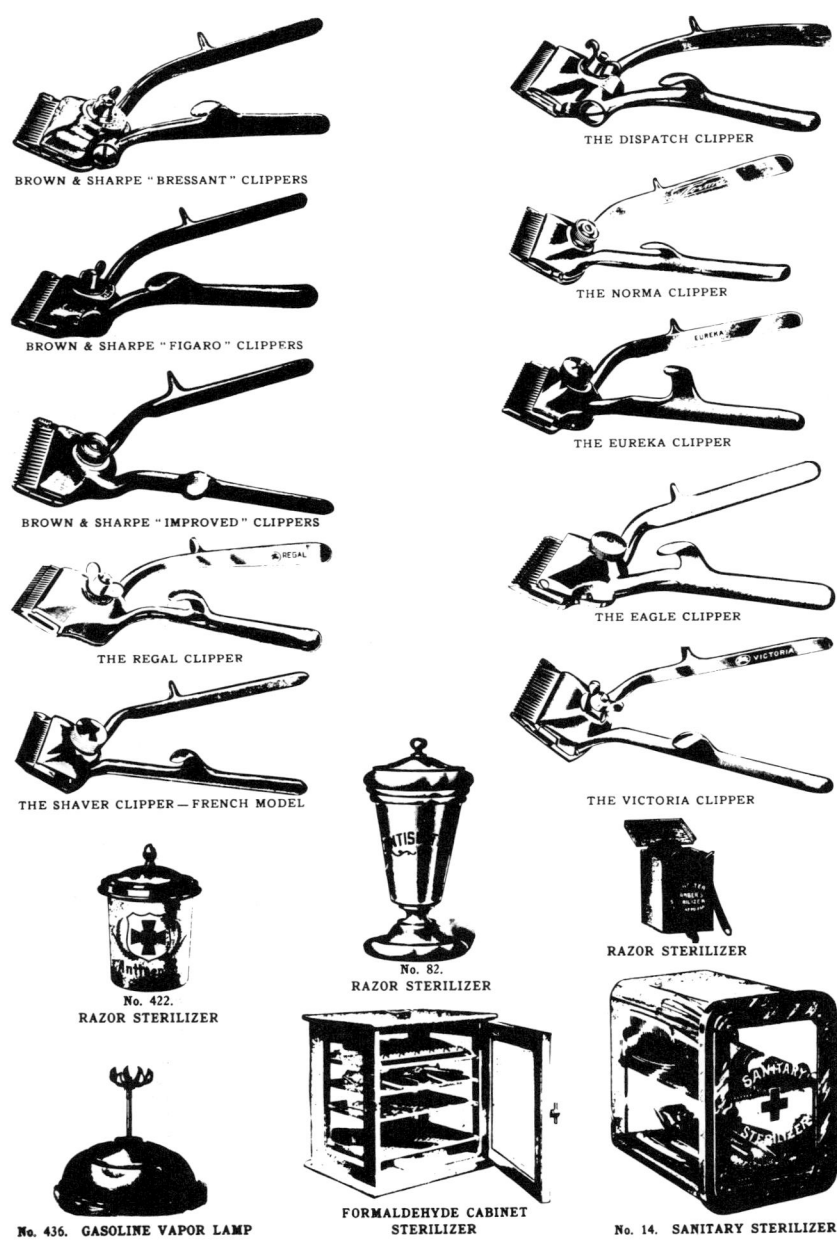

STEAM STERILIZERS

RED CROSS STERILIZER

VULCAN STERILIZERS

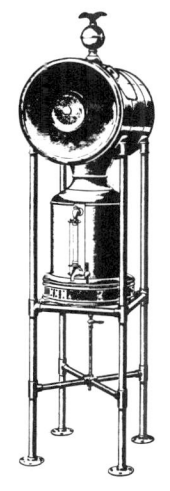
SIMPLEX STERILIZERS

PEERLESS STERILIZER

CABINET STERILIZERS

No. 845.
HOT WATER URN

THE COMMON-SENSE
STERILIZER
No. 80.

BUFFALO SANITARY
STERILIZERS

LAMP STOVE

COPPER BOILERS

LATHER BRUSHES

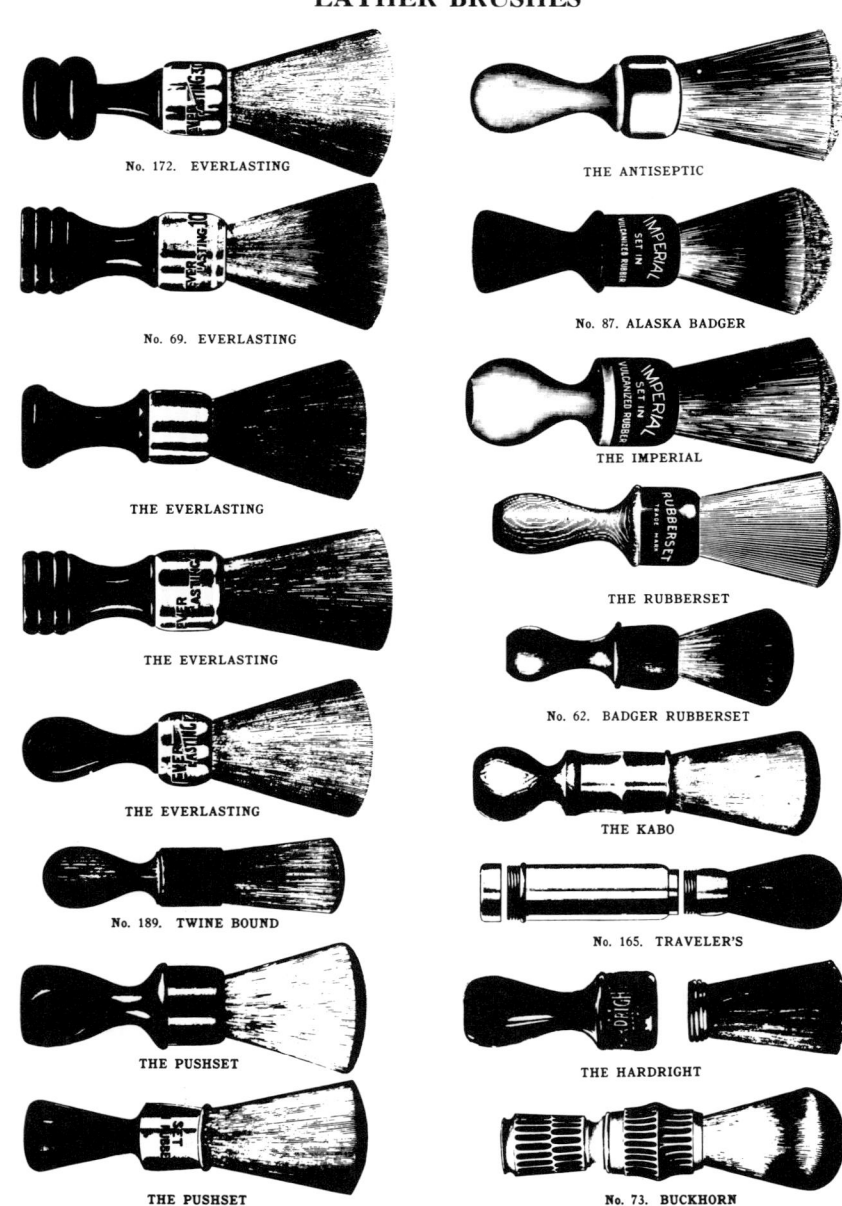

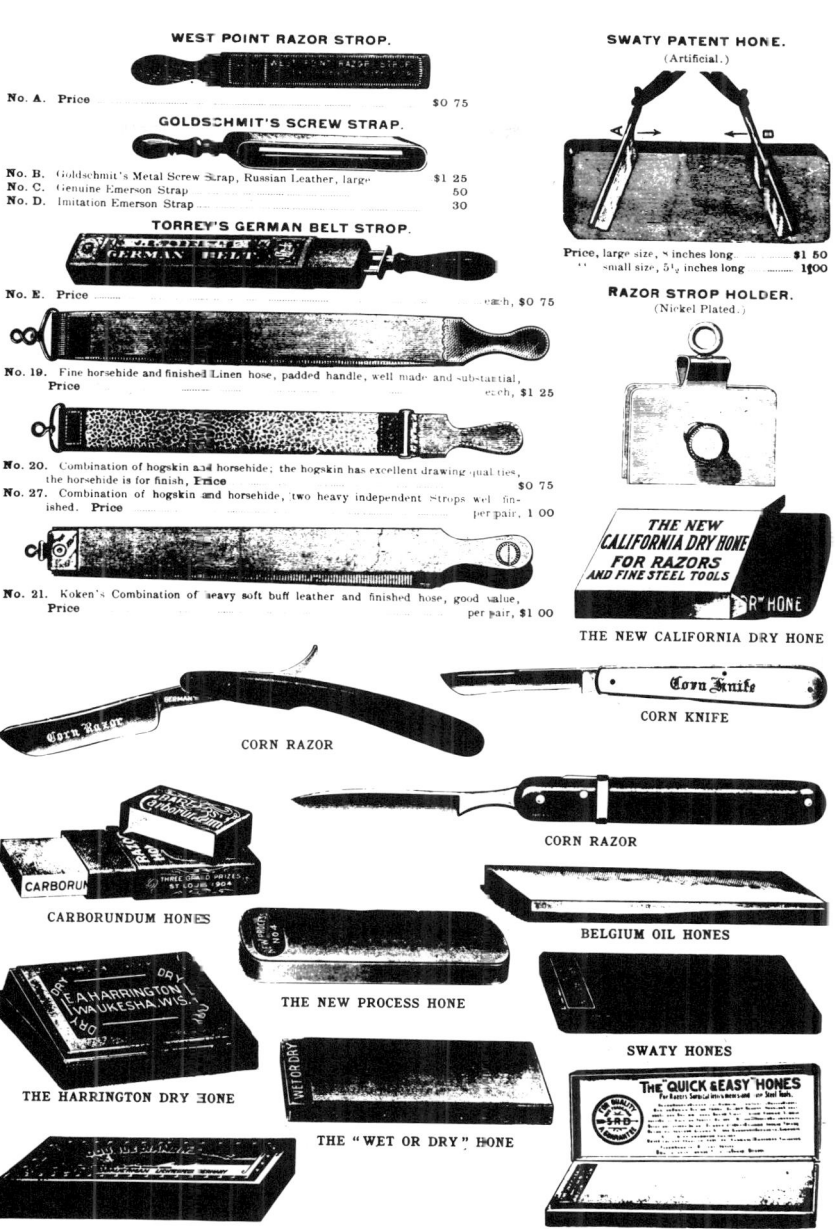

WEST POINT RAZOR STROP.

No. A. Price $0 75

GOLDSCHMIT'S SCREW STRAP.

No. B. Goldschmit's Metal Screw Strap, Russian Leather, large $1 25
No. C. Genuine Emerson Strap 50
No. D. Imitation Emerson Strap 30

TORREY'S GERMAN BELT STROP.

No. E. Price .... each, $0 75

No. 19. Fine horsehide and finished Linen hose, padded handle, well made and substantial, Price .... each, $1 25

No. 20. Combination of hogskin and horsehide; the hogskin has excellent drawing qualities, the horsehide is for finish, Price $0 75
No. 27. Combination of hogskin and horsehide, two heavy independent straps well finished. Price .... per pair, 1 00

No. 21. Koken's Combination of heavy soft buff leather and finished hose, good value, Price .... per pair, $1 00

SWATY PATENT HONE.
(Artificial.)

Price, large size, 8 inches long $1 50
" small size, 5½ inches long 1 00

RAZOR STROP HOLDER.
(Nickel Plated.)

THE NEW CALIFORNIA DRY HONE

CORN RAZOR

CORN KNIFE

CORN RAZOR

CARBORUNDUM HONES

THE NEW PROCESS HONE

BELGIUM OIL HONES

THE HARRINGTON DRY HONE

SWATY HONES

THE "WET OR DRY" HONE

THE DOUBLE DIAMOND WATER HONE

THE QUICK AND EASY HONE

RAZOR CASES AND TOOL BAGS

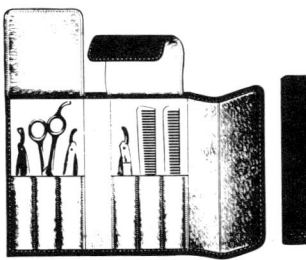

No. 739. TOOL POCKET

Made of fine seal-grain leather. Lined with leather. Holds three razors, one shear and two combs. Very flexible.

Each, case only.. $1.50

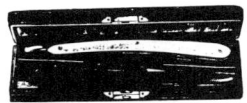

Morocco Razor Cases.

No. 400—Case only for one razor............each, $0.50
No. 500—Case only for two razors............ " .75
No. 600—Case only for two razors, plush and silk lined, extra fine .... " 1.00

No. 744. RAZOR CASE

For two razors. Covered with seal-grain leather. Silk lined with silk cushion inside of cover. Nickel-plated lock.
Price of case, empty $1.00

No. 755. RAZOR CASE

Holds seven razors. Very elaborately covered with seal-grain leather. Silk cushion inside of cover. Balance trimmed with fine velvet. Nickel-plated lock and invisible spring hinges on cover.
Price of case, empty $2.50

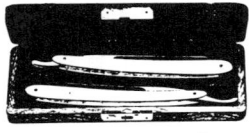

Polished Oak Razor Case.

Satin and plush lined, case only for two razors.
No. 800 ....each, $1.50

No. 746. BARBERS' COMBINATION BOX

Made to hold razors, shears and combs. Covered with leatherette and lined with velvet. Fitted with lock and key.

Each $1.25

No. 708. TOOL BAG

Made of genuine leather, raised alligator pattern, fitted with patent lock and key. Very substantial and extraordinary value for the money.

Each $2.25

No. 754. TOOL CASE

Made of wood, covered with leatherette, alligator pattern. Fitted with nickel-plated trimmings, snaplock and key.

Each $1.75

TRAVELING CASE WHEN OPEN

No. 756.
BARBERS' TRAVELING CASE

This traveling case is lined with velvet throughout, furnished with a good nickel-plated lock and key, and is put together substantially. The arrangement is very compact, and the case measures upon the outside only 11½ inches long, 6½ inches wide and 9 inches high.

Price, case only, with three empty bottles $5.00

TRAVELING CASE WHEN CLOSED

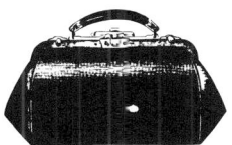

No. 706. TOOL BAG
Made of imitation leather and fitted with patent lock and key.
Each $1.15

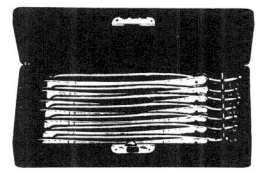

Seven Day Razor Case.
No. 700—Case only for seven razors .... each, $2.50

Corn Razor.
No. 203 .... each, $0.65
No. 204—Pearl handle .... " 1.25

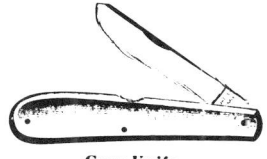

Corn Knife.
Made of fine steel, handsome white bone handle.
No. 202 .... each, $0.75

SAFETY GUARD RAZORS.

Curley's Reversible Safety Guard.
Can be attached to any razor.
No. 205 .... each, $0.25

Curley's Safety Guard Razors.
No. 200—With one blade .... each, $1.75
No. 201—With two blades .... " 2.75

Gem Safety Razor.
This razor has the latest improvement. It opens by means of a hinge for easy removal of lather.
No. 206 .... each, $1.50

235

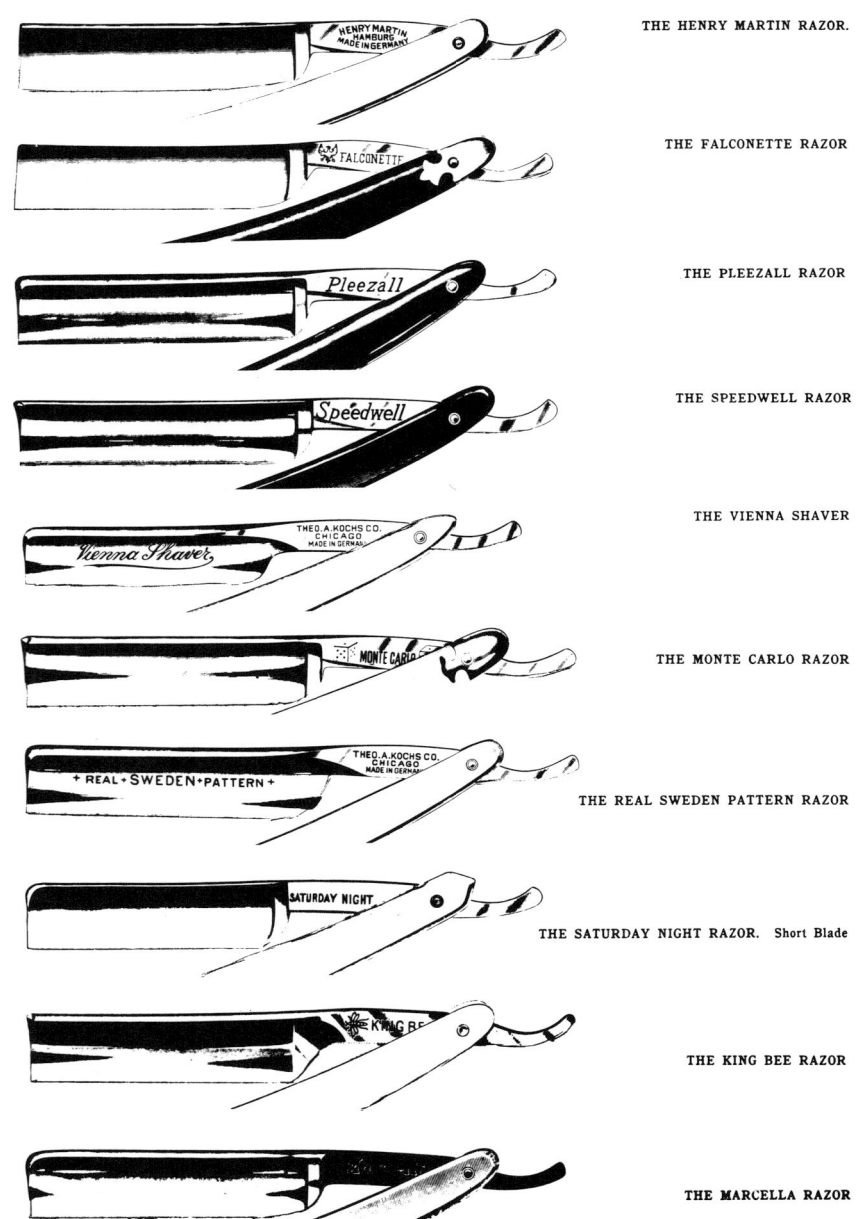

RAZOR HANDLES

Razor Racks and Pockets.

RAZOR RACK.

RAZOR POCKETS.
An Article every Barber should have

No. **452.** Black rubber, round, 4-8, 5-8, 6-8 and 7-8, each 20c

No. **451.** Black rubber, flat, 4-8, 5-8 and 6-8, each 20c

No. **453.** Black, with German-silver tips, 4-8 and 5-8, each 35c

No. **466.** Black, fancy, 5-8 only, each 30c

No. **458.** White ivorine, 4-8, 5-8 and 6-8, each 25c

No. **459.** White ivorine, with German silver tips, 4-8 and 5-8, each 35c

No. **461.** Imitation mock turtle, 4-8, 5-8 and 6-8, each 30c

No. **467.** Imitation tortoise shell, with German silver tips, 4-8 and 5-8, each 35c

No. **462.** Imitation tortoise shell, lined with German silver and with German-silver edge, 4-8 and 5-8, each 20c

No. **468.** White ivorine, light antique finish, 5-8 only, each 25c

No. **469.** Imitation smoked pearl, 5-8 only, each 25c

No. **450.** Aluminum, fancy, 4-8 and 5-8, each ... 30c
No. **464.** Aluminum, plain, 4-8 and 5-8, each ... 25c

Price, Razor Rack, as shown above $2 50

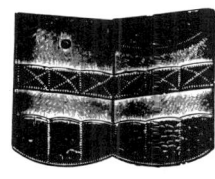

No. **724. RAZOR POCKET**
Made of sheepskin, stamped alligator pattern. Very handy to carry in pocket. Holds 6 razors. Lined with velvet.
Each 65c

No. **733.**
RAZOR POCKET
Made of fine seal grain leather. Lined with velvet. Holds two razors.
Each 55c

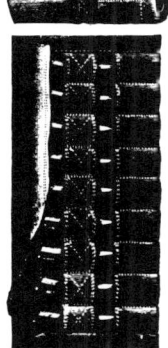

	Price.
Razor Pocket, Calf Skin, 6 Loop	$1 00
Razor Pocket, Calf Skin, 9 Loop	1 25
Razor Pocket, Calf Skin, 12 Loop	1 50
Razor Pocket, Alligator Skin, 6 Loop	75
Razor Pocket, Alligator Skin, 9 Loop	1 00
Razor Pocket, Alligator Skin, 12 Loop	1 25

No. **727. RAZOR ROLL**

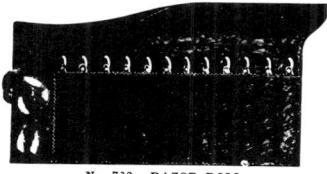

No. **732. RAZOR ROLL**

No. 1101.
Silver Plated.
Each $1.10

No. 1104.
Heavy White Metal Nickel Plated.
Each $1.25

No. 1103.
Aluminum, handsomely engraved.
Each $1.00

No. 993. SHAVING MUG
A substantial shop mug, heavily nickel-plated.
Each $1.00

No. 995. SHAVING MUG
Made of aluminum.
Each .... 60c.

No. 997. SHAVING MUG
Made of aluminum.
Each .... 70c.

No. 1218.
GLASS SHAVING MUG
Gold band top and bottom.
Each .... 35c.

No. 1216.
GLASS SHAVING MUG
Clear glass.
Each 25c

No. 1217.
GLASS SHAVING MUG
Ribbed, clear glass.
Each .... 25c.

PLAIN CHINA MUGS

NUMBERED CHINA MUGS
With gold stripes.

GOLD BAND CHINA MUGS

Bottle Tubes.

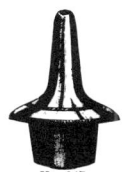

No. 347.
NICKEL-PLATED
BOTTLE TUBE
Per dozen .... 30c.
Each .... 3c.

No. 352.
CROWN STOPPER
Gilt finish.
Per dozen .... 60c.
Each .... 6c.

No. 348. SELF-CLOSING BOTTLE TUBE
Per dozen .... 40c.
Each .... 4c.

No. 1.
OPAL TUBE.
Price, each $0 10

No. 3.
BRITANNIA.
Price, each $0 05

No. 2.
BRITANNIA TUBE.
Nickel Plated, Long Neck.
Price, each $0 10

No. 713. ALUMINUM TALCUM SHAKER
Screw top.
Each .... 25c.

Aluminum Talcum Sifter.
No. 400 ..... each, $0.35

No. 715. SOAP POWDER SHAKER
Made of aluminum. Screw top.
Each .... 20c.

No. 419. ALUMINUM STAND BOTTLE
Satin finish.
Each .... 50c.

No. 423. ALUMINUM STAND BOTTLE
Highly polished.
Each .... 65c.

No. 719. TALCUM SHAKER
Silver-plated.
Each .... 85c.

No. 916. ATOMIZER
Continuous spray. Fitted with rubber cork.
Each .... 50c.

No. 209.
CLEAR GLASS STAND BOTTLE
Each .... 25c.

No. 211.
CLEAR GLASS STAND BOTTLE
Each .... 25c.

DECORATED SHAVING MUGS

241

No. 653.

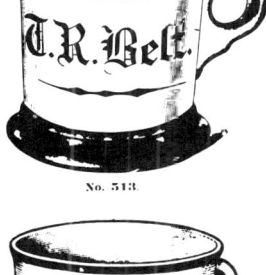

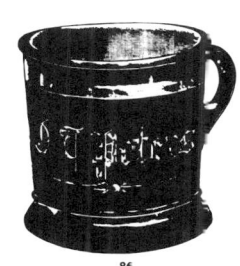

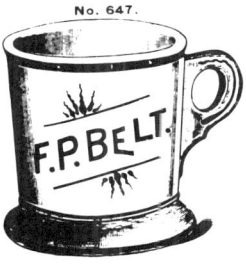

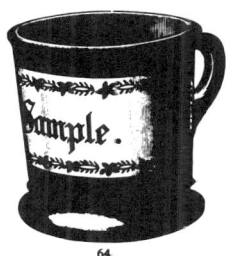

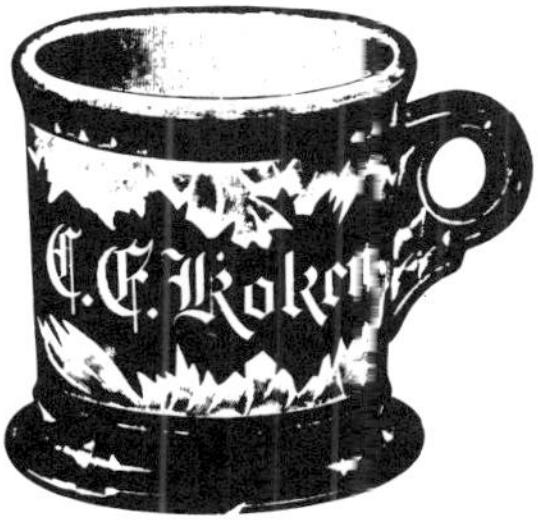

No. 625.

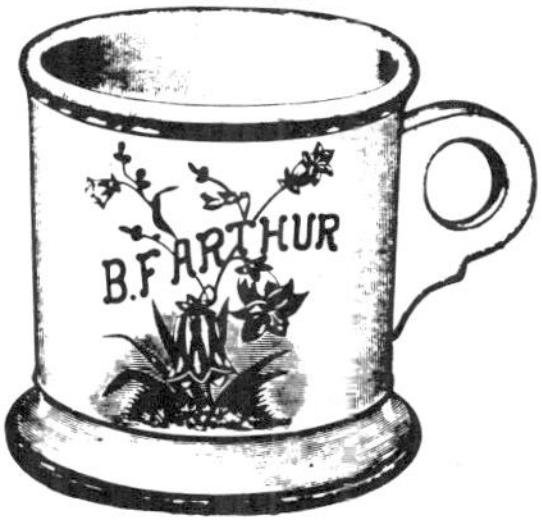

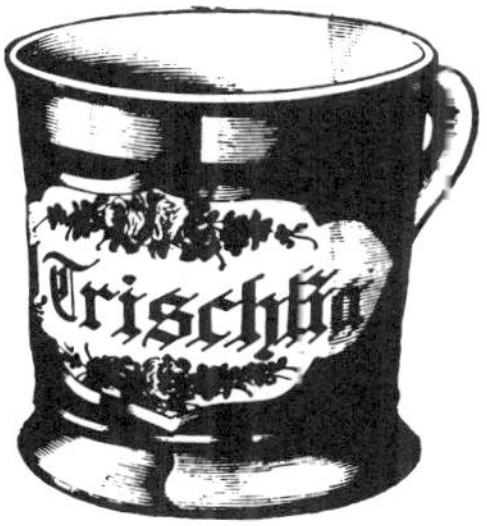

25

No. 665.

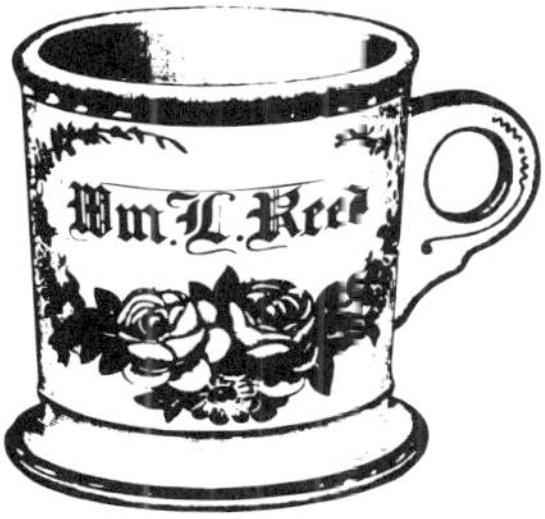

No. 594.

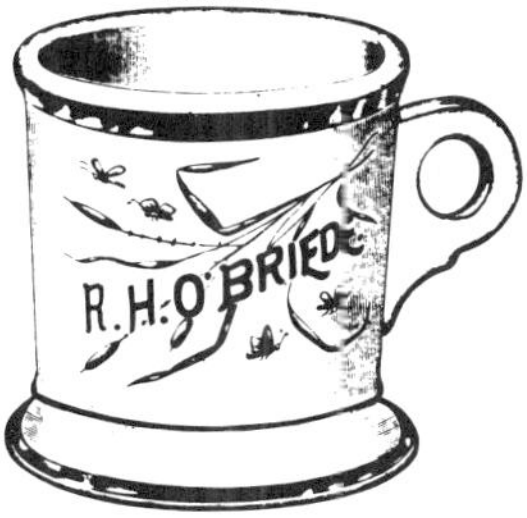

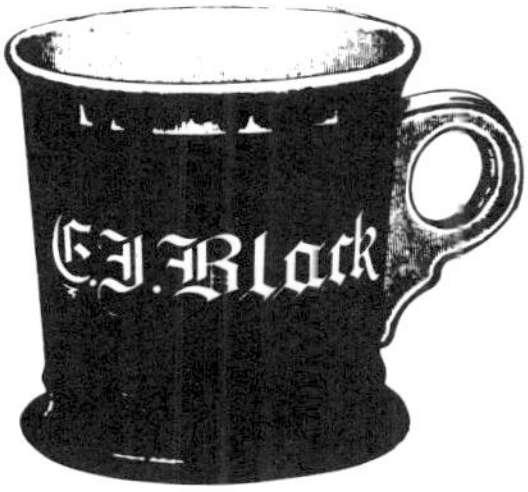

No. 748.

No. 513.

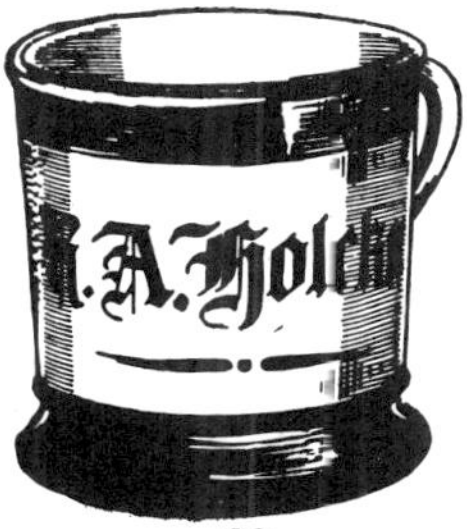

30

86

No. 647.

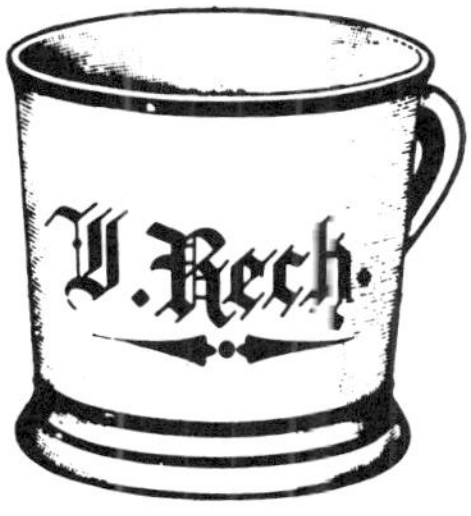

1

64

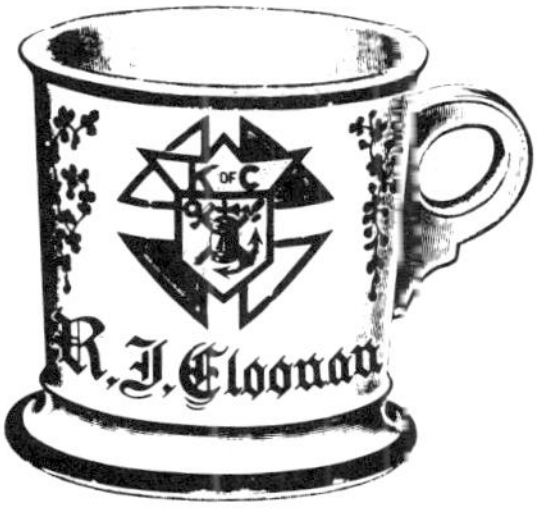

No. 785.

No. 634.

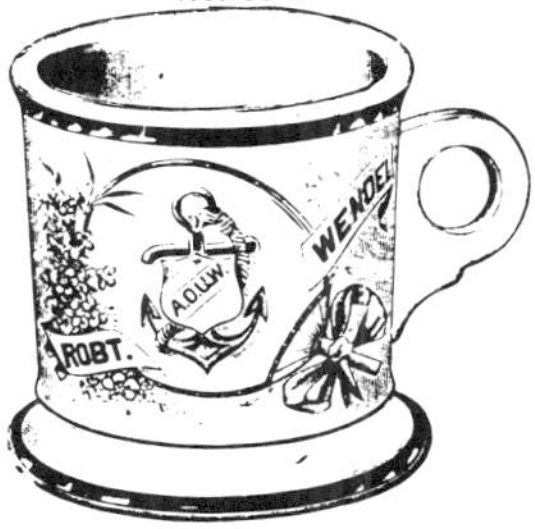

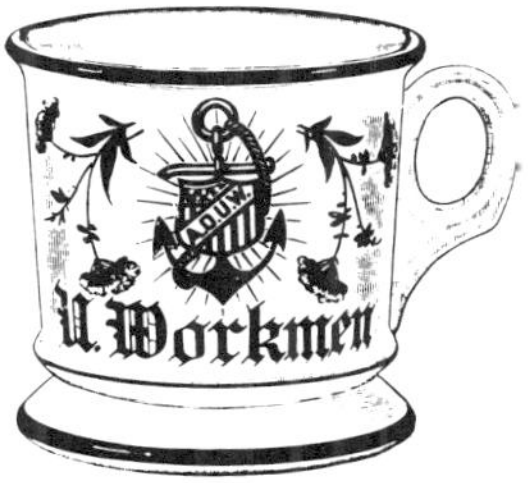

301

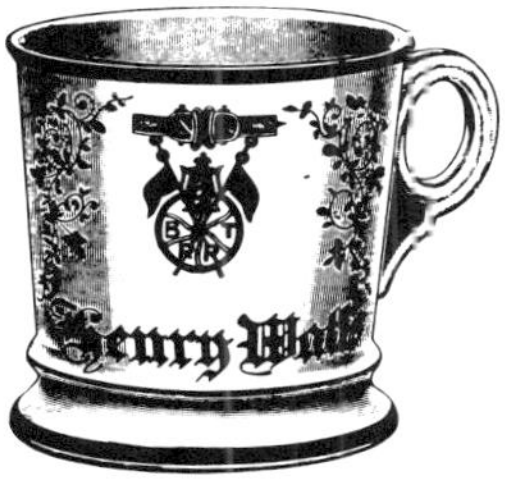

343

No. 644.

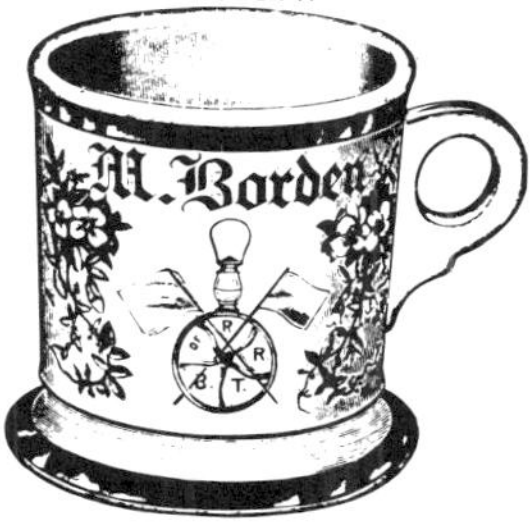

No. 643.

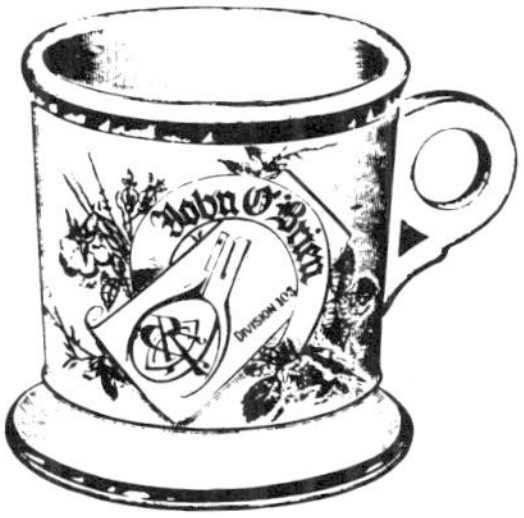

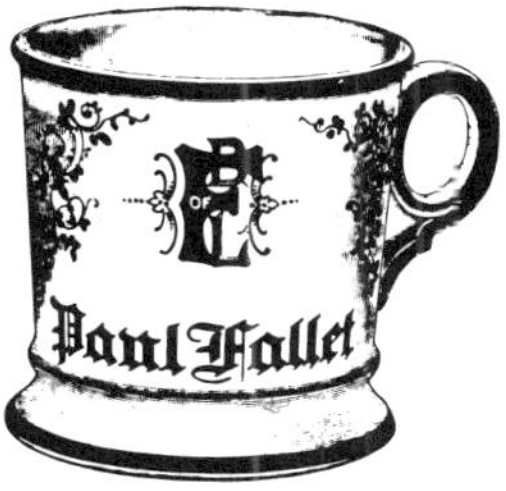

364

No. 641.

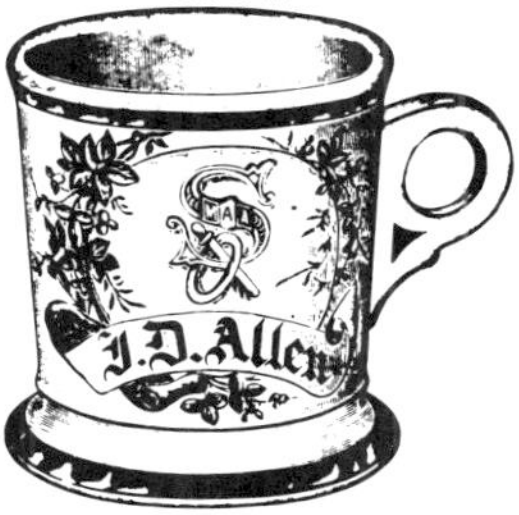

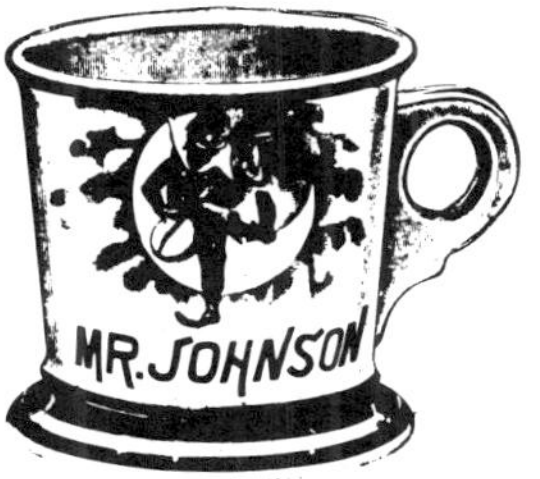

No. 735.

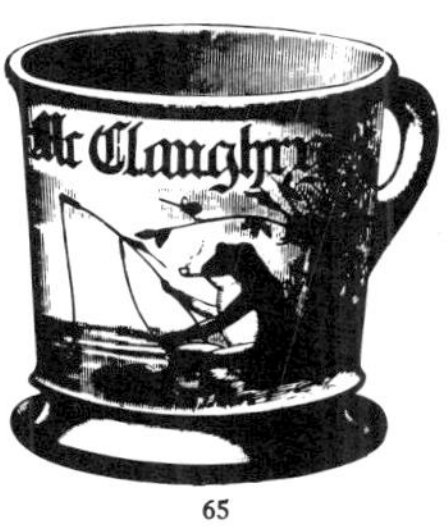

65

256

No. 642.

No. 667.

No. 557.

New Design.
Solid Iron Barber Pole.
No. 17.

BOX POLES, Nos 1 AND 2.

POLE No. 14.

| No. 1. Price | $ 9 00 |
| No. 2. " | 12 00 |

| 10 inch Pole | $16 00 |
| 12 inch Pole | 20 00 |

10 in. diameter; height 8 ft.
Price.......... $24 00

KOKEN BARBERS' SUPPLY CO., ST. LOUIS.

Wooden Barber Poles.

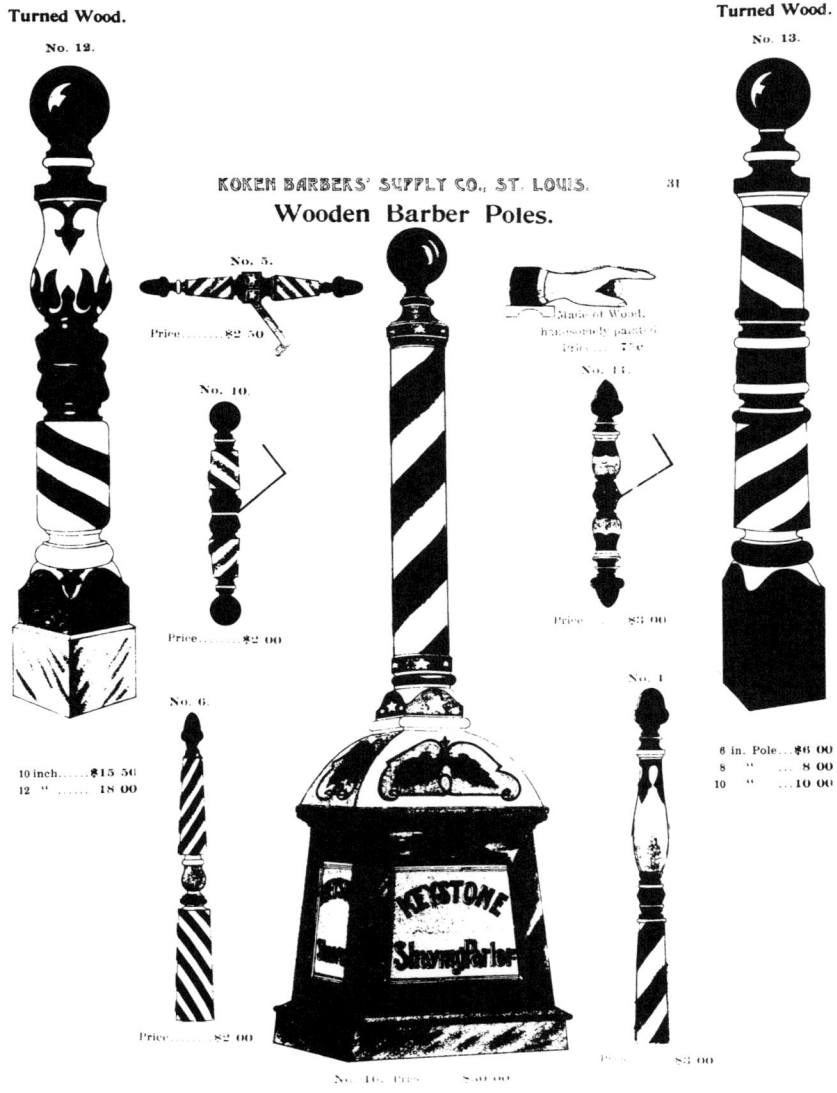

First barber shop in Comanche, Oklahoma. *Permission of Mr. and Mrs. L. M. Zigler.*

First Barber Shop in Comanche, Okla.

This early photograph, of the first barber shop in Comanche, Oklahoma, was taken by a travelling photographer, in 1916, just nine years after the Territory of Oklahoma had become the 46th STATE (admitted Nov. 16, 1907).

The shop owner, "Boss" Jennings never went to a Barber College to learn the trade, and as his brother-in-law, Mr. L. M. Zigler explains, "he probably had never heard of a barber college in those days." "He simply decided he wanted to become a barber, saved his money, bought the shop as a young man, and worked at the trade for 48 years, until his death in 1964.

During the early days of Oklahoma statehood people were pouring into the state from everywhere. At the time this picture was taken, Comanche, Oklahoma boasted a population of about 600. Events happened almost daily, which would make a lasting impression on the mind of a youngster, shining shoes in the town barber shop. But of all the things which occurred, one fact remained indelibly painted in the lad's mind. And, that was the travelling Carnival which came to town each August for a week (from Monday thru Saturday). On those occasions Indian tribes numbering some 400 to 600 also came to town to see the carnival. The Federal Government furnished them with beef, which they slaughtered and cooked right at the edge of town, where they set up their camps. The town's population was further swelled to an additional 7,000 to 8,000 for the Carnival by the crowds that came from all over that part of the territory. The Rock Island Railroad ran special trains to accomodate the crowds. The gala carnival atmosphere prevailed the entire week, and there were horse races daily. This affair was further livened by the Wild West Show which was presented by the famed *One Hundred And One Ranch*, an Oklahoma institution known throughout the world during that era.

Author's collection.

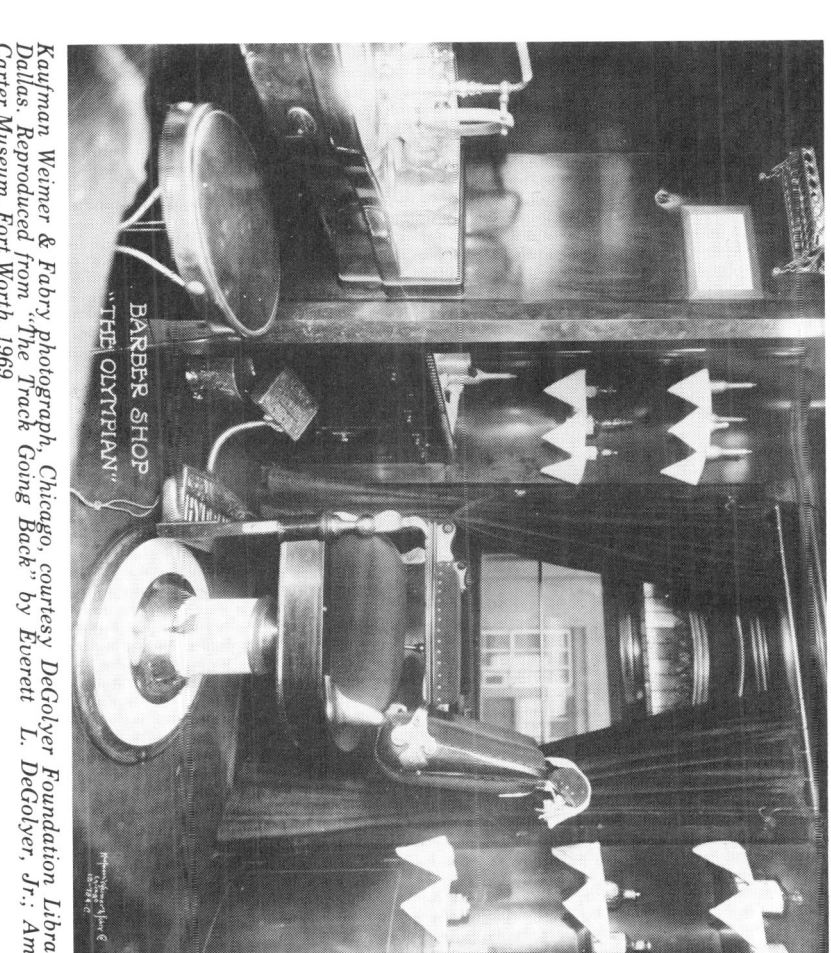

Kaufman Weimer & Fabry, photograph, Chicago, courtesy DeGolyer Foundation Library, Dallas. Reproduced from "The Track Going Back" by Everett L. DeGolyer, Jr.; Amon Carter Museum, Fort Worth, 1969.

Railroad Barber Shop aboard the Milwaukee Roads' "The Olympian" —early western transcontinental train (between Chicago and the Pacific Coast — a 3-day trip).

SEITZ

The name Oscar Seitz is well known in Salina, Kansas, as one of its earliest settlers. When he was 18 he came to New York from Kassell, Germany. After working in New York for awhile, he went to Columbus, Ohio and then to St. Louis. About that time the Civil War broke out and he joined the Northern Army to become a hospital steward. After the war he was mustered out of the army at Paducah, Kentucky. Soon afterward he went to Leavenworth where he and another man opened a drug store and called it "Gurdan — Seitz Drug."

Being both ambitious and adventurous, Oscar Seitz next moved all his belongings by ox-cart to Junction City (at that time located at the end of the railroad line) to open a drug store of his own. Arriving there he discovered that the building he was to occupy had been sold from under him. So he kept traveling (another 50 miles west) till he got to the next town of Salina — population not quite 100 people, there he opened the first drug store in Salina, Kansas, in 1866 and later stores in Wilson and Ellsworth. This was the wisest business move he had ever made because the next year the railroad came to Salina. In 1869 he traveled back to Staten Island to marry his childhood sweetheart, Joanna Wulp who came back to Salina with him. Soon afterwards he bought the location where the Seitz drug store was — until about 1946.

Seitz Drug Store, 1884. First drug store in Salina or Saline County, Kansas. Left to right: Oscar Seitz, N. M. Curry, John Gustafson, Charles F. W. Seitz, Theo Wary.

Author's collection.

In 1869 the covered wagons started rolling through Salina, and Oscar Seitz was on his way to amassing his fortune. (At that time there wasn't another drug store between Salina and Texas and everyone had to stock up at his drug store.) His store was a shopping place for Indians as well as early settlers.

By 1888 when he built a mansion for his family he had made a fortune of at least $100,000 from his drug store. The house cost over $21,000. This home contained among all its finery the first grand piano in Salina. Mrs. Seitz was an accomplished musician and she taught Christie Campbell (the first white child born in Salina County) to play the piano — in exchange for lessons to speak English. The Seitz' also brought the first upright piano to Salina; it was easy to load on a wagon when needed for entertainment elsewhere, because it had a handle on each side.

Author's collection.

Favorite Barber Shop Joke

About the time America 23-skidoo-ed into the 20th century, many barber shop jokes made their debut from the sanctuary or many local barber shops.

One such joke, although bearing a full growth of chin whiskers by now, was a long-time favorite in Tom Cowsar's Tonsorial Parlor in Wichita Falls, Texas.

Tom relates the experience a local farmer had while shaving with an old straight razor one summer morning. He was barefooted, and was shaving on the back porch. There was a large hole in the window screen.

After lathering his face, and while he was stropping his razor, a large horsefly flew in through the hole in the screen. It landed right on his nose.

Instinctively he slapped at it with the hand holding the razor.

The result was natural — he cut off his nose.

The sharp pain caused him to drop the razor — which fell to the floor, cutting off the big toe on his right foot.

In all this pain he still had the presence of mind to know if you replace a dismembered part of your body immediately, there was a good chance it would heal satisfactory.

The sight of blood so excited him that he made the mistake of putting his toe where his nose had been and his nose on his foot, after which he fainted.

Several hours later his wife found him, still unconscious. She hitched up the team of horses and rushed him to the nearest doctor, who decided that because so much time had elapsed since the accident it would be unwise to correct the mistake.

Tom then relates with a wry smile and then a chuckle, how the farmer fully recovered from the accident, but was forced to live the remainder of his life with a terrible inconvenience. Every time he had to sneeze, it was necessary for him to take off his right shoe.

INDEX:
Page numbers in *italics* indicate photographs.

Abel, Mr. A. Lawrence, MS, MD, FRCS, 20
Adams & Co., 58
Adelph Silverplate Co., *45*
Advertising signs, 22, 24
After shaving lotion 39
Alexander The Great, 9
Alexandria, 9
Aluminum Stand Bottle, 239
Amber color glass mugs, 57
American Belleek shaving mugs, *106-109*
American Patent System, 63
"Amole Cup" glass mug, *61*
Antiseptic Jars, 152
"Antiseptilene", 192
Aqua Velva Lotion, 3⅝
Arlequin Tooveraar er Barbier, *31*
Arnart — 5th Ave., 163
Arrowheads, 7
Art glassware (imported & domestic), 152
Art Pottery Urns, 151
Art Pottery Vases, 151
Asklepios (god of medicine), 9
Atomizer, 239
Atterbury & Co., 64

Barber basins: (same as bowls)
 Aluminum, 14, 26, *28*
 Barber tools decoration, 17
 Delft, *21*
 Delft faience, 23
 Dutch, glazed Delft, *12, 14, 15*
 Enamelware, 30
 Faience, *19*
 French, *12, 14, 17, 19*
 French faience, 23
 French Majolica, *31*
 French pottery, 27
 Half-moon indentation, 29
 London (Lambeth) English Delft, *13, 14*
 made of (composition), *13*, 29
 miniatures, *14*
 notch, 20
 Oriental Export, 25
 Pewter, *12, 17, 27*, 38
 Pennsylvania pottery, *26*
 Portuguese, *17*
 Sgraffito, 24
 shapes & sizes, 29
 silver decorated, *26*
 silver on brass, *28*
 slip decoration, 24
 soap receptacle, 13
 Spanish, *17, 25*
 Spanish copper, *26*
 Swiss, *15*
 Tin, *17*
 Turkey, 25
Barber advertising signs, 18, 22
Barber Assn. in Germany, 22

Barberbaekkener, 18
Barber/Beauty shop, 195
Barber Bottles: *135-145*
 European imports, *135-140*
 fraternal emblems, *140*
 glass labels, 99, *140-142*
 handpainted, *144*
 list of types, 137
 litho labels, 141
 made in USA, *141*
 melon shaped, *144*
 new opalescent, *145*
 owner's name on, *140, 141*
 reverse painted, *140-142*
 square style, *144*
 Venetian or spiral, *145*
Barber bowls (see barber basins)
Barber bowl in use, *31*
Barber chairs, *224, 225*
Barber chair, folding, *227*
Barber customs, 18
Barber, Edwin Atlee, 13, 24
Barber Figurine, I, 5
Barbering equip., supplies, furniture, *224-260*
Barbering profession today, 195
Barbers, 16, 22, 24
Barbery, 7
Barber Shop, French, *10*
Barber shop, Henry Ford Museum, *176*
Barber shop, 1st in Comanche, Okla, *261,262*
Barber shop, 1st transcontinental RR, *263*
Barbershop furniture, equipment & supplies:
 Atomizer, *239*
 barber poles, *260, 261*
 bottle tubes, *239*
 brushes (lather), *232*
 clippers, *230*
 column racks, *228*
 copper boilers, *231*
 corn knife or razor, *233*
 hat & coat racks, *228*
 hones, *233*
 hot water urn, *231*
 lamp stove, *231*
 powder shaker, *239*
 razors, *236*
 razor cases, *234, 235*
 razor handles, *237*
 razor pockets, *237*
 razor rack, *237*
 razor rolls, *237*
 razor sterilizers, *230*
 razor strops, *233*
 razor strop holder, *233*
 safety razors, 235
 stand bottles, *239*
 sterilizer cabinet, *230*, 231
 sterilizers, steam, *231*
 talcom sifter, *239*
 tool bags & cases, *234, 235*
 washstand, *226*
 water bowl, *138*
 workstands, *229*

Barber merchant display cases, *147-150*
Barber poles, 13, *259-260*
Barber pole decal mug, 164
Barber pole, handle on mug, 57
Barber seats (child's), 227
Barbershop Mug sheets, *128,* 129
Barbers' Signs, 13, *14,*
Barber skare, 18
Barber Supply Company:
 alphabetical index, 209, 210
 alphabetical list of decoraged mugs, 215-223
 catalogs list of mugs, 215-221
 decorated shaving mugs, 212-223, 240-259
 Shaving mugs:
  extra decorations, 212
  fancy decoration, 212
  extra fancy decoration, 212
  lettering on mugs, 213, 214
  marks on mugs, 209, 210
  numbered, 213
  sizes, 212
 Trade designs, society emblems, 213
Barber-Surgeon, 7
Barber-Surgeon basins,
 (see Barber basins), *10*, 11
Barber-Surgeon bowls (see Barber basins)
Barber Trade Signs, 18
Barnum, P.T., shaving mug, 54, *55*
Basins (Barber-Surgeon), 10
Bathhouse operators, 16
Bathing sign (advertising), 22
Bay rum bottles (see barber bottles) 144, 145
Bazin, X. (see soaps), *36*
Bear Grease (porcelain box), 36
Bearded Man pattern, *57*
Bench bottles (see barber bottles)
Bench mug, 53
Bennington shaving mug, *43*
Berninghaus, Eugene, *128*
Biggins-Rogers Co., *46*
bleeding dishes, (See barber basins), 22
bleeding & surgery, 11
bloodletting: 7, *8,* 20
 first illustration, *6*
 first written record of, 9
 instruments, *6*
 techniques, *8,* 24
bloodtapping (see bloodletting)
blood tapper rod (spear rod), 18
blood tappers, 22
blue glass (litho label) shaving mug, *99*
blue milk glass shaving mug, 99
bobbed hair, 193
Bohemia glassware (see barber bottles)
Bohemian ware. decorated, *152*
Boppert, Mr., *182*
bottle tubes, *239*
bottles (see barber bottles)
Brandenburg over anchor mark, 163, *165*
brass basin, (see barber basins), *28*
brass bekken, 18
Bronze Age, 7
Brooks, Geo. P., 64

brown slipware shaving mug, *43*
brushes, lather, *232*
brushless shave creams, 39

Castle, Irene, 193
catalog, list of mugs, 215-221
"Centennial Flower", 69
"Centennial Pattern", *57*
Chairs:
 barber, *224, 225*
 child's haircutting, 227
 folding, barber, *227*
 waiting, 227
character type mug (reproduction), 158
Cherubs & Arches opalescent glass mug, *59*
child's haircutting chair, 227
child's seat, 227
China decorators, 128
Chinese export, 29
Chircurgeon, 22, 24
Christ, 9
Civil War, 50, 52
Civil War Drum, decal, 164
Civil War tin shaving mugs, *50, 51*
clambroth or clamwater glass mugs, *58-62*
Claudius Galen, 11Cleveland, Grover, 100
Cleveland, Grover, 100
clippers (hair), *230*
coffee mug as fake, *160*
column racks, *228*
cologne bottle (see barbers bottles) *144,145*
Cook Ceramic Mfg. Co. 168
"Combination Mug", *66*
comic design mugs, *125-127*
conestoga wagon decal, 165
copper boilers, *231*
corn knife and corn razors, *233, 235*
cream pitcher (see Yankee Shaving Mug), *56*
crystal opalescent sponge bowl, *152*
Currier & Ives reproductions, *161*
cut glass stand bottles, 143, *144*
cutler, 131

Davis, Hugo H., 180, 188, 209
Decorated Bohemian ware, *152*
Decorated shaving cups
 (see shaving mugs), *128, 129*
Decorated shaving mugs, *240-259*
 alphabetical list, 215-223
Decoy shaving bowl, *173*
Delft, *21*
Dentist-barber-surgeon, 16, 20
"Devil Head" glass shaving mug, *59*
DeZemblers barber shop, 168
display cases, *146-150*
Doctors (or surgeons), 16, 22, 24
Doublecap shaving stick, 37

Ear dishes, 22
Eghpt, 7, 9
European marks, 211
"Excelsior" mug, *66*
 used as a fake, *156*

Faience, 11, 23
Fake decal-type mugs, 155
Fakes & reproductions, etc., 153-173
Fancy Globe Bottle, 143
Fireman's insignia decal, 165
Flint (glass) splinters, 6, 7
Folding barber chair, *227*
Formaldehyde cabinet sterilizer, *230*
Franklin
  Institute of Penna., 41
  Institute Fair 1848, 41
Fraternal shaving mugs, *253-255*
French barber shop, *10*
French cut-glass bottle, 143
French opaline glass (shaving glass, 54, *55*

Galen, Claudius, 11, 20
gallipot, 22
Gem safety razor, *235*
German marks, 211
German white metal, 44
Gillette safety razor, 131
glass:
  bottles (see barber bottles)
  Decoy Shaving Bowl, *173*
  Label shaving mugs, 60, 98, 99
  opal, 64
  powder bowls, *152*
  powder stands, *143*
  shaving paper vase, X, 151
glass shaving mugs: 54
  Blue glass, 99
  clear glass, 62
  historical milk glass, *58, 59*
  milk glass, 55, *58, 62,* 65
  patented, *55,* 56, *61,* 63-70
  pattern, *55, 69*
glass:
  sponge bowls, *152*
  stand bottles, *239*
  white opal, 64
  white opal ware, 64, 65
Golden Duck shaving mug, 168-173
Gorgon Medusa head, *56,* 57
Gospel of St. Luke, 11
Greece, 9
Grimm, Curt, 189, 196-203, 206-209

Hairfertilizer, 192
Hair oil bottle, *144, 145*
Handel, J., pat'd. mug, *62*
handles (razors), *237*
hat & coat racks, *228*
Hauel, Jules, (see soaps)
Hearst, Wm. Randolph, collection, *27*
Heimerdinger B. S. Co., 104
Henry VIII decree, 20
Heston, David, 64
Hinge and Scroll, 69
Hingecap shaving stick, 37
Hinged Handle and Scroll, *69*
Hinge Pattern, *69*

Hippocrates, 9
historical: 100
  glass shaving mugs, *58, 59*
  glass mug (fake), *162*
History of Signboards, 16, 22
Hobbs, Brochunier & CO., 65
Hobnail bottle (see barber bottles)
Holder Top Stick, 37
Holsager Antiseptic shaving cup, *60*
Holy Bible, 9
hones, *233*
hot cast porcelain, 64
hot water urn, *231*
Howland & Jones, Importers, *65, 66*
Hughes, Thomas E. (1st shave mug patent), 63
humorous design mugs, *125, 126, 127*

Imported Bohemian bottles, *144*
Imported glassware, *152,*
Ironstone pat'd. shaving mugs, *65, 66*

James Dixon & Sons Sheffield shaving mug, *48*
James Kent, Ltd. — England, 163
Japanese Export, 29
Japanese new imports, silk screen mugs, *166*
Johnson, Oliver T., 189

Koken:
  advertising shaving mug, *113*
  Antiseptilene, 192
  attempts to unionize, 187
  author's note: 177
  barber bottles, 141, 205
  barber chair, 67, 181, 184, 185, 191, *224, 225*
  barber poles, 191, *259, 260*
  The Beginning 1874, *178*
  catalogs, 191
  cellar drama, 186
  china decorating dept. 191
  china decorators, 205
  "Congress" barber chair, 182
  Davis, H. H. (office boy to President), 193-195, 202, 203
  decorating mugs, 104, 181
  departments in 1917, 130, 194, 195
  E. E. Koken apprenticeship, 181
  E. E. Koken, 98, 137, 177, *179,* 187
  evolution, 178-208
  exhibit at 1904 exposition, *184*
  factories, *178, 179*
  family: Wm. Theodore, Charles E., Frank, Ernest Edward, John Charles, Theodore, W. W., Walter F., 180, 181, 187, 189
  first patented barber chair, 182
  gasoline engine, 187
  giant barber chair, 184
  Golden anniversary (1924) catalog, 208
  Greene, A. B., 183
  Hairfertilizer, 192
  Hydraulic barber chair, 182
  Johnson, Oliver T., 186

mug decorating/process, 198-*203, 205-208*
mug decorators: 197, *200,* 201, 203, *206-208*
mugs (see shaving mugs)
marks on mugs, 104
number employees in 1917, 193
orthodontist chairs, 195
photographic mugs, 205
Purity shaving soap, 192
razor grinding dept. 208
shaving mug decorating ended, 188
stand bottles,202
subtle humor on mugs, 192
Sutherland, George, 183
toiletry items, 192
Kokenites, 189, 190
Koken & Boppert, 188, 190
Kidney-dish, 11, 22
knives, 7
Koch, Barber Supply Co., 100, 187

Lamp stove, *231*
Lancets, *6*
Larkin, Bill, Lt. Col., USAF, 50
lather brushes, *232*
lather shaving cream, 37
lead-glaze, 11
"Leader" glass shaving mug, *62*
leeching, 24
leech-books, 11
Lefton China, 165
Lenox Company, 105-112
Lenox shaving mugs, *105-*112
  belleek shaving mugs, 105-112
Lenox shaving mug decorators, 109
litho label (glass shaving mug), 60, *99*
Lord Nelson Pottery —England, 158
Louvre, 9
Lucan (ships surgeon), 9

Mary Gregory:
  powder and sponge bowls, *152*
majolica, 11
McGrady, James, 64
McKinley Tariff Act, 211
medicine, 9
melon shaped bowl, 152
memorial glass mugs (see historical)
Mephistopheless glass shaving mug, *59*
milk glass insert, *47*
milk glass mustard jar as fake mug: *160*
milk glass shaving mugs, *55, 58, 62, 65*
Missouri Historical Society, 191
Mohawk Co., 164
monasteries, 11
monks (European), *10*
Moore, John Hudson, company, 168
Morley, William, 109
Mt. Vernon Silversmiths, Inc., 111
Mug cabinet, case or rack, *146-150*
mug decorating room, *197, 206*
mug posters *128*-129

Nelson Lebo Co., 168
New England glass mfgrs., 64
new shaving mugs, *162,* 167
Nosek, H., 109
number mugs (see gilt number shaving mugs)

Occupational Types or Trade Designs shaving mugs, *71-89,* 256-259
Old Foley Staffordshire, *161,* 163
Old Spice replica coffee mugs,*162*
old style shaving mugs, *169*
opalescent glass mugs, 56, *59, 69*
Oriental export, 29

painted toilet bottles, 143
Paris Barber Assn. Law of 1371, 18
patented glass shaving mugs, *55, 60-70*
pattern glass mugs, *55, 57, 61, 65, 69*
peach blow bottle, *144, 145*
pedestal base mug, *57*
Penna. Farm Museum of Landis Valley, 51
Penna, German potters, 13
Penna. Redware, 29, *30*
Penna. slipware (oldest), 24
personalized barber bottles, *139*
personalized barber shop towels, 140
phlebotomes, 6
phlebotomy bow, *8*
photograph under glass label, 99
pineapple bottle (also see barber bottles), 143
pineapple bowls, 143, *145,* 152
pink clambroth glass mug, 57
pole (barber), 22, 191, *259, 260*
political glass (see historical)
Pomade jar, *152*
Pope Leo barber basin, *27*
porcelain soap boxes, *33*
porringer, 11, 22
portable washstand, *229*
portable workcabinet, 229
powder bowls, *152*
powder shakers, *239*
Presidents (U.S.) Lincoln, McKinley, Garfield, Cleveland, Wilson, *58, 59,* 100, 109, 131
Proctor & Gamble, 37
Purity Shaving Soap, 192

quadruple-plate (see silverplate or shaving mugs silver-plate)

Rack (mug), 146, *147, 148*
Razors, 48, *130-134, 236*
Razors (alphabetical list) 133, 134
Razor Cases, *234, 235*
Razor handles, 132, *237*
Razor imports, 131
Razor pockets, *237*
Razor rack, *237*
Razor rolls, *237*
Razor sterilizer, *230*
Razor strops, 233

270

Redware shaving mugs, *42, 43*
Redware (Penna.), 29, *30*
replicas (see fakes and reproductions)
reverse painted glass labels, 98
Robin & wheat pattern glass, 57
Rockingham type shaving mugs, 42
Royal Crown — Imperial 164, 165
Royal Porcelain, 164
Royal Bowl, 12
Royal College of Surgeons for England, 12

Safety Guard Razors, 235
Sandwich Historical Society, 54
Sanitary sterilizers, *230, 231*
Sawyer, Wm., 64
saponaceous shaving compound (see soaps), 40, 41
sea foam bottle, *144, 145*
Sears-Roebuck catalog razors, 132
Secret Society emblems, 130
Seitz (1st drug store), shaving mug, *264, 265*
settees, *227*
sgraffito (decoration), 13, *43*
shampoo stools, *227*
shaving basins in America, 24
 (also see barber basins)
shaving box, 33
shaving compound (see soaps)
shaving cream (see soap), 35
shaving cups (see shaving mugs)
shaving glasses, 54, *55*
shaving pots, 49
shaving soaps (see soaps), 192
shaving stands, 49
shaving stick (Williams) 37
shaving mug:
  cabinet, 146, *147*
  cases, *146-150*
  display cases, 146, *147*
  rack, *146-148*
  sheets, *128*-129
  toilet goods & mug case, *148*
  values, 174, 175
shaving mugs: *212-223, 240-259*
  advertising types, 113
  aluminum, 44 53, 238
  Bennington, *43*
  blank imported, 109, 199
  Brittania, 44, *48*
  brown slipware, *43*
  character types, *119-124*
  current Japanese imports, *156*, 163
  decal mugs, *114-116*
  decoration, 104
  evolution, 1-5
  fakes & reproductions 153-*173*
  fraternal emblem designs, 91-97, 100 253-255
  German imports, 114
  gilt number, 103, *104*
  glass, 54, 238 (see also pat'd mugs)
  glass labels, *98*, 99
  gold band china, 238

goldplated, 47
humorous or comic designs, *125-127*
Japanese reproduction, *159, 166*
left-handed, 207
ladies, 207
Lenox:
  blank china mugs (white wares), 110
  china marks on mugs, 112
  exports to Europe, 110
  factory decorated, 110
  silver mark, *111*
  silver overlay, 110, 111
  stock molds, 110, *111*
Litho labels, 99
  mfgrs. mark, 211
new English imports, 158, *159*
nickel-plated, *238*
numbered china mugs, 238
occupational types, *256-259*
occupational mis-nomers, 154
pewter, 44, *48*
photographic, *100-201*
plain, 213, *238*
primitive pottery types, *42, 43*
  redware, *42, 43*
  Rockingham, *42*
  scuttles, *117, 118*
  scuttle reproductions, 161
  Secret Societies, 91-97, 100
  semi-characters 123
  sgraffito, *43*
  silverplated, 44-*47*, 49, *238*
  spongeware, *43*
  sports designs, *251, 252*
  stoneware, *43*
  tin, 44, *50, 51,* 52
  trade unions, 91-97
  Virginia pottery, 42
Shaving paper vase, X, *151*
Shining stands, *226*
ships surgeon, 9
shoeshining stands, *226*
signboard, 16, 22
silver-deposit on glass mug, *60, 61*
slip decoration, 13
Smith Brothers, Cutlers, 67, 68
Smith Brothers patent mark, *70*
Smith Brothers patent mug, *68*
soap boxes, personalized, *33,* 34
soap containers, 32, *33*
soap depression (in basins), 29, *30*
soap mfgrs., 32
soap (shaving), 32
spear rod, 18, 22
spongeware shaving mug, *43*
Sportsman Brand Shaving Mugs, 168, 173
stand bottles (see barber bottles), 145, *239*
Statute of Liberty, 131
steam sterilizers, *231*
sterilizer cabinet, *230, 231*
sterilizer (razor), *230*
stoneware shaving mug, *43*
stools, *227*

271

Straight razors, 130-134
  alphabetical list, 133, 134
strops (razor), *233*
Stuebner's Sons, *128*
surgeons advertising sign, 20, 22, 24
Surgeons Inc. Bill, 22
Surgeons of the Long Robe, 18
Surgeons of the Short Robe, 18
Swan design mug, *57*
Swiss Violet Shaving Cream (see soaps)

talcom sifter, 152, *239*
taster, 22
Tatler, Inc., 168
Taylor, H. P. & W. C., H. P & C. R. 40, 41
Temesvar, Rumania, *26, 28*
terra cotta clay, 11
Three Crown Germany, 114
Tiffany Co., 111
tin-glaze, 11
tombstone photo plaques, 207
Tonique de Luxe, *113, 190,* 202, 205
toilet goods & mug case, *148*
toilet-shape glass shaving mug, *58, 59*
tonsores, 20
tool bags, *234, 235*
tool cases, *234, 235*
towels, personalized, 140
towel urns, *151*
trade designs (see shaving mugs) 130
transfer prints on mugs, 68
Travelers leatherette, 37
tree-bark barber bottles, *142*
Trenton Potteries Co. decal mug, *116*
Tufts, James W., *45, 46*
Turkish Pomade, 190, *191*

"Unique" shaving mug, *59*
U. S. Patent Office, 63
"Utility Shaving Cup", *46*

Vases (shaving paper), *X, 151*
vein surgeon, 22
Viking Pattern, 1, 2, *55, 57, 61,* 65
Virginia pottery mug, *42*

waiting chairs, *227*
wall cases, *146-148*
Warner-Lambert Co., 168
Washington, George, *60,* 63,131 *223*
washstand, *226*
Wendel, Robert F. & Edgar, 104, 189, 203-208
white agate glass, 70
white enamel for barber chair, 196
white metal (German), 44
white opal ware glass mugs, 56, 64, *69,* 70
white opaque milk glass (see shaving mugs), *57, 65, 69*
wigmakers, 16, 22
Wild Root advertising mug, *113*
Wilson, Woodrow, 100, 109
Williams Co., The J. B., *32*-35, 37
  1892 ad, *38*
  advertising shaving mug, *38,* 113
  Genuine Yankee Soap, 35
workstands, *229*
World's Fair, 1851, 41
Wright's soap box, *36*
Yackey, Mrs. Olive (Koken), 180
Yankee shaving mug, *56*
Yankee soap, 35, 37

Robinson Township Public
Library District
606 N. Jefferson Street
Robinson, IL 62454